SPEAKER

SPEAKER

LESSONS FROM FORTY YEARS IN COACHING AND POLITICS

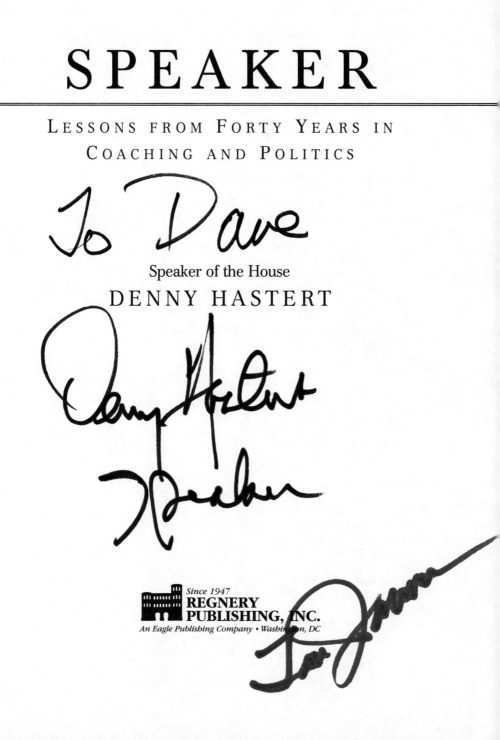

Speaker of the House

DENNY HASTERT

Since 1947
**REGNERY
PUBLISHING, INC.**
An Eagle Publishing Company • Washington, DC

Copyright © 2004 by J. Dennis Hastert

Photos taken by the House photographer were purchased for use in this book at fair market value.

Library of Congress Cataloging-in-Publication Data

Hastert, Dennis, 1942–
    Speaker : lessons from forty years in coaching and politics / J. Dennis Hastert.
        p. cm.
    Includes bibliographical references and index.
    ISBN 0-89526-126-X (alk. paper)
    1. Hastert, Dennis, 1942– 2. Legislators–United States–Biography. 3. United States. Congress. House–Speakers–Biography. 4. United States–Politics and government–1945–1989. 5. United States–Politics and government–1989– 6. Wrestling coaches–Illinois–Biography. 7. Hastert, Dennis, 1942–Philosophy. 8. United States–Politics and government–Philosophy. I. Title.
E840.8.H288A3 2004
328.73'092–dc22

2004014246

Published in the United States by
Regnery Publishing, Inc.
An Eagle Publishing Company
One Massachusetts Avenue, NW
Washington, DC 20001

Visit us at www.regnery.com

Distributed to the trade by
National Book Network
4720-A Boston Way
Lanham, MD 20706

Printed on acid-free paper
Manufactured in the United States of America

10 9 8 7 6 5 4 3 2 1

Books are available in quantity for promotional or premium use. Write to Director of Special Sales, Regnery Publishing, Inc., One Massachusetts Avenue, NW, Washington, DC 20001, for information on discounts and terms or call (202) 216-0600.

I would like to specially dedicate this to my wife, Jean, our son Josh, and our son Ethan and his new bride, Heidi.

Jean, you have been a tremendous source of strength and support over the years. Without your love, patience, and encouragement, I couldn't have run for the Illinois State legislature, let alone Congress. Truly, I would not be Speaker today if not for you.

To my sons Josh and Ethan, you both have grown to be upstanding, independent-minded men, of whom I am very proud. You both have learned that education is a lifelong process, no matter how many degrees you have hanging on your wall.

∾

To THE YORKVILLE FOXES OF 1976:
While many of our teams did well, you were the very best. For me, winning the state championship was among the finest moments of my life. So many of the fine athletes I had the good fortune to coach are today raising and coaching boys and girls of their own. They're mentoring the next generation. For me, it doesn't get any better than that.

∾

To THE PEOPLE OF THE FOURTEENTH CONGRESSIONAL DISTRICT OF ILLINOIS:
You have honored me by selecting me as your representative in Congress since 1986. While I have the chance to travel this great country often now, I'm always happiest when I can be at home with you along the Fox River. I'll always be truly grateful to you for placing your trust in me.

∾

To THE MEMBERS OF THE U.S. HOUSE OF REPRESENTATIVES:
We are the oldest continuous democracy in the world. A true democracy can only work when people can come together and debate the issues of the day. We don't always agree, and our philosophy on many things is very different. But it is a measure of our success and maturity as a nation that we can have these debates. And yet, we will stand together when we are attacked and to protect the rights of others around the world. You have honored me as your Speaker. I strive every day for this beloved country of ours. Thanks to all of you for your faith in, belief in, and service to our nation.

Contents

INTRODUCTION

Short words are best, and the old words,
when short, are the best of all.
—Winston S. Churchill

Twenty-five years ago, I was a high school wrestling coach in northern Illinois. Occasionally, I drove the school bus. In between, I taught history, economics, and social studies.

Today I'm Speaker of the United States House of Representatives, the third highest position in our government. Now, I'm not the most articulate guy or a great speech master; I'm not pretty, and I didn't go to Harvard or Yale. How did I wind up where I am?

"Illness, illness, scandal, and dumb luck," suggests Scott Palmer, my longtime chief of staff.

He's right—up to a point. (Six years ago, if someone had asked me to predict Newt Gingrich's successor as Speaker of the House, I wouldn't have been on my own list.) I did learn very early that you play the cards you're dealt, remain focused, and that there's always a way to win. And at the same time I always knew what my strengths—and limitations—were.

They call me "Speaker," but I like to think of myself as a listener. I have always believed that if people can discuss their problems and have someone listen to them carefully, then those problems can be solved.

Another distinction, perhaps, is that although the home I share with my wife, Jean, is on a river, it's not the Potomac. I'm referring to the Fox that creases and caresses northern Illinois. That's where my roots are. I draw sustenance, strength, and inspiration from the people in my congressional district. I still have my hair cut at Chuck's Barbershop in Yorkville; I still wander over to Loren Miller's auto body shop for coffee at least one morning a week—even though I have to have security accompany me. And I love to hop on my old International tractor to set out and survey our farm with our two pet Labs, Bud and Zander, yapping in my wake.

Because I view my job as serving *all* Members of the House of Representatives, I don't have an agenda of my own. If you have to deal with a lot of egos, I've found, it's best not to let your own get in the way. So I don't have to be on television every week; I'm not looking to get my name in the paper every day or otherwise seek celebrity. The revelation that fewer than one-third of respondents asked by Gallup know who I am or what I do doesn't bother me one bit. My motto has always been: Under-promise and over-produce. So if someone wants to underestimate me, that's great.

The U.S. House, I found, is a far more partisan place than the Illinois General Assembly, where I served for six years. In Springfield, you could go out for drinks or dinner with friends from across the aisle. In Washington, that's tough to do. Distinct philosophical differences separate Republicans from Democrats. The incivility—and both parties share blame—has reached such a low that I don't know how we'll ever bring it back up again. But I pledge again: I have done—and will continue to do—everything I can to bridge the gap that divides us today.

That's one reason why this book is not going to be what they call a tell-all. (All of you on Capitol Hill thumbing through the index now to see if your names are included—and you and I know who you are—can breathe a sigh of relief.) I have to live and get along with people here. I have no scores to settle and too much mud has been flung about by too many people for too long.

There's another reason as well. Years ago, when I was serving in the Illinois State legislature, I took a train to St. Louis. The train passed through the southwestern Illinois towns of Alton, Bethalto, and Granite City. Jim McPike, a Democrat, represented that area in Springfield, and he would lambaste us at every opportunity. When I was a freshman, I thought he was a jerk—until I saw where he was coming from. As the train rolled through, I counted broken windows, dilapidated factories, and abandoned buildings everywhere. The people having those hard times were *his* constituents, and that's why he was upset. He was echoing their concerns. He was representing *them.*

The lesson I learned from that: No matter what your opinion is of a Member of the U.S. House of Representatives, that person has been elected by the majority of 600,000-plus voters who have been convinced that he or she shares their views. Otherwise, he or she wouldn't be here; it's as simple as that.

The premise of democracy is that a lot of people—collectively—try to make the right decisions for the rest of us. No one individual has the ultimate truth, so collecting that truth is a process. It is, in fact, a slow and messy process. But you try to get to what's right and do it again and again.

How I came to be in a position to do that is the story that follows.

PROLOGUE

"MR. SPEAKER, MR. SPEAKER." I HEARD A QUICK, INSISTENT KNOCK at the door on the first floor of the U.S. Capitol—It was just past nine on the morning of September 11, 2001, and I was visiting the House physician for a routine appointment. I recognized the voice of Sam Lancaster, the "gatekeeper," who is a trusted aide. "Something's happened to the World Trade Center in New York," he said. "Either a small plane or a helicopter, we don't know which yet, has flown into the north tower and there's a big fire in the upper stories."

"I'll be upstairs in just a minute," I said.

As soon as I entered my office suite on the Capitol's second floor, I turned to the television. I could see the fire and the black smoke rising from the burning building. Then, my God, coming rapidly into view at the left side of the screen, a second plane. No doubt that this was a commercial airliner, and I watched it fly directly into the second Trade Center tower. It struck the south tower building at five hundred miles per hour and disappeared. The cameras focused on people in the street below running for their lives.

Immediately, I thought that this was not an accident, that this was terrorism. Scott Palmer, my chief of staff, was working in an adjacent room. "My God," I called to him. "Did you *see* this?"

Two other planes were missing, apparently hijacked. Nobody knew who was responsible. Just that something was drastically wrong.

The television showed President George W. Bush listening to young students at an elementary school in Florida. Then Andy Card, his chief of staff, whispered to him, and the look on the President's face confirmed my worst suspicions of what we were dealing with. It was while I was watching that moment on television that Sam Lancaster said Vice President Dick Cheney was trying to reach me on the secure phone.

There are three phones on my desk: my regular phone, the White House phone, and the secure phone. The secure phone is black and sits quietly in a corner next to photographs of my family. It's an ever-present reminder of the dangers we face, and I pray that it forever sits silent—that I never have to use it. On this morning, my prayers were not answered. It was set to ring.

To use the secure phone, you have to push a button and turn a key. On that dreadful day I couldn't make the thing work. No matter what I did, I couldn't connect with the Vice President. As the minutes passed, my frustrations grew.

Then a yellow light started flashing on the regular phone console. Normally, I don't pick up when it's flashing like that because someone always screens my calls. But I thought: Cheney's got to be as frustrated as I am by this non-functioning secure phone. The flashing light must be his call. They must have put him through. So I answered the phone. I was fully expecting to hear Cheney's smooth baritone.

"What the heck are you guys doing on Capitol Hill?" a strange voice asked. "I can't get a hold of Bush. Colin Powell won't return my phone calls. The economy is going to hell. You guys can't make a decision up there. Your appropriations aren't done. What are you guys doing?" he screamed.

I didn't recognize the voice. "Whoa, whoa, wait a minute, slow down," I said. "Who is this?"

"What do you mean, 'Who is this?' I'm just a citizen. Who in the hell is this?"

"This is the Speaker of the House," I said. "Just calm down, will you?"

The view of the National Mall and the Washington Monument from my office window is one of the best in the city. As I hung up the phone, I saw a huge plume of black smoke rolling across the Mall's far end. "Sam," I called out, "find out where that smoke is coming from." He returned minutes later to tell me that a third plane had crashed into the Pentagon's west wall, leaving a gaping wound. The building was on fire, and hundreds were believed dead.

All of this was happening so fast; events were threatening to spin out of control, and we didn't seem to have a lot of time to think. Quickly, I tried to assess what we knew: Two planes hit the World Trade Center in New York, another hit the Pentagon. I didn't know what else was out there, but it seemed clear that the Capitol building–the very symbol of freedom and democracy– was an obvious target.

Here in the Capitol complex of the House of Representatives and Senate, we have 535 lawmakers; some thirty thousand men and women work on Capitol Hill; and while there's no way of telling how many tourists we have at any given time, the number is always large. All of these people were my responsibility.

"Sam," I hollered, "Call the Chaplain and have him meet me on the House floor. I'm going to have him say a prayer, and then we're going to adjourn the House. We're at risk, and we need to get everyone out of here."

I had opened the House at nine o'clock–something I'm obliged to do myself at least every fourth legislative day–and now I'd be closing it an hour later, just ten minutes away. I hadn't been on the House floor more than a minute when two of my security detail, Jack DeWolfe and Bo Singleton, entered the chamber and started running directly toward me. "We think there's another plane heading for the Capitol," Jack was saying. "We're going to evacuate the Capitol, and you're going to a secure location."

I'm a large man and not easy to lift or move, but those security guys, one on each side of me, scooped me up and hoisted me off my feet. The next thing I knew I was whizzing through the back halls of the Capitol, down the elevator, and through the long tunnel to the Rayburn House Office Building. We dashed into the garage, climbed into a waiting Chevy Suburban, and soon went hurtling through the back streets of Washington, D.C., at ninety miles per hour or some other unholy speed. Then we turned onto the Suitland Parkway. "Where are we going?" I asked.

"Andrews," was the reply. Our driver kept his gaze straight ahead and his foot on the gas. When we reached Andrews Air Force base in suburban Maryland, our communications people finally succeeded in hooking me up to the Vice President.

"I have the Secretary of Transportation with me," Cheney said. "We're bringing all planes down, landing all planes. This is certainly a terrorist attack." There was one plane down on the West Virginia–Kentucky border, he continued, and another plane had crashed in Pennsylvania. We didn't have contact with four or five separate planes coming across the Atlantic or with another civilian jet that was somewhere over the middle of Canada. "There's a real danger," Cheney said. "I want you to go to a secure location."

Our helicopter lifted off the tarmac at Andrews and flew over Anacostia and the southern half of Washington, D.C. Looking down, I saw no cars or people in the streets. Everything was deserted. By this time it was almost eleven o'clock on a crisp September morning with a deep blue sky and puffy white clouds. To the east, I saw the empty runways at Reagan National Airport, no people moving, everything shut down and nothing happening.

Looking down from the other side of the chopper, I saw blue-black smoke pouring out of the Pentagon and obscuring the bright day. And I thought to myself: As a history teacher for sixteen years back in Illinois, I'd taught my students about the British invasion of Washington during the War of 1812 and the burning of our capital. Now here I was, Speaker of the House in 2001, and our country and capital were being attacked again. Never in my lifetime had I dreamt that something like this could happen in America.

At our secure location, rooms had been set up for us to use. First I tried to reach my wife, Jean, who was due to join me in Washington that afternoon. When she didn't respond, I had to assume she was still in transit somewhere. Next I got a hold of Cheney, who told me the President was in a safe location and brought me up to date.

The initial report of a plane down on the West Virginia–Kentucky border had been wrong, he said. He confirmed that a commercial airliner had indeed crashed in central Pennsylvania, and the four or five non-responding jets flying across the Atlantic were still heading our way. Ditto for the jet crossing southern Canada, bound for Dulles International Airport outside Washington, D.C. We had fighters in the air trying to provide cover for our major cities, the Vice President said. He did not have any idea at that moment who was behind all this. Cheney is usually low-key, but I couldn't miss the outrage in his voice.

As the day passed, other Members of Congress appeared at the secure location: House Majority Leader Dick Armey (R-Tex.) and Majority Whip Tom DeLay (R-Tex.); Minority Leader Dick Gephardt (D-Mo.) and Minority Whip David Bonior (D-Mich.); Senate Majority Leader Tom Daschle (D-S.D.) and Minority Leader Trent Lott (R-Miss.); Assistant Majority Leader Harry Reid (D-Nev.) and Minority Whip Don Nickles (R-Okla.).

All of us were milling about, saying very little as we watched those shocking, riveting, ghastly images on television. There were huge losses, we knew, in New York City and the Pentagon. We had no idea what the extent of the damage was, nor could we even guess the number of casualties. Yet we knew that this was no mere terrorist strike. America had been dealt a horrific blow. Other attacks might be in the offing, and we'd have to respond. We needed leadership to get the job done, and that started with the President. We heard reports that he was heading back to Washington.

We were accomplishing nothing where we were; I decided it was time to move out. Addressing my colleagues, I said, "Hey, it's up to us. We need to stand together, go back to Washington and show people that we are standing together." So we returned to the Capitol around six o'clock. Daschle and I agreed that we needed to go to the press and announce that we'd be back in session the next day. Evidently, word of our intentions spread quickly, for when we stepped around to the other side of the building I saw what appeared to be a crowd of several hundred Members of Congress already standing on the East Capitol steps.

Both Daschle and I, standing shoulder to shoulder, spoke briefly; we said what we felt about sorrow, prayer, and resolve. As we turned to leave, someone—later, I found out that it was the irrepressible Dana Rohrabacher (R-Calif.)—began singing "God Bless America." Everyone began joining him, and at that moment, chills went down my spine. "We're going to be okay," I thought. "This country is going to pull together, and everything's going to be fine."

∽

Every time I look out the window of my office at the stunning view of the city, down the expanse of the National Mall, I can't help but think about the plane that went down in Pennsylvania—the plane assigned to fly straight down the Mall and into the middle of the Capitol, directly into my office. It is a constant reminder to me of the heroes of September 11—not only our heroes in uniform but also our citizen heroes. It is a reminder of the great strength and conviction of the men and women of United Airlines Flight 93—voting to attack the hijackers and regain control of the airplane, filling pitchers with boiling water, and taking the struggle to the cockpit. I think of the timeline a lot. In hindsight, I realized that were it not for the heroes of Flight 93, the plane would have struck the Capitol at the very moment that I was making decisions about evacuating the buildings. Their desperate courage saved us from a great wound. And they saved the lives of many people.

Over the next several weeks, in the very room where the plane would have struck, we crafted bills that would help heal our wounds and aid us in preventing other attacks on our great nation.

CHAPTER ONE

JUST CALL ME DENNY

The White Rabbit put on his spectacles. "Where shall
I begin, please your majesty?" he asked. "Begin
at the beginning," the King said gravely, "and go
on till you come to the end: then stop."
—LEWIS CARROLL, *ALICE IN WONDERLAND*

ON JANUARY 2, 1942, THE NEWS WAS GRIM ALMOST EVERYWHERE.
An article on the front page of the *Washington Post* warned JAPS
MAY TRY TO SHELL CITIES ON WEST COAST. The headline of the
Christian Science Monitor screamed JAPANESE TAKE MANILA, while
the *New York Times* announced that rationing was set to begin
here at home on January 15. The temperatures in Chicago that
January 2 ranged from a low of nine to a high of sixteen degrees.
And there was just one other piece of news to report—of interest
only to family and friends: at 7:55 PM at St. Joseph's Mercy Hospital in Aurora, Illinois, some forty-five miles southwest of
Chicago's Loop, John Dennis Hastert, weighing seven pounds
and eleven ounces, came into this world. I was "a chubby baby,"
my aunt Doral Swan says. Some things—like some people—never
change.

My parents were Jack and Naomi Hastert, and I was the first
of their three sons. David would come along in 1948, Chris in

13

1953. Their ancestors, the first Hasterts in America, had emigrated from Osweiler, Luxembourg, in the 1860s, fearing that the tiny nation was about to get gobbled up by one of its hungry European neighbors, and they had settled in an immigrant neighborhood on Aurora's northeast side called Pigeon Hill.

Those ancestors, my great-grandfather Christian Hastert and his brother Matteus, were blacksmiths, wheelwrights, and wagon-builders. They soon found jobs, probably building rail cars, in the Chicago-Burlington Railroad's yards and shops. At the turn of the century, there was a strike on the Burlington, so my great-grandfather went to work for the Elgin, Joliet & Eastern Railway Company (EJ&E), owned by U.S. Steel, which was hauling coal from Coal City to the steel mills in Joliet. Both Christian and Matteus wound up as engineers. Hasterts have always been railroad people.

My grandfather on my dad's side, John "Dutch" Hastert, was a short, bald-headed guy who smoked a pipe or cigar and whose shoes were always impeccably shined. A machinist by trade, he had started out as a boilermaker and worked his way up to be superintendent of the EJ&E shops. Dutch's wife, my grandmother, was Borghild Lund Hastert, a nurse from Alpena, Michigan, who met her future husband at Silver Cross Hospital in Joliet. She was of Norwegian descent, and everyone called her "Borg."

On my mother's side, my grandparents were of German descent. They had come to Illinois from an industrial section of Philadelphia called Bridesburg. My grandfather John, who was tall and graceful, had played semi-professional basketball for an ammunition company in or near Wilkes-Barre, Pennsylvania. His playing name was Jack Russell; he and his teammates traveled

with drop-net cages—that's how basketball players got to be
called cagers—and they used old military armories for games. My
grandfather had played semi-pro baseball as well and by the time
I got to know him, he also worked for the EJ&E as a switchman
and was a bookbinder by trade.

What I remember most about him was his wonderful sense of
humor. An amateur magician, he carried a bag full of tricks. He
was always juggling balls in the air, pulling a quarter out of your
ear, or making things hop over your knuckles, smiling and saying,
"Now you see it, now you don't." All the kids loved him because
he made us laugh. John was married to Laura, my grandmother
on my mother's side, who was a fabulous German-style cook.
"The noodle girl," he called her.

After a few years in Chicago, he and Laura moved to Joliet.
John and a business partner were going to start a cement block fac-
tory to produce building blocks for home construction, but when
the Depression hit, no one needed foundations. All home building stopped, and the business failed. John and Laura lost almost
everything. He found a job as a switchman on the EJ&E, and that's
how he hoped to feed his family. Unfortunately, he lost that job.
He started selling things—paper products, for the most part—door
to door. He had to walk some distance each morning and check in
to see if he could work that day. Most of the time the answer was
no, so he'd walk home with no money in his pockets.

My two sets of grandparents had a friendly relationship. How
did they get to know each other? In today's world the answer may
seem quaint: They lived next door to each other on Fairbanks
Avenue in Joliet in a neighborhood called Ridgewood, near the
railroad yards.

So my parents' love story is literally boy falls in love with the girl next door. It just took my dad, Jack, a while to figure it out. He was twenty-seven when he married—old by Depression-era standards. Dad, who was born in 1913, graduated from Joliet Township High School and then attended the Worsham College of Mortuary Science. After his graduation, he taught embalming there. An uncle owned a funeral parlor in Aurora, so Dad worked there for a while and then switched to the Fred Dames Funeral Parlor in Joliet and worked there until about 1939. Then in 1940, the same year he married Mom, he started Hastert Farm Supply at 1421 New York Street on Aurora's east side. He hoped to sell a lot of Purina feed.

Six feet tall, blond, with glasses and a slightly receding hairline, Dad was a pretty good-looking guy who didn't say too much. Some people called him gruff, but he taught me a lot about many things. I always thought he was incredibly wise. He was a workaholic—his most enduring characteristic—and he was never home.

In his absence, my mother, Naomi Hastert, pretty much ran the show. She stood about five feet eight and was a strong woman. During the Depression, she quit high school to work in a grocery store in Joliet where she could buy food at a discount. She was the only one in the family with a full-time job. Because she had worried constantly about money and debt, she continued to pinch every penny, and we lived a pretty frugal life. And she kept working long after her own kids were born. She'd put on a pair of khakis and work all day in and around the chicken houses, and then she'd mind the store when Dad had to go out into the country to call on customers and deliver feed.

Mom had a sense of humor and was radiantly happy when she was around her family. And she had a remarkable gift for making friends. She was also the family disciplinarian. She wouldn't tolerate lies or unkind words, and she could put you in your place, reminding you where you came from if she sensed your ego was getting out of hand. As a youngster, I was a little mouthy; I talked back sometimes, and I learned pretty quickly that if I broke the rules, I'd probably get a smack across the face.

Because I was born in 1942, I don't remember too much about World War II. I do remember my uncle John Nussle, Mom's brother, going off to war, and I also remember looking at the war cartoon that appeared on the front page of the *Chicago Tribune* every morning. On our way to the feed store, which we opened at 8:30 AM every day, we stopped at a gas station and picked up the *Tribune* for five cents.

I grew up in that store. I was there working with my dad every Saturday and every day during the summertime. Customers would come in and I'd bag feed for them—I was probably in the third or fourth grade when I started doing that. You really learn a lot about people that way. The person I learned most about was Dad. When I was a kid, I spent a lot of time with him. From the age of four or five, I was in the country with him whenever he called on his customers. So I'm not kidding when I say that I grew up on the back of a feed truck. It was a 1936 Dodge. During the war and even afterwards, you couldn't buy a truck. You couldn't buy tires. This was an old truck, but it had decent tires. It had once been a beer truck, so it had high sides.

We used that truck to haul feed. It didn't have a heater, and the seats were shot. You could look down through the floorboards and actually see the road. So we'd be driving through the country, both of us freezing in the cab of that truck. The temperature outside would be zero, and Dad would be teaching me the ABCs to take my mind off the cold. Even as a little kid, I was pulling bags off the end of that truck. The next truck he bought was a 1948 Chevrolet. He bought it brand new. It had a heater that worked, and when I stepped inside, I thought I had died and gone to heaven. My dad needed trucks to earn a living, but I think I loved trucks even more than he did—and I still do. (I have a 1954 Mack fire engine that I keep in the barn at home that I love to drive; it's just a great old truck.)

"I'm not going to give you an allowance," Dad said when I was in the third grade, "but if you want to earn some money I'm going to give you twenty chickens. You have to take care of them every day." We had a little hen house, and the chickens were mine. I went to pick up those eggs three times every day. I could sell them for about thirty cents a dozen and earn a few extra bucks each week. When you collected the eggs the chickens would peck at you. Bravery for a kid, I decided then, was sticking your hand in a chicken's nest knowing she's going to peck at you three or four times and then extracting the egg without breaking it.

Next door we also had a thousand chickens in a long chicken house, and I had to clean out under the roosts. It was a messy business and a tough job for a kid. In the winter when it was cold, the air would carry a heavy ammonia scent from the roosts.

As I grew older, I baled hay all summer long, despite having allergies, including hay fever. I'd be sneezing, and my eyes would be running. But if you were going to make any money at all, you had to take the jobs that were available.

Although my grandparents on both sides were Democrats—that came from the men working on the railroad and being with the union—Mom and Dad came out of the Depression as Republicans. Growing up, I heard about politics around the dinner table all the time. Our home county, I learned, was named for Amos Kendall, who had been President Andrew Jackson's first postmaster general. Originally, the county name had been Orange—to honor the first settlers who had come from upstate New York in the 1830s and 1840s—and they wanted a post office. So the Jackson administration, being the good patronage machine it was, proposed a deal. If the settlers wanted their wish fulfilled, they would have to change the county's name. Reluctantly, they agreed, and the evidence was there for all to see: a good Republican county bullied by Democrats just because its people wanted to exercise their rights. That's the kind of story that could stir emotions in a seven- or eight-year-old.

If you grew up in Kendall County, the odds are that you were a Republican. I was just a kid when Truman was in the White House, but nobody where I lived was enamored with Truman. Now Eisenhower, he came down to the crossroads in Yorkville, and that was a big deal in 1952. Adlai Stevenson, who was opposing him, had been governor of Illinois. But he raised taxes on the small business guys, the truckers and the farmers; he was pretty much a liberal, and that didn't win him a lot of support in Kendall County.

Throughout the 1950s, after the stockyards moved away from Chicago, the farm-supply business began a long, steady decline. Our family moved the store from Aurora to our home on Plainfield Road in Oswego Township five miles away. The walk-in business wasn't important anymore, so we concentrated on warehousing and hauling. Since the business was in our backyard, we were open all the time, and I'd deliver feed early in the morning or after I got home from school.

Dad and I were the delivery team, so we spent a lot of time together out in the country. Because of this, we had a great understanding of each other. Back then, kids grew up in the family business and shared in whatever the family did. The family connection seemed much stronger than it is today. There were mentors in each family then, and everyone acknowledged the importance of their role.

When I was in junior high school, I delivered feed with the help of our neighbor Vern Wheeler. We delivered feed after school. He would drive; I'd help him load and unload, and I knew where all the customers lived. I was a big kid with big shoulders and a broad back–the right build for lugging feedbags. By the time I was in high school, I'd get up at four o'clock in the morning during the summer, drive the truck down to the mill in Bloomington, Illinois, and load eight or nine tons of feed on it, drive back, deliver it–twenty hundred-pound bags equaled one ton–and be home by one o'clock that afternoon. Starting when I was a sophomore in high school, I would come home after practice at least two nights a week, and there would be a semi-trailer with tons of feed to unload. No one told me; I just knew it was my job to unload that truck, and I never complained. At one time, Purina shipped feed in cotton print bags. Farm wives would come to the warehouse and want ten bags of the same print to make matching curtains or a dress. I could tell where some families got their feed by the dresses their daughters wore to school.

Because everyone in our family was so busy, we just didn't have time for vacations. But there were exceptions. In the early 1950s, for example, before my youngest brother, Chris, was born, we drove to Leach Lake, Minnesota, in my dad's 1941 Lincoln to spend a week with my grandparents. Back then there was no such thing as reservations. Since we couldn't find a motel, we stayed in an old rooming house in Red Wing, Minnesota, that overlooked the Mississippi River. That was my first night away from home. My younger brother David and I went fishing and swimming. Staying there for one whole week was a big deal.

∾

In his novel *Crossing to Safety*, American writer Wallace Stegner pointed out that "Friendship is a relationship that has no formal shape; there are no rules or obligations or bonds as in marriage or the family. It is held together by neither law nor property nor blood; there is no glue in it but mutual liking. It is therefore rare."

I've always liked that passage because it helps explain one of the most important, and enduring, relationships of my life. When I was in seventh grade, I met Tom Jarman. Tom moved in from St. Louis. I was fascinated by Tom because he said he knew judo, and I had never known anyone who knew judo. Tom became my best friend. I don't know how to explain it other than to say that we just clicked. Just about all of my friends called me Denny; Tom always called me Dennis. But that didn't matter. Our aspirations matched, and so did our values. Soon we were inseparable. He came with me when I delivered feed. Tom was a town boy and hadn't yet learned to drive. Our old GMC feed truck had a four-speed shift plus reverse, and I taught him to drive by having him shift gears while I steered and worked the clutch. That was before driver's education, and his parents never quite figured out how he learned to drive a stick shift.

When it came to possessions, we Hasterts didn't have very much. (No one in our family, for example, had a bicycle until long after the end of the war. Dad bought me a Schwinn right out of the hardware store's front window when I was in fifth grade and that was my prized possession, the first new thing I'd ever had in my life.) We didn't have a lot of money, but I never thought about it. Still, a quarter was a precious commodity.

The Jarman family, however, was clearly better off; they had a place in Wisconsin. They opened their doors to me and I went up to Wisconsin a lot with them. Even though we're the same age—and were born in the same town of Aurora—Tom is someone I've always looked up to and considered a mentor. As kids, we spent a lot of time together. Both of us were asking questions that all teenagers raise: What's it all about, and what are you going to do with the rest of your life?

I was a pretty serious kid, and in my early teenage years I can remember feeling a great uneasiness. I was just unsettled and needed to have something happen to me. Sure enough, it did. We were in a cabin by a lake camping out overnight. Some kids might have produced a six-pack of beer or a pack of cigarettes. Jarman pulled out a Bible. Suddenly, I had a yearning to accept Christ as my savior, and I did. Almost instantly, my uneasiness disappeared. Later, I joined Tom at the Claim Street Baptist Church in Aurora, where his parents sang in the choir. This experience isn't something I discuss publicly, but it really changed my life and it has focused my life ever since.

What happy times they were. Jarman and I went to youth group Sunday afternoon and church every Sunday night. That's when they had these Baptist hymn-sings. The choruses were there, and I can still hear them belting out such majestic old favorites as "Great is Thy Faithfulness" or "The Church's One Foundation."

Sunday night was also date night for us, and after church we'd go to Oberweis Dairy, which had the best ice cream in town. Jarman and I observed the same ritual every week: We'd check to see if we had enough money to take our dates to Oberweis Dairy. Sometimes we didn't have enough for a date, but we always seemed to have enough to wind up there ourselves. I guess that shows what our priorities were.

By the time I was thirteen or fourteen, I was a big kid, still in the eighth grade, and about to be a freshman in high school. It was time for me to buy my first pair of football shoes. "Make sure they're big enough, so you can grow into them," my mother cautioned me. So I went down to the Hayden & Swasey Sporting Goods store in Aurora. Half a size is one size too big, as I was about to learn. I wobbled around in those shoes, turned my ankles in them, and had to wear three pairs of socks so I didn't get blisters from them. Mom was tight with a nickel, but being frugal had its price.

We had four acres in this little subdivision called Gastville. We lived in a Sears prefab house, really just one story. We put a dormer on it, and my brothers and I shared the room upstairs. We had chicken houses on the property, a barbecue pit in the back, and one hundred apple trees—which were the bane of our existence because we had to pick those apples up. Dad wanted me to learn about animals, so he would bring home every runt pig he could find. I joined 4-H and raised pigs as my project.

Dad bought a sow from the executive vice president of Armour & Co., who owned a farm in Naperville. The sow was a purebred Hampshire, and she farrowed nine pigs. I raised those pigs myself and took them to the 4-H fair in Sandwich, Illinois.

The judge placed my hogs in the first prize position because the pigs were younger and larger than any other hogs in the market class.

A 4-H leader from Yorkville, Illinois, jumped up. My pigs were too big, he objected; they couldn't have been born when I'd claimed they were. Therefore, they didn't deserve first place. The judge heard him out and dropped me down to fourth place. My dad was outraged. The next year I was in a different 4-H club. I learned at an early age about some kinds of political influence.

In my new 4-H club, I had Black Angus calves. The first year I had one calf–Clancy was his name–and I took him to the International Livestock Show in Chicago and sold him there. He was only about two years old at the time, but when you raise a steer, he almost becomes a member of the family. At eleven years old, saying goodbye to him was one of the hardest partings I had ever experienced.

My mentor here was Percy Rebhorn, the leader of the Trojan 4-H Club, who was just a great guy. He took me to a sale, and we bought some sheep. Soon I had about thirty head of ewes, and Percy taught me how to show them, to block them off, and get them ready to show. I became a young leader in this 4-H club and helped other kids do the same. The great thing about 4-H is that it teaches you responsibility. You know those animals can't take care of themselves. Someone has to feed them at night and again in the morning. So you got up before you went to school and you fed and watered them. Then you had to repeat that cycle at night. If you didn't do it, nobody else would. Their lives were in your hands, a fact that was impressed upon me particularly when I had bred some Southdown ewes to a Shropshire ram, and the ewe was having trouble lambing (giving birth). I called the local vet, who promptly came out and said he'd perform a cesarean. "Watch what I'm doing because you can't afford to have me come over again," he cautioned. So he did the cesarean, showed me how to do it, and said the rest I'd have to do on my own. I had no idea then how much I would need to remember the details of that experience.

Because I wasn't involved in sports in junior high, my mother urged me to concentrate on the books. My life took on a routine: come home, study, do chores. (And at six o'clock the next morning, there would be additional chores). But Oswego High School, which I entered with the class of 1960, was a whole new experience, for this was about the time that I met and got to know Ken Pickerill, the athletic director at OHS—who was also the coach for the football, baseball, and wrestling teams. He also taught biology, human anatomy, and physical education.

Here's a man who made a huge difference, not only in my life but also in the lives of many young men in northern Illinois. Imagine having a football stadium named after you—and living long enough to accept a large crowd's thunderous applause for everything you had done. That's what happens to legends, and Ken has always been a living legend for me. Tom Jarman agrees with me that he was probably the single most influential person in our lives. We learned about inspiration and discipline and saw those lessons fleshed out in our coach. Pickerill wasn't a deeply religious man, but he lived by his ideals. He was very disciplined, and he really cared about his players' lives.

Initially, Jarman and I didn't do much to merit his attention. In the fall of 1956, our first year at OHS, one of Pickerill's assistant coaches, Jim Aird, picked the two of us—Jarman at quarterback and me at tackle—to co-captain the freshman-sophomore team. In the first football game we had ever played, he told us what to do: "If there's a penalty, look over to the sidelines," he said. "If I take my cap off, refuse the penalty. If I put my cap on, take the penalty."

Every time we looked over to the sidelines, Aird's hat was on the ground. We never knew whether or not to take the penalty. We lost the first game.

It got better after that.

No matter what sport he coached, Pickerill operated the same way. Both he and his wife, Jackie, always tried to see the best in everybody. He was a quiet guy who didn't yell at his kids a lot. There was none of this shouting from the sidelines for him. But he had high expectations; he demanded and received total loyalty. He was smart, a good teacher, and believed in discipline. He was a fierce competitor, but there was one principle he never violated. He'd push, push, push, but he would never invade an athlete's dignity. His boys loved him for that, and it taught me a lesson I've tried to remember ever since: There's never sufficient reason to try to strip away another person's dignity.

With him as our coach, the Oswego Panthers football and wrestling teams were undefeated in our junior and senior years, and we were the smallest high school in the state to field a wrestling team. Out of that bunch of country farm kids, this guy created believers who learned how to win.

As I began to wrestle under Coach Pickerill, I found that it takes a lot of practice, but practice has its rewards. The more you do it, the better you become. Jarman and I would go at it all the time. He was a tough kid; he weighed 157 pounds, while I was a heavyweight. One day during Christmas vacation in December 1958, my junior year at OHS, I was working out with this older guy who had graduated the year before and was home on break. We were rolling around on the mat. I was riding him, and he rolled me. My right shoulder hit the mat hard, and I blacked out. The next thing I knew, my clavicle was bent way out of shape, and it really hurt.

I remember sitting at home on my seventeenth birthday, January 2, 1959, watching the bowl games on television. I'd had a very good junior year playing football, and the wrestling season was just beginning. My right shoulder was killing me; the clavicle couldn't heal, we discovered, because the tendons had snapped, and I had to wait another month before I could have surgery. They inserted a pin to hold the shoulder down and sewed the tendons back together. The doctor said I'd probably never be able to wrestle or play football or do anything else again, and I was thinking, "There's the rest of my life–gone." Finally, they took the pin out, and the doctor said, "Maybe you can get a special kind of shoulder pad."

I was supposed to be co-captain of the football team senior year, so I went to the coach, who said he could find some professional shoulder pads that I could wear so all the pressure would be on my chest and not on my shoulders. The big pads worked, but toward the end of the season, my shoulder started acting up again. The doctor had used the wrong kind of suture, the kind that didn't disintegrate over time, so I developed an infection. In no time at all, that shoulder became septic. It grew bigger and angrier and it really hurt.

Jarman and I didn't know what to do. We thought if I went to the doctor that he would say I couldn't play football or wrestle anymore, and that I would have to have surgery again. Well, I'd already had surgery and just look at me. With the supreme confidence that most kids can muster when they're seventeen, we decided to do it on our own. Jarman had worked for a vet and knew something about surgery, while I had done cesareans on my ewes. We heated up a razor blade and found some hydrogen peroxide to apply. We had no anesthetic. I told Tom that I had a high threshold for pain, so he just cut and opened up the infected shoulder.

There must have been quarts of that foul stuff that poured out of my right shoulder. It was gory, and I remember using towels to sop it up. The "operation" succeeded; I played football with a patch over my shoulder, and after every practice and game, I'd remove the patch. All that stuff would come oozing out, and I'd have to clean it up again. Finally, after football and wrestling seasons were over, I had surgery again. Doctors had to scrape the infection out and hope it would heal. I learned from the experience that when bad things happen, don't complain. You play the cards you're dealt and remember there is a way to win.

Years later, as a coach, I didn't have a lot of sympathy for someone who complained that his finger or foot hurt. I coached with an older guy named Gordon Campbell—he was forty while I was twenty-two, so I called him "Gramps." Every time a player would come up with a gripe, Campbell would say, "Spit on it and rub it," and send the player away. Because of my shoulder experience, I understood and agreed.

In mid-August of my senior year, one of our assistant football coaches, John Bednarcik, left to take a job as a grade school principal. The district superintendent wouldn't let him keep coaching on the side and wouldn't allow Pickerill to hire a replacement. So when his remaining assistant coach, Jim Aird, had to work with the freshmen and sophomores, Pickerill asked me to coach the line. Already, I was playing both offensive and defensive tackle, what they used to call a sixty-minute man, and I felt honored by the request to coach.

Our Oswego Panthers won eight games and tied one that fall of 1959. We were undefeated conference champions, and I was named first string tackle on the all-state team. I wasn't our most skilled athlete—not by any stretch of the imagination. I was a lineman with a lineman's speed. But I carried my load because I worked hard and took a lot of responsibility on defense. I was the guy who pulled everybody into the huddles and said, "Okay, here's what we have to do." And they listened to me.

I want to make one thing clear. Sports stories notwithstanding, we *did* go to class at OHS, and we had some fine teachers there. Mrs. Thompson and Miss Obidizinski were unrelenting in English. Terry Workman was a wonderful history and business law professor. (Years later, he would claim that Jarman and I "used to try to get me off the subject... [and] bring up discussions that had nothing to do" with the lessons. We plead guilty as charged.)

∾

Normally, at OHS, we had wrestling practice on the stage of the gym, but they were remodeling that part of the school my senior year. So I got to drive our feed truck to school every morning because we didn't know from one day to the next where we were going to practice. We had to roll up these ancient horsehair mats, load them onto the truck, find out where we were going to wrestle, drive over there and unload the mats, tie them together, stretch the tarp over them, have a two-hour practice, reload the truck, and then haul them back to the high school. Without our feed truck, we wouldn't have been able to do that. I'm not sure kids would do that today, but we were a bunch of farm kids used to hard work.

When wrestling season began, I was tagged to be our heavyweight. I only weighed 190-odd pounds, and I'd be coming up against opponents who outweighed me by forty or fifty pounds. I was the biggest guy on our squad, so I wrestled last. In matches where we were far ahead, the winner of the heavyweight competition didn't matter that much. But in most of our meets, where the outcome was on the line until the very end, the result of my match made the difference between victory and defeat. I knew that to succeed, I'd have to remain focused and never, ever give up. Of our twelve dual meets that year, at least six came down to the final match, and I'm proud that I won them all.

I wasn't terribly agile on my feet, but once I was down on the mat I could think through what my opponent was likely to do and develop a plan to counter it. Sometimes that was harder than it appeared. I remember we came up against DeKalb, which placed second in the state that year. One of our guys got pinned—a big six points for them right there—and soon we were behind by one point. I came up against their heavyweight, who was pretty good, but I was ahead of the guy on points. He started using an illegal move, but the referee wouldn't call it—some refs were notorious "homers" in those days. Pickerill stood up to object, "You gotta watch that guy."

The ref just glared at him. "Sit down," he barked.

Pickerill threw his keys on the floor, and the keychain broke. Keys flew every which way, and he was *so* upset. He turned and was gone.

I pinned my opponent, and we won the match. Everybody was celebrating until we went down to the locker room. There was Pickerill flat on his back, passed out cold. All twelve of us on the OHS team were scared to death. The press was clamoring to come inside. Parents were trying to push in the door. I held everyone out until the doctor arrived. Eventually, Pickerill came to and rode back with us on the school bus. Only then did I begin to appreciate how much pressure he was under that year. He was teaching a full load of courses, coaching three demanding sports, serving as athletic director, working on his master's degree, and building a house at the same time. In small schools like Oswego, they did everything on a shoestring back then; sometimes that string got pretty thin.

One reason Pickerill was so successful was his insistence on competing against the biggest and best schools in the state. He felt our wrestlers would never improve if we only came up against people we could beat easily. He wanted to challenge us, force us to grapple with the toughest opponents he could find. Joliet, with four thousand kids, was one of the largest schools in Illinois. Pekin, in Senator Everett Dirksen's hometown, was big, too. Then there was Morton of Cicero, our only tie that year. They had three thousand students to our three hundred; they had almost as many teachers as we had students. No wonder we felt proud to be coming up against them. Among the teams we beat were some of national caliber: Oak Lawn, St. Charles, Carl Sandburg, Lockport, and Naperville were all very tough.

What was so thrilling about our success that year was that it was a team effort. Jarman, who wrestled at 157 pounds for us, later became a National Collegiate Athletic Association (NCAA)

champion and a very successful college coach and athletic director. Neil McCauley ranked third in the nationals when he was in
college, and Bobby Plaskas, who graduated from Northwestern,
was a Big Ten champ.

Of the twelve wrestlers on our varsity squad, seven later
became coaches, and three wound up as athletic directors. And
our student body of three hundred kids also included Rita Gar-
man, a future state supreme court justice; John Wheeler, a Viet-
nam War hero; and John Kellogg, the president of the National
Pork Producers Association. Not too bad for a bunch of kids from
the cornfields, I'd say.

∾

Our family feed business was on its last legs now, and even Dad
was losing interest in it. Once the stockyards left, the livestock
feeders just disappeared. Nobody was feeding cattle or hogs anymore because their markets were gone, and we just didn't have
a business anymore. To be sure, my mother and I were still running the store. By the time I was ready to graduate from high
school, she sold the truck, and we were out of it. That's how
small business is from time to time—you adjust. As a family, we
had to find something else to do.

Dad was about forty-three then. He had a wife and three kids
to support, and he basically had to start life all over again. His
brother had started a restaurant called the Harmony House which
was next to our old feed store. Dad got involved in it, too, and
soon he was managing the place.

He wasn't home nights. I never saw him from one weekend to
the next because in that business you go to work at three o'clock

in the afternoon, and you get home at eleven or twelve o'clock at night. Then you work all weekend long. People asked me if I was going to go into the restaurant business. "No," I replied. "In that business, you're never home."

The Harmony House was a family restaurant, and chicken was its specialty. (I couldn't order, eat, or even look at fried chicken for twenty years afterward.) Dad and his waitresses served more and more chicken, and more and more customers came to enjoy their meals. Soon one restaurant turned into three restaurants. After he left the Harmony House, my dad started the Will-O-Way Manor in Naperville. Later he opened the Clock Tower in Plainfield, which was an upscale establishment with linen tablecloths. My uncle had the White Fence Farm in Lemont. Even in the middle of this success, Dad wasn't willing to rest on his laurels. To make sure his income stream continued, he also managed the food operation for St. Joseph's Hospital in Joliet.

The restaurant business offered me the opportunity to work my way through college. Some of my jobs were good; others were not so good. At the Harmony House, my first job was to park cars. I parked cars on Saturdays and Sundays. Five or six dollars in tips was big money. At Will-O-Way Manor, my first inside job was dishwashing. That was horrendous—it was one of the worst jobs I've ever had. The dirty dishes just kept coming, and you thought you'd never catch up. You'd be elbow-deep in garbage trying to wash and sort stuff out for about one dollar an hour. That gave me lots of incentive to do something else.

Will-O-Way Manor had a boiler chef for lobsters, steaks, and chops, but I got to be a fry cook maybe one night a week. I'd fry trout, wall-eyed pike, and chicken; you had to bring the french fries and other orders up at the same time, so you worked hard. On Sundays you'd start at ten o'clock in the morning to open up at noon, and you'd go until nine or ten at night.

At our next restaurant in Plainfield, the Clock Tower, I cooked everything Saturday and Sunday and a couple of nights a week while I was in college.

At these restaurants, I learned some lessons that I'll never forget. I know what it is like to get up early in the morning and start the line going and be there at ten or eleven o'clock at night making sure that everything is swept out before you lock the door—because if you don't do it, no one else is going to do it for you the next day. Even when our restaurant business was prospering, I remember my mother making sure the salad dressings were right and the condiments were there, making sure that whoever closed the kitchen—sometimes me—did it the right way. If it didn't get done correctly, I heard about it the next day.

In the summer of 1960, I wound up in the first job that ever provided a paycheck. The people Dad was working with at Will-O-Way Manor owned the Will-O-Way Dairy, so I started a milk route and earned twenty-five dollars a day. I had to get up at 3:30 AM in order to start loading trucks with milk in the truck yard by 4:30 AM. I had to drive fifteen miles to get there. I was afraid to ask any girl out for a date because I knew that if I stayed out past 9:00 PM, I'd never be able to get up in the morning.

To get up at 3:30 in the morning, I had to go to bed at 8:30 the night before. I'd spend the first two and a half hours asleep, then wake up in the middle of the night to see what time it was. It was always 11:00 or 12:00 or even 1:00, and by the time 3:30 rolled around, I was dead to the world. Mom would get me up, make some breakfast, and make sure I got out of the house. I remember driving over to Naperville at four o'clock in the morning trying to keep the car on the road. Before, I'd picked up three dollars here or five dollars there, enough to put gas in the car. Now I was earning a paycheck, and that felt pretty good.

∾

At that time, to be honest, I hadn't thought about my future very much. With my experience in 4-H and the farm service business, my initial plan was to go to the University of Illinois and become a veterinarian. Mom thought it would be great if I continued my education because no one in her family had ever gone to college. No one in Dad's family had ever gone to college either, but he wanted me to go to a restaurant school. With all due respect, I didn't want to do that. I wanted to play college football. So I applied to North Central and Wheaton and was accepted at both schools.

Because North Central was in Naperville, where Dad's Will-O-Way Manor restaurant was, he wanted me to go there. His partner in the restaurant was a North Central graduate, he said. So I agreed to go there and started paying my way by working at the restaurant and delivering milk. In my freshman year, I was president of the dorm.

North Central was a nice school, and the football team did well that fall; but our coach was a raucous guy. He was recruiting talent from the military—we had an almost semi-pro situation there. And on top of that, we had a team physician who was doing things that I thought were questionable. I decided that was not where I wanted to play ball. It was not my style.

My first semester there, I was running the milk route and then going to class. I was just eighteen. I had a hard time staying awake in my afternoon classes, and if I'd stayed there any longer, I probably would have flunked out. Finally, I decided that if I was serious about college—and I was—I needed to get out of Naperville.

At the semester break in January in the middle of my freshman year—and over Dad's protests—I transferred to Wheaton College in Wheaton, Illinois. My roommate at North Central, Jim Parmelee from Hopkins, Michigan, was transferring to Wheaton, too, and my old buddy Tom Jarman was already there. Wheaton was a pretty strict and pretty conservative Christian school—a good place for me. At Wheaton, you had to be pretty serious about your faith and your grades or you didn't belong.

In those days Wheaton students took about thirty hours of religious instruction—Old Testament, New Testament, theology, canons, etc. Those courses gave me a foundation, and my education was centered around the Christian values they stressed there. And I was tested both in and out of class.

As we approached the Memorial Day holiday of my freshmen year, Jarman and I realized that we'd been chained to our desks too long studying for final exams. We needed to blow off some steam, so we headed out to Oswego "to study." We found a couple sets of boxing gloves in an old barn. We started messing around and soon we really got into it.

Jarman was fast on his feet, and he had technique. He was moving around, jabbing at me repeatedly, and I didn't appreciate that at all. I pursued him more aggressively, throwing punches and landing a few, when suddenly he stepped underneath one of my roundhouse swings. I felt this solid THWACK on the bridge of my nose. "What was that?" I asked as my nose started to bleed.

My nose was pointing west while I was facing south, Jarman pointed out. That, he said, was "not good."

Jarman's dad had forbidden him to box, and my parents weren't keen on the rough stuff either. So we decided to keep what had happened a secret from everyone. We thought we were so slick. We stopped the bleeding, put the gloves away, and scraped together enough cash—we emptied our pockets and the glove compartment of my old Ford—until we had enough to pay for a visit to the doctor. We told him that we didn't want anyone to know and that we'd pay his bill up front. He smiled and said he'd send us the bill. He straightened my nose and packed it with all this gauze. It was really uncomfortable. For the next four or five days, we laid low while we took our exams. We thought we'd gotten away without anyone finding out. Then one of the secretaries in the medical office sent the bill to my home.

Mom knew I didn't box, so she stopped by Jarman's home. "I know Denny didn't break his nose," she began. "Did Tom break his nose?"

"No," Jarman's dad replied, "but something's going on here."

The conversation continued at the Hastert kitchen table when Jarman was visiting me. "Boys, I just got a medical bill from the clinic," Mom said, ever the cross-examiner. "Someone broke their nose. Do either of you know anything about that?"

There was no getting away from her. I blurted out the truth. I was never a very good liar. Maybe I wasn't smart enough. I could never get away with it, so I made up my mind as a kid to tell the truth and pay the consequences. And that's what we did.

I wasn't a part of the social culture at Wheaton—everyone else
stayed on campus and participated in college activities on weekends. I worked at Dad's restaurant, the Clock Tower, in Plainfield
one or two nights a week and every weekend—sweeping the floor
and cooking on both fryers. My next summer job was running a
Pepsi-Cola route. Picking up the empty bottles was a dirty job, but
it paid twenty-five dollars a day. I needed that for tuition and living expenses.

I was a business major because I thought I would become a
businessman after college. We were all in Reserve Officer Training Corps (ROTC) our first two years. The agreement was that if
you passed, you could join Advanced ROTC, and the military
would pay tuition the final two years. When I took the final physical exam for Advanced ROTC, the Army doctor said I had a cal-
cium deposit on my right shoulder and couldn't carry a rifle.
"What do you mean?" I asked. "I'm playing football; I'm
wrestling." And he said, "You flunked the physical."

He was right. I could do a lot of things, but I couldn't pass that
physical.

When I washed out of ROTC, I thought I'd give five years to
coaching because some of the people I admired most—my old
coach at Wheaton, George Olson, and Ken Pickerill, for example—
had been coaches, and I really enjoyed it. But if you were going to
coach, you also had to teach and that meant earning an advanced
degree. At Wheaton, Dr. Rung taught me political science and had
gotten me interested in both politics and teaching. I thought I
could teach politics. So I signed up for some education courses at
Northern Illinois University in DeKalb about sixty miles west of
Chicago. To complete this dash around the triangle, I was coaching the freshman football team at Wheaton and working at Dad's

restaurant in Plainfield. I was still living at home, getting along on a shoestring, and I needed money. "Why don't you get a real job?" Dad kept asking me.

The truth was that I still didn't know what I wanted to do. I just knew I had to get enough hours for my teaching certificate.

Still, my course was set. I drove over to Oswego High School, my alma mater, but they didn't have any job openings. Next I headed to Yorkville High School a few miles away, wearing an old flannel shirt with a pair of blue jeans. When Charles Ellis, the guidance counselor, asked if he could help, I said I was looking for a job application form.

"We have some openings," he said. "Let me have you talk to the superintendent."

I said I wasn't dressed for an interview.

"Come on in," Charles insisted. "Just talk to him."

I was a live body, and they needed one. By the time I left that day, I had a teaching job. I had also signed up to be head wrestling coach and assistant football coach. I didn't have all my required hours yet, so I didn't have my teaching certificate. But back in 1965 you could still teach if you were on your way to getting that degree.

Before I stepped into a Yorkville classroom that fall, I made two trips that left lasting impressions on me. The first, in June 1964, was to New Jersey for Jarman's wedding to Jan Lisk, a girl he met at Wheaton who had been his sweetheart for years. On my way home, I stopped in Bethesda, Maryland, to see my aunt Doral Swan and to spend a day walking around the Capitol. Back then, if you wore a suit, you could go anywhere. In the Senate chamber gallery, I listened to a debate between Arizona Republican Barry Goldwater and Montana Democrat Mike Mansfield. They were discussing one of our missile programs. There were only five or

six senators there, so it wasn't a full-dress debate. Yet to be able to
sit in the gallery and watch that was inspiring to me. Anyone could
go to the U.S. Capitol, walk through the vast corridors, and rub
shoulders with those guys.

Next I flew to Japan. The way that trip fell into my lap amazes
me to this day. Many executives who worked in Chicago lived in
suburbs like Plainfield, and the director of Chicago's Duncan
YMCA used to bring his wife to our restaurant. He had an opportunity to work with the International YMCA, he told me one
night. "How would you like to go on a trip to Japan?"

I was in my first year of grad school at the time, and I had
never been out of the country before. "Yeah," I replied.

Tony Podesta, president of the Young Democrats at the University of Illinois (Chicago Circle), was a member of our group.
We didn't see eye-to-eye politically, but the trip was interesting.
During my nearly three months there, I really fell in love with
Japanese culture. We were part of a People to People program; our
group consisted of eighteen Americans and eighteen Japanese,
and we got to know each other well as we built a small amphithe-
ater on the side of a mountain way out in the boondocks in the
Kansai area. (Today, I return to Japan, and those kids aren't kids
anymore; they're dentists, diplomats, and architects—and we're still
good friends.)

The YMCA back then was big on listening to people say what
their problems were and then walking through those problems
with them step by step. That just exasperated me. I had always
thought that if a problem existed, you just went out and solved it,
boom, like that, you know? My approach, they told me in what
we called "T-sessions," wasn't sensitive. The YMCA believed in

sensitivity training; if there were a disagreement in the group, we'd sit for hours until we hashed the thing out. It was a skill I learned in later years to be time-consuming but invaluable.

We found there was also a basic difference in our cultures. Americans are rugged individualists, an *I* people—I'm going to do this, I'm going to do that. The Japanese are a *We* culture—everything is, "We're going to do this." The conflict is huge.

But from that experience, I learned that the Japanese were on to something. You *can* sit down with people who have divergent views and come out with something that everyone will agree on. And I learned as well that we do resolve problems by listening to what people's concerns are. If people talk about their problems and someone else is actually listening, they can communicate and you can solve the problem. But you don't enter the conversation with preconceived ideas. That's what has worked for me.

Because I didn't obtain my master's degree at NIU until 1967, I taught my first two years at Yorkville High School with a provisional teaching certificate. Other teachers were in the same boat, and no one made a fuss. The first year I was there, I lived at home and commuted. The next year I moved into a house in town.

In 1967, my third year at school, I moved into a farmhouse in the country with three other teachers—Bob Evans, Dave Manning, and Frank Hammelman. I was the cook, and Evans, who had played football at Iowa State and was then (as he is today) coaching the Yorkville Foxes, cleaned up after most meals. By that time I'd developed a real taste for Asian food, and I kept urging him to try it as a change of pace. But Evans was a meat and potatoes man.

Most of our time was consumed with teaching and coaching. As bachelors, we weren't as bad as Oscar and Felix from *The Odd*

Couple. We just enjoyed each other's company. From time to time, we also had fun with practical jokes. There was a little tavern out in the country, about five miles south and west of us, and I remember one time when Dave Manning volunteered to make the beer run. As soon as he drove away, I called Torry Balou, a teacher friend, and asked her to phone the tavern. Once she got the bartender, I asked her to say, "My husband's coming to buy beer. Please don't serve him. Don't let him buy any beer because he's using the money we need to feed the kids."

Manning walked into that tavern, and the bartender fixed him with a frosty glare. "Your wife just called," he said, and refused to sell him the six-pack and then told him why. "You take that money and go home and feed your kids," he said.

"But I'm not married," Manning insisted. "This just isn't true." None of that did him any good. The bartender told him to go. Manning's face turned bright red, and by the time he reached home, he was really smoked. He blamed Evans and me—I caught the brunt of it—and we did our best to suppress a real belly laugh.

In most subjects I taught, I tried not to teach by the book. I wanted my courses to be unique, and I hope they were. In American history, for example, I started by having the kids draw a map of the U.S. from memory that included all the states and their capitals. That was so they could better understand relationships and remember, say, that Alabama was down south, while Idaho was up north. I asked the kids to read books like *The Jungle*, by Upton Sinclair, and John Steinbeck's *Cannery Row* and *Grapes of Wrath* because I wanted them to understand the social situations that drove historical events. When we discussed world history, I tried to focus on relationships. Who was Columbus and why did he discover America? What was happening in Spain at the time? I wanted those kids to know more than just where he sailed and the names of his ships. I rarely flunked a kid, and if I did it was to give him or her a wake up call.

In economics, I asked my kids, "How do you make money?" Or "What's wealth?" I had them make a list of everything they spent, figure out what percentage of the total household expense was theirs, and then calculate on an annual basis what their consumption was. Over a period of six weeks, I drew up a series of cards that created a business situation. We formed companies—five kids to a group—and put them in business. Each of these groups then chose a president whose grade depended on how well the company performed.

This wasn't just academic. This was a real-life exercise. We made plastic pipes and everyone competed against each other. I'd give them a business prognosis every week that covered three months and then they had to react with a strategy of their own. They could issue stock or raise capital by borrowing on a combination. They had the option of investing in trucks or machinery, or they could buy finished goods from other companies. Another possibility was selling the stock to buy bonds. If they felt aggressive, they could become raiders and buy out other companies. Some kids did very well. Others didn't have the slightest idea what it took to succeed, but most of them eventually got it.

Sociology was fun, too. I didn't teach it out of the book because academic sociology can lead you into social theory and statistical theories that sixteen-year-old kids really don't relate to. What I taught was values and value formation—not my personal values but what core values were and why they were important.

That included how you deal with your problems and with other people—conflict resolution, some might call it today.

∾

We'd sit in a semi-circle—as I'd done in Japan—and talk. I'd say, "Here's a problem. Why do you think this problem exists and how can you solve it?" Then we'd ask about how kids could get along with their parents and how they could resolve problems they had with teachers; about where values come from and how they're relevant. I'd spend hours and hours listening to the kids talk and trying to pull their thoughts together. Every now and then, I'd sense that light bulbs were starting to flick on in their minds and that made spending all that time worthwhile.

What I loved about teaching was that it gave me a chance to travel; I've always had wanderlust. (Tom Jarman likes to say that my mistress is an atlas.) Thanks to the International YMCA, I visited both Venezuela and Colombia to work on projects there in 1966. In 1967, I returned to Japan. The next year I traveled to Europe and then, in 1970, I went with a National Education Association tour group to the Soviet Union. I had to pay about four hundred dollars, but that took care of the airfare and the six weeks I spent there. One group leader with whom I got along especially well was Stewart Frazier of George Peabody College (part of Vanderbilt University in Nashville, Tennessee). "Listen," he suggested at the end of our Russian trip, "I have some fellowships coming from the National Defense Education Act. Why don't you come to Nashville and work on your doctorate?"

Talk about an opportunity falling in my lap. This was my big chance to earn a Ph.D. And once I had my doctorate, who knew what opportunities would open up? I flew to Nashville to start the interview process. Then I had second thoughts. "If I do this, I won't be coaching anymore," I said. The next obvious question was: What do you do if your doctorate is in international education? Answer: You become a professor of international education. At that moment, my inner compass said, "I don't want to do that for the rest of my life."

Soon after I had decided to stay where I was, Jean Kahl came into—and became—my life. A slim, auburn-haired woman with big blue eyes, she had grown up in a close, loving farm family in Shipman, Illinois. When she was in eighth grade, her school principal had said to her, "If you want to go on in school, you can either be a nurse or a teacher." Those were the options, and Jean knew she didn't want to be a nurse. After graduating from Southern Illinois University in Carbondale, she taught at a junior high in the small town of Mascoutah, Illinois, and then went on to earn her master's degree at the University of Colorado in Boulder.

And now at the midpoint of 1970, she was stepping into a real hornet's nest. The class of senior girls at Yorkville High had almost literally run Jean's predecessor out of school. Everyone wondered if calm, unflappable Jean could meet the challenges that would be thrown at her and show those tough girls who was really in charge. She did it without raising her voice or even breaking her stride. She just exercised quiet discipline, made it through that year, and then—because she wanted to teach in a small community—decided to stay.

We noticed each other right away, but at first nothing clicked. I was enjoying life as a bachelor and driving around in a Porsche, whose upkeep pretty much devoured a young teacher's extra cash.

The next summer, a year and a half after we first met, she spent six weeks in Europe, and I found myself feeling surprisingly alone.

"You know, I really miss Jean," I told Jarman on the phone. "I think Jean is just about perfect for me."

I could hear Jarman's laugh even before his reply: "Dennis, no kidding. Are you just realizing that? You're the last person on the planet to know it."

"Well, I have known it," I said defensively. "We're just... you know." (I was really talking myself into working up the courage to pop the question.) Then I said, "So, do you want to be in a wedding or not?"

"Well, if it happens," Jarman replied.

"Well, I think it's going to," I said.

As soon as Jean returned, we started doing things together—not expensive things because we didn't have much money then. But we went to the movies, attended sports events, and talked and talked. And the more we were together, the more obvious it seemed to me that we complemented each other perfectly.

Over Christmas vacation in 1972, in the kitchen of the little home she had rented on River Road in Yorkville, I popped the question to her. Actually, instead of going down on bended knee to ask, "Will you marry me?" I used an indirect, elliptical approach. "Well, people think we ought to get married," I said. Men can be such verbal stumblebums when it comes to matters of the heart. Fortunately for me, Jean sensed how I really felt and what I was trying to say. She said she'd need some time to think about it. She didn't need that much time and we were married in her hometown of Shipman, Illinois, on April 21, 1973. After a honeymoon on the beach near Sarasota, Florida, we moved into our first home, a one-bedroom cottage in Yorkville that's not there anymore. Jean had no idea—nor did I—of what lay ahead for us. As she put it years later, "He enjoyed coaching so much that I thought he was going to teach and coach for the rest of his life. That was fine with me."

CHAPTER TWO

CHAIRS IN THE HALL

He that wrestles with us strengthens our nerves
and sharpens our skill. Our antagonist is our helper.
—EDMUND BURKE, 1790

IN 1966, MY SECOND YEAR AT YORKVILLE HIGH SCHOOL, THEY offered me the job of head football coach. I was just twenty-four. The responsibility of a head football coaching job was enormous. I never had enough time to do everything. There were so many things to teach, so little time to teach them, and every week marked a different campaign.

The Yorkville Foxes were a good team and our fans were great—but they had a way of reminding you that your job was always in jeopardy. I remember once during a homecoming game, our opponent scored a go-ahead touchdown, and the two score-keepers up in the press box moved a hangman's noose into position right over my head. The not-so-subtle message: one mistake, one losing season, and you can be gone.

I held that job for four years. To be honest, I was a mediocre performer, and our record was even. Then the school board changed the rules so that a teacher could only be head coach of one sport. I had no trouble at all deciding that coaching wrestling was what I could do best.

Wrestling is a tough sport that demands individual responsibility. Nobody else is going to take the blame for anything you do out there, but the harder you work at it, the better you become.

The school really hadn't had a program in the sport before I arrived, so that gave me a free hand. The Yorkville Foxes' colors were red and white; I wanted to accent them, so I added black. Our uniforms consisted of red and white tops with the big Y in front and black tights. They looked pretty good. Then I introduced wrestlers' robes—white with a red trim and a black belt. Some of the sport's powerhouses at that time—Iowa State and the Colorado School of Mines—had their wrestlers wear robes, and that seemed to boost their confidence. Put kids in a robe, I thought, and it'll make them feel special. They'll have something no one else has, and, because they perform so well, that robe will become a symbol of excellence. We were the first high school team in Illinois to have robes. Within a year, many schools on our schedule had them.

The sport of wrestling may have its roots in ancient Mesopotamia (now Iraq) and be five thousand years old, but the basic challenge facing every grappler has remained the same: Take the other guy down, roll him over on his back until his shoulders touch the mat, and then wait for the referee to slap the mat for a "pin." It is, of course, much easier said than done.

If you had a good takedown, you could ride a guy while you worked for the pin. And if you could jam his elbows and break him down or push him off his base, you might set him up for that pin. If you were on the bottom, you'd try to escape. A short sit out might do: You could push back into him hard, then pivot right or left, stand up, and turn in. A takedown was two points; so was a reversal. An escape was one point; a near-fall was three; and a pin was six team points.

Because takedowns are so important, everyone focused on them. We worked on knee snatches and double-leg takedowns. When you're in the upright position circling each other on the mat, the quickest link from any part of your body to your opponent is your hands to his knee. With the single leg snatch, you use both hands to grab behind the knee, bring that knee to your chest, and then how he reacts determines what you do. If he tries to turn away, you attack and double-leg him. (That means tackle both legs.) If he attempts to kick that knee out, you come up with your hips underneath, pick him up, put him in a "turk," and take him to the mat, sometimes directly to a pinning situation.

In wrestling, I knew you could do a lot of fancy stuff and still never win, so I tried to keep it simple and focused on five or six moves. If you could do a few things well, it would take you a long way toward being very good.

Because I knew our opponents were drilling the same fundamentals we were, I was always looking for something that would give us an edge. I found what I was looking for in our own backyard. First was the intensity and duration of the practice we conducted after school every day. I wanted to make those sessions—and we're talking two or two and a half hours each—as tough and as profitable as possible.

I didn't have our guys do a lot of running around the track. Instead, we conditioned on the mat, and at the end of each practice, I had them climb ropes ten or fifteen times without using their feet. I didn't want to wear them out, so I told them that if they could tell a joke that would make me laugh, I'd knock off one rope climb.

We wrestled in the "Pit," our nickname for the old gymnasium that was the site of our home matches. It was an old-style arena that held five hundred and fifty people at most. Our matches would start at six o'clock, but by five o'clock, the Pit was full of red and white. It would be so hot in there that you could hardly breathe. I rigged up an old-fashioned, high-wattage floodlight directly above the mat that framed the warriors for each match. When the competition began and the two wrestlers went after each other out there, every other light in the house went dark and the flickering shadows of those warring grapplers filled the arena along with the whooping and hollering of the Yorkville fans. It was a sight to behold, and every little brother or grade school boy in the crowd wanted to be under that light in a Yorkville uniform someday.

We had been winning too many matches by a score of 3–0 or 4–1, something like that. And that could be boring for the fans to watch. I decided to have my kids experiment with something new. Billy Martin, the legendary wrestling coach at Granby High School in Norfolk, Virginia, had developed a new system that allowed the wrestler in the bottom position to score or even pin his opponent from there. Imagine you're a wrestler and your opponent has you moving in an arc at about twenty miles per hour. You try to stop it, but you can't. That's what the Granby does. Talk about revolutionizing a sport. This put the top guy on defense, and our kids loved it. Learning, developing, and practicing the Granby 150 or even 200 times a day made us a much better team.

Once you've built a winning program, everyone wants to be on that team. Of the four hundred students who attended Yorkville at any given time, about two hundred of them were boys. At one time I had eighty-two of them out for wrestling. Not all made the squad, but we fielded a full freshman, sophomore, junior varsity, and varsity team. And then we had the "mat maids," female students who decorated wrestlers' lockers, cleaned the mats, kept a running score of all matches, and promoted team spirit. Sometimes I had more mat maids than wrestlers.

Another program attraction was the trips we took. I piled some kids into the van and drove nine hundred miles to a Granby clinic in Hampton Roads, Virginia. My kids, flatlanders all, had never seen a coast or an ocean or Navy ships before. They'd be looking out the hotel windows at the submarines and aircraft carriers below, and it was just amazing for them. I remember one young man, standing there watching the cars disappear into the Chesapeake Bay Tunnel, turning to me and asking, "Coach, what *happened* to those cars?"

The Norfolk area wasn't our only port of call. For almost a dozen years, I drove my kids to the Rocky Mountain Wrestling Camp in Gunnison, Colorado, on the Rockies' western slope. We carried ten or twelve kids in the van each time and everyone chipped in fifteen dollars for gas. We removed the seats so they could pack their sleeping bags and gear and then sit on them. The more kids you had in the van, the less trouble they'd get into. They'd tell stories, have contests to see who could hold their legs out straight the longest, or amuse themselves in other ways, and the trip itself was always interesting. For some reason, those kids knew better than to ask, "Are we there yet, coach?"

Finally, about the middle of Kansas, I would announce, "Hey, we're getting close to Colorado. First guy who sees a mountain, I'll buy him an ice cream cone." For the next five hundred miles, those kids would be transfixed as they looked for mountains. And they'd imagine they saw a mountain in every cloud on the horizon. We didn't have mountains back in Illinois.

Because history was one of the courses I taught, I wanted to have the kids visit important historical sites—Gettysburg or Yorktown—every time we came east. And I'd always take them to Washington, D.C., to the U.S. Capitol and the museums, no matter what they said they wanted to do. Once, we found ourselves eyewitnesses of history unfolding right in front of us. It was August 9, 1974, the day Richard M. Nixon resigned as president. You could drive around the White House back then, and I was doing that in the van just as Nixon was leaving in his helicopter. That night we stopped in a motel in Maryland and watched his departure from the White House lawn again on TV. As a history teacher, I knew this was important and that I'd be talking about it for years to come. At the time I didn't think the kids shared my view.

As a coach, I realized that no two kids are exactly alike. My job was to figure out what each kid could do and get him to produce. I wanted to help each kid exercise his capabilities to achieve, and I set the standard as high as I could. But, of course, you have to deal with different personalities in different ways. Some kids, you just have to get on their case. I could walk up to them and say, "Hey, this is what I expect. Go out and do it, one-two-three." Other kids, you'd kind of back off and say, "Maybe if you do this, this, and this." There's no textbook for that. Either you know it or you don't.

I felt a special bond with our wrestlers, and I think they felt one with me. In my talks with them, I stressed how important it was that they learned to do a few things well. That was better than trying to do everything halfway. "It's work and not talk that wins championships," I kept telling them. "Perseverance is the key in whatever you do."

In 1973, I had my first state champion, Gary Matlock, at 112 pounds. He would be followed by nearly a dozen more. In 1973, among six hundred schools, Yorkville ranked tenth in the state. The next year we came in second, a point and a half from first place behind Savanna. In 1975 we fell to fifth, but then we came back in 1976 and took nine (of our starting twelve) kids to the state tournament. That in itself was pretty spectacular because you had to qualify in a district and sectional meet and there was a lot of winnowing down before you got to the state tournament. Each of the nine kids scored in that tournament, and we had five in the finals.

They held the tournament at Assembly Hall, the field house for the University of Illinois at Champaign-Urbana. You could have shot a cannon down Yorkville's main street and not hit anyone at state tournament time because everyone showed up at Assembly Hall. And when our Foxes won the Class A state title, it was a great community event. We had ordinary kids who had developed into an extraordinary *team.* I had the honor of raising the team championship trophy high above their heads. That was probably the greatest experience I'd ever had in my life.

In my years as a coach, I developed half a dozen guiding principles that affect how I think, plan, react to disappointment, and feel about victory and defeat. They apply not only to sports but also to life itself:

(1) You never win the big match the night before. So never go into a contest unprepared. Focus, discipline,

patience, courage, and diligence are virtues in this respect.

(2) Never underestimate your opponent. No matter how experienced or rich or important you are, you can be beaten. The unforeseen can and will happen every time. It's how prepared and flexible you are that counts.

(3) Always under-promise and try to over-produce. (As a coach, when asked what kind of a team I was going to produce, I always said, "Oh, man, terrible year, we lost so many of our good kids." I knew what we had coming up, but I never advertised it. I'd rather say we were going to have a so-so year and wind up being conference champs than say we were going to win the title and then not do it.)

(4) Do your coaching during practice; coaching from the sidelines in front of the fans is too late.

(5) Never rely on your opponent to help you win.

(6) When you are in a position to score, you had better put points on the board. You may never be there again.

After we won the state championship (and I was named coach of the year), I received several job offers. Clinton, Illinois, is a little town with a nuclear plant. The high school asked me to become head wrestling coach and chairman of the social sciences department. There were similar expressions of interest from schools in Montrose, Colorado, and Coeur d'Alene, Idaho. Then there was an opening for head wrestling coach at the University of Illinois.

That was just for a coach; there was no teaching position associated with it, and it paid only twelve thousand a year. To be a Big Ten head coach would be an ego boost, but it would be hard to feed the family (Josh, our first son, came along in 1975; Ethan was born three years later). So I didn't do that. I turned the other offers down as well. At this point I didn't know how much longer I wanted to teach, but it occurred to me that if I ever intended to do anything political, I should stay where I was. The Yorkville area was my whole life, where I grew up and where my roots were. So I stayed.

I was serving as president of the Illinois Wrestling Coaches and Officials Association (IWCOA)—later, I would become president of the National Wrestling Coaches Congress—and Steve Combs, my predecessor as IWCOA president and then head of the U.S. Wrestling Federation, convinced me that it was important for our group to become more involved in the growth of the sport. We built that coaches association into a leadership organization. We sponsored banquets, including one for our Hall of Fame, gave out "outstanding wrestler" awards, and published a wrestling newspaper called *The Word* that came out half a dozen times a year. It ranked wrestlers by weight class and let coaches and officials know what was going on in the sport around the state.

In the late 1970s, lawmakers in Washington, D.C., were wrestling—the right word—with a piece of legislation that everyone called the National Sports Act. It would establish a national sports training area in Colorado Springs and end a lengthy dispute over money and power that had been festering between the NCAA and the Amateur Athletic Union (AAU). Specifically, it would strip power from the AAU, the governing body of amateur sports, and return it to the grass roots, the high school and college coaches who'd been shut out of the decision-making process for years and weren't getting a fair hearing. What Steve and I both wanted as part of this transformation was to have the U.S. Wrestling Federation—it's called USA Wrestling today—be the governing body for our sport. Witnesses were appearing before a Senate committee, and Steve asked me to fly to Washington, meet people, and talk about grassroots wrestling.

At that point I'd taught government, history, and economics for more than a dozen years. I'd always been in awe of the U.S. Capitol and the people who worked there. But this trip was a great opportunity for a kid from the Illinois cornfields. I found out that people in the Capitol were just the same as the folks back home. They weren't overwhelming intellects and they weren't ten feet tall; they were flesh and blood people like everyone else. I talked to them and watched them operate, and I thought I could do that myself. That thought stayed in the back of my mind.

In 1978 and 1979, when we were still discussing implementation of the National Sports Act, I took stock of myself and my job prospects. I was thirty-seven and had a family. I liked kids. I liked teaching and coaching, but did I want to do that for the rest of my life? I just couldn't say. I didn't necessarily want to be a principal or get into administration, where a lot of coaches wind up at the end of their careers. I just wanted more than what I saw facing me at the end of that road.

One day I was talking to the superintendent of the Yorkville School District. "I need a little help on this," I began. "I'm teaching full time—government, history, and economics; five or six classes a day. I've been head football coach, and I'm now head wrestling coach. I'm a department chairman, and I drive a school bus when I have to. My wife works; I work part-time in a restaurant; and we have two kids." Our combined income was about thirty thousand dollars and I told him that. "I just need a little better economic placement.... I need to get on a better income track."

I was concluding that pitch when he said, "Well, you have a master's degree, don't you?"

"Yeah, sure."

"What's it in?"

"History of philosophy of education."

He stepped back, took a closer look at me, cocked his head, and then said, "Well, that won't do you any good." Then he added, "Tell you what I'm going to do. We're going to have an opening next fall, an assistant principal's job, in the junior high school. If you go back to school this summer and pick up the supervisory certificate, six or seven hours, I'll start you out as assistant principal over in the junior high."

"Supervisory hours" didn't sound too appealing to me, but I thanked him and said I'd get back to him.

Some time later, I stopped in to see Bill Carpenter, a good friend (now deceased) who was Yorkville's principal. He was a real sports fan, and I'd go down to his office once or twice a week to chew the fat with him. There were seven or eight chairs in the hallway just outside his office, and those chairs were always full of kids in line to see the principal. Carpenter had to deal with those kids every day. On the other side of his office was the teachers' lounge. Teachers always had problems. I watched as those teachers came to Carpenter looking for him to solve their problems. I looked at those chairs in the hall and at the teachers' lounge and thought to myself, "You know, I don't want to do that for the next twenty

years of my life. I don't want chairs in my hall." That realization
helped lead me toward a career in the state legislature.

∾

Late one afternoon in October 1979, I came home from school,
picked up the *Aurora Beacon News* and read that Bill Kempiners,
our state representative, was resigning his seat in the Illinois General Assembly. So there would be a vacancy in Springfield soon. I
asked myself, could I do that?

While I had thought about it, I never dreamed that I could actually get into politics. First, because I thought you had to have so
much money—funds I knew I'd never be able to raise on my own.
Also because I'd have to give up a teaching career that meant a lot
to me. But there it was, a vacant seat, an opportunity that might not
come again. When Barry Goldwater had decided to enter politics,
he had said, according to columnist George F. Will, "It ain't for life
and it might be fun." I wondered if that could be true for me.

Suzanne Deuchler, a county board member from Aurora, said
she was going to run for Kempiners's seat. She was well known in
that district, and she had a large organization with a lot of active
women behind her. There was talk that Don Gould from Joliet
might run, plus George Wendt from Batavia. Jean and I talked
about it; time was running short. It was almost mid-November,
and I'd have to have at least three hundred signatures on petitions
delivered by the end of December's second week to qualify for the
primary coming up in March. I sent the petitions out and didn't
know enough to include a stamped, self-addressed envelope.

The Kendall County Republican chairman, Dallas Ingemunson, was state attorney then, so I thought I ought to go to him to
talk about my plans. "I'm not sure I can back you," he told me. "I

don't know anything about you. But I encourage everyone, so go ahead and run." That first part wasn't true. He had lived in the community since 1965, and he did know me through wrestling. What he was trying to tell me, I thought, was that he had already cut a deal.

I'd taught government and history, and I knew economics; yet people were perplexed when I said I wanted to run. I got my three hundred or so petitions signed, and people asked, "What are you doing?" And my kids and parents said, "You can't leave us."

The budget for that first race was about $3,500, and we didn't get off to an auspicious start. I remember our first fund-raiser at the Toll Gate Inn in North Aurora. Of the sixteen people who attended, eight were relatives. As a candidate, I wasn't any great shakes. Every time I made a speech, I made a gaffe. But I learned.

Soon some local women came to my support. One, from Yorkville, was Phyl Oldenberg; I had taught her kids at school. Phyl was a political operative. She had a friend, Bev Wright, who had run Tom Corcoran's campaign. Tom was our Congressman. Phyl sent me over to talk to Bev, who gave me some good advice. Late one night we were sitting and talking and, on impulse, she called Scott Palmer, the registrar and director of public information at Aurora University, who was then twenty-nine years old and a talented artist. "Oh, Scott," she said, when he picked up the phone. "I'm glad I caught you at home."

Scott was used to this. "Bev, at one or two o'clock in the morning, where else would I be?"

"Come on over here," she replied. "I have a job for you."

Amazingly, Scott did, and Bev told him to design a yard sign for me.

Until reapportionment came along in 1982, each legislative district in the state had three representatives, with two belonging to the majority party and one to the minority. The thinking behind that was that each minority—Republicans in Chicago, Democrats in the suburbs or downstate—deserved a voice in their part of the state. Both political parties in Illinois had functioned that way since the end of the Civil War. The important thing, everyone agreed, was that minority representation be preserved.

Realistically, what this meant was that in a county like Kendall, which is one of the smallest in the state, a Republican would need seven or eight thousand votes to win while a Democrat could prevail with four hundred votes. In Chicago, the reverse would be true: a Republican could win with two hundred votes. A Democrat would need many times that number to emerge victorious.

For the past several years, two Republicans, Kempiners and the "old bull," eighty-two-year-old Alan Schoeberlein, had, along with Democrat Laz (Lazarus) Murphy, represented our 39th legislative district (which included parts of Kane, Kendall, Will, and DuPage counties). Now with Kempiners gone, Suzanne Deuchler and I were battling for his seat. On Primary Day in March 1980, I fell about five hundred votes short and came in third behind Deuchler and Schoeberlein. I was odd man out in a three-person district; the Democrat won with a small number of votes.

"Denny, you did one helluva job for a guy who was just starting out," Scott Palmer told me the next day. "You were in a difficult situation against some pretty talented, capable, and well-known people, and you kept your powder dry. There will be other opportunities."

"Here I go," I thought, "it's back to teaching now." But the political bug had bitten me for sure.

CHAPTER THREE

MOVERS AND SHAKERS

The only reward of virtue is virtue;
the only way to have a friend is to be one.
—RALPH WALDO EMERSON

BY MID-AUGUST, I WAS BACK HOME, AND IT WAS CLEAR THAT OLD Al Schoeberlein was not feeling well. We had our annual Kendall County pig roast the week before Labor Day, and Kempiners told me, "You ought to be ready. I don't know what's going to happen to Schoeberlein." Five days later, he suffered a stroke and was incapacitated.

His managers decided that he should give up his nomination.

The four county chairmen came together to pick Schoeberlein's successor at a golf outing in DuPage County a few weeks later. The DuPage County boss, James F. (Pate) Philip, was a gruff, hard-boiled character who seemed to have serious reservations about me. Lou Yangus, the Will County chairman, just wanted to put his man, Don Gould, in the job. Because I had run for office respectably and also because I had a good relationship with him, John Grotberg, the state senator who was also party chairman for Kane County, threw in with me. And Dallas Ingemunson was pushing hard for me.

I don't know how many ballots they cast, but it boiled down to a race between Gould and me, and we were tied at 2–2 for a

very long time. Pate Philip couldn't vote for me. Finally, Dallas
took him to the bar. "Pate, what's the problem with Denny?" he
asked. "You were talking with the guys from Will County, and
Denny's a good guy."

Philip snorted and spat out the words: "He's a schoolteacher."
Philip didn't like lawyers either.

"Pate," Dallas insisted. "The guy is a coach. He knows what
sports are about. He's your kind of guy. I don't care if he's a
schoolteacher or not."

Philip mulled it over for a while. Finally, he said, "Okay, I'll
just abstain."

The chairmen went back to vote again, and the result was two
to one with one abstention. Finally, I had the nomination, and on
Election Day in November 1980, I won.

∾

After hiring the superbly competent Marilyn Marklein to run my
district office ("Denny, I've never done this," she protested. "Neither have I," was my response. "We'll learn together." And we
did.), I drove the 161 miles to our state capital and moved into a
townhouse with John Hallock, a representative from Rockford,
and Jim Riley of Jacksonville, who later became Deputy Governor.

That first year in the General Assembly, I mostly sat and listened. I didn't get up and speak a lot, but I was watching carefully.
I tried to identify the movers and shakers and figure out how
things worked.

There wasn't a lot to do in Springfield, but you didn't go
there for recreation. Because the state constitution required that
we complete our work by June 30, the end of the fiscal year, we

were facing deadlines almost from the moment the legislative session began. There would be so many votes and so many second and third readings of bills to sit through that you remained at your desk in that chamber almost all the time. If you were up against deadlines, you could be there until two or three o'clock in the morning. We had a vote on something new every three to five minutes so you didn't slip out to your office or go do something else.

Once we passed all the House bills and sent them over to the Senate, the Senate's bills came over to the 177-member House, and we were up against the same sorts of deadlines again. With that constant interaction, you got to know people on the other side of the aisle. Over time you'd argue with them, laugh, and joke with them. A collegiality developed that was, frankly, wonderful. I made some good friends there, Democrats from the southwest side of Chicago. We'd go out at night for dinner or a beer. In Springfield, you could do that.

When I first got into politics, even after being in front of people all the time as a teacher and coach, I used to get nervous if I had to give a speech. Then I discovered it was like wrestling. If I practiced enough, I'd get used to it. Initially, I had two types of speeches: a five-minute pep talk and a forty-minute lecture. I prefer the pep talk. I really hate reading speeches—I just hate *reading* them. I'd rather have an idea and be able to take it, develop it, and talk about it rather than put it in a written speech. As a teacher, I think I developed an ability to communicate. Ninety-five percent of all learning is a result of the students relating to you and having them understand and follow you. If you read a speech, you risk losing people; their minds wander off. I'm not a funny person, not a joketeller, but I think it's good in a speech to make fun of myself. That recaptures the audience.

What I remember most about my freshman year is that we had something like seventeen votes on the Equal Rights Amendment (ERA). Emotions were red hot on that issue–I opposed it because I thought the U.S. Constitution protected women's rights more than adequately–and we had people throwing blood on the door of the House. George Ryan was House Speaker. He was also running for Lieutenant Governor, and the women's caucus was in full rebellion against him.

Because Speaker Ryan couldn't trust some members of his leadership–they were friends of his, but they had to vote with the Democrats because they were City of Chicago guys–and because he knew that I was dependable and had a sound philosophical position, he put me on the House Rules Committee and the Revenue Committee as well.

Talk about being in the right place at the right time. Tom Ewing, a lawyer then serving his fourth term in Springfield, was chairing the Revenue Committee, and we were voting on the floor every night. One evening, Ewing had to take off to go speak at a graduation exercise in his district. Lee Daniels, the assistant leader, decided to pull an end run and move the vote on an inheritance tax measure to later that evening when Ewing wasn't there. I rose to object. They wouldn't recognize me. So I lassoed some of our committee members, marched over to Speaker Ryan's office, and raised the roof with him. To reverse Daniels's action was a big deal. But I stood up and said, "We're *not* going to do this," and that was a signal to the leadership that they would have to deal with me.

We were in the majority that first term, and we passed lots of legislation to tie in with the Reagan tax cuts. That was fun indeed, but then in the mid-term election of 1982, a constitutional amendment cut the number of House seats from 177 to 118; we Republicans lost and descended into the minority.

The Democrats in Springfield, I figured, could be divided into one of four different constituencies. First were the throwbacks from the 1960s revolutionaries; they formed the party's liberal wing. Next were the traditional Democrats who came out of the union movement. Third was the Chicago Democratic Machine and, finally, you had the quasi-intellectual college professor types.

As Republicans, we were in the minority now. And it was tough to do business in Springfield because the majority was run by the Chicago Machine. Sometimes you had to go around them or behind them or underneath them to succeed. But most of the time, to get anything done, you had to deal with them. It was a great training ground for me.

Halfway through my second term, my seatmate (and housemate) Jim Reilly resigned to become Governor Thompson's Deputy Governor. I was asked to become Republican leader on appropriations. In that post, I was in charge of the whole human services side of the appropriations process on the Republican side. What a great learning experience that was.

One important truth that dawned on me early was that zeroes really count, because some lawmakers, like real people, don't always grasp how large some dollar amounts really are. They can tell the difference between thousands, tens of thousands, or even maybe hundreds of thousands, but millions and billions and trillions are beyond comprehension. You have to break the numbers down into figures that average people can understand. If you don't, you don't win the support you need, and eventually you lose. So you have to lay out your arguments very carefully.

What brings this to mind was a series of votes we held on the floor one day. Doris C. Karpiel, a state representative from Carol Stream, Illinois, sat next to me in the chamber, and she had a bill to fix the roof of the rabbit hutch at the state fairgrounds for fifteen thousand dollars. The members understood how much fifteen thousand was and what it should or shouldn't cost to repair that roof. We had a forty-five-minute debate on the House floor; it became very spirited, and Doris's bill got defeated.

The next measure up for discussion was mine: $3.2 *billion* for public aid. People don't like welfare, so I began by saying that we had cut as much as we could from the bill. In fact, I learned, we had cut too much—about $6 million too much. Greg Coler, director of the Illinois Department of Public Aid, had told me, "You cut too much out of my bill," and I had replied, "Wait a minute; the bill is on third reading. What do you expect me to do now?"

"Well, you're going to have to bring it back," he said. "We can't get our federal matching funds unless we get that money." Federal dollars as opposed to state dollars—somehow, that attached a new urgency to the bill. I said I'd do what I could.

"Mr. Speaker," I began, "I have the annual appropriation for public aid for the state of Illinois, for $3.2 billion. I ask that we move the bill back to second reading to amend the bill to add an additional $6 million to it so we can get our state share of federal matching funds for the state of Illinois. And I ask unanimous consent to add $6 million to the bill." Unanimous consent was granted. All it took was for one member out of 118 to object to block the bill. No one did.

By that time, I was on a roll: "Mr. Speaker, I have this bill for public aid, $3.2 billion plus $6 million that we just added onto it, for welfare payments for people in the state of Illinois. I ask that we move it from second reading to third reading." And they did. But I wasn't finished yet. "Mr. Speaker," I said, "I have a bill on third reading for public aid for the state of Illinois, welfare money that will go to families and mothers and people in need. If you convert this bill into five-dollar bills, the resulting stacks of money wouldn't fit under the dome of this State Capitol. I just wanted to let you know how much money it is." They passed the measure in forty-five seconds flat. Which is precisely my point: Lawmakers needed forty-five minutes to decide that $15,000 was too much for a rabbit hutch while $3.2 billion was just too much for them to comprehend. So they passed it in a flash.

In the final days of each session, the tradition is that our female lawmakers have candy or fruit baskets or bouquets of flowers delivered to their desks. And Doris Karpiel, the author of the bill to repair the rabbit hutch, was upset because no one had sent her anything. Doris, who was a single mother with four children and five grandchildren, was always in my ear complaining about this or that. One day I turned to her and said, "Doris, for crying out loud, I already have a wife. I'm not married to *you*. I don't have to listen to all your problems."

"Look," Doris kept grousing, "nobody's sending me anything."

I thought back to the episode with the rabbit hutch and that gave me an idea. Turning to my friend and colleague Tom Ewing, I suggested, "Let's get a couple of rabbits."

Easier said than done. This was late June and all of the little bunny rabbits that had been around at Easter time were not available. Tom and I called pet shops, but we had no luck. Finally, we found a farm supply guy with grown rabbits for sale. Then we obtained a big fruit box complete with flaps and holes. We put the rabbits inside the box, tied it up with a big pink ribbon, brought it onto the floor of the General Assembly, and placed it squarely on Doris Karpiel's desk.

Doris strolled into the chamber, spotted this box on her desk, and squealed, "Oh, look, somebody sent me some fruit." Quickly, she untied the pink ribbons and pulled at one of the flaps. She was beaming. Two rabbit heads popped out like Jacks in the Box, and I heard this "Ahhhhhh..."

Somehow, the press had been alerted to this, and Judy Baar Topinka, who's currently the Republican Party chair in Illinois, was sitting one row behind us. "Oh, bunnies," she shrieked; she grabbed each rabbit by the nape of its neck and held it up for the photographer. Doris, of course, was furious. Not only did she not get her fruit, but she didn't get her picture with the rabbits on the front page of the *Chicago Tribune*.

And worse, they were her rabbits now, and she didn't know what to do with them. She put the rabbits in the back seat of her Oldsmobile and started driving home to DuPage County on Interstate 55. Somehow the cover fell off the top of the box. These were huge rabbits, white with pink eyes, and Doris could hear them scratching to get out. Every time they stood up and seemed ready to jump, she slammed on the brakes or jerked the wheel of her car, and they fell back down into the box. Eventually, Doris left them in a nursing home. She suspected, of course, that Ewing and I were responsible, but we never confessed.

The wonderful thing about Doris was that she could—and would—laugh at herself. (Even today, she's still telling the "Doris,

I already have a wife" story in her speeches.) Once she saw the humor in a situation, she'd join in the merriment. We did our best to provide opportunities. In 1984, after four years in the House, she ran for and won a seat in the state senate. Eventually, she became chair of the Executive Committee—a very important committee over there. A few years later when I was in the U.S. Congress, she wrote letters to me and Ewing complaining that in our effort to cut congressional spending, we were posing a threat to public television. Well, she wanted me to know that she and her grandchildren sat down together and watched Big Bird all the time. By God, it was a good thing, and from that moment on, she wanted me to vote for public television.

Ewing and I knew Dick Miller, a lobbyist for the telephone company in Springfield, so we called him and asked, "Can you find someone who can rent you a Big Bird suit?"

Miller did, and we hired the guy to wait until Doris was chairing her important committee and then to show up in a Big Bird suit with a bouquet of flowers and a big sign that read, "I love you, Senator Karpiel, for lobbying Congress to save my job." He walked down the center aisle of that committee room, kissed her on the top of the head, gave her the flowers, and she just went bananas in front of everyone.

Although we were in the minority, the fact that Governor Thompson was a Republican made my job of pushing his appropriation bills through easier. Here is how it worked: The Democrats would propose fat budgets. I would set the parameters of where I thought the budget ought to go to be balanced—as it had to be—and lay out amendments that would specify where we had to cut. The Governor would come along with a mandatory veto pen and follow my amendment trail, slicing things to balance the budget. I thought this was great, and I was just forty-two years old.

My counterpart in the House, a Democrat from the northwest suburbs of Chicago, had his own agenda of more spending and seemed not to care about anything else. The Republican on the Senate side was not real effective. So that left just two of us to make the decisions. Howie Carroll, a Democrat from Chicago's north side, was Chairman of Appropriations in the Senate chamber, and I remember sitting up in his office on the top floor of the Capitol as we cut the deals.

We'd start the arguments about the end of June, right before the Fourth of July, and we'd be there at this big table. Howie would bring in the directors of all the state departments and agencies and just beat them up for jobs. Before we'd ever get any appropriations bills set in real numbers, he would talk about jobs. He'd already rubber-hosed all the agency directors for jobs. Once he got what he wanted, then we'd sit down and try to figure out the real appropriation numbers. Howie was an amazing guy. He had his staffer Garret Deacon sit next to him. Garret was from southern Illinois, and I got along with him really well because he raised sheep and, of course, I had too when I was a kid. I would watch Garret carefully. He would grab Howie's coat and give it a tug and then whisper in his ear. Then I knew the negotiating had begun. I'd ask, "How much should we put into this project?"

"Well, they want $360,000," was the reply.

Howie settled that: "Well, my daughter's going to be thirteen this year, so let's make it $213,000." I would say "Let's cut the difference in half." Howie would say okay, it's a deal. There wasn't a lot of science to it, but it was fun working with him because you could get things done.

During my years in Springfield, probably the most important thing I worked on was an effort to make property taxes more equitable across the state. That's dull stuff, but then, quite unexpectedly, a new and challenging opportunity fell right into my lap. While I served as Republican leader on Appropriations, I was also on a small panel called the Sunset Commission. Like groups of the same name elsewhere in the U.S., our mandate was to eradicate government waste and do away with bodies that had outlived their usefulness.

In 1984, some good friends in Springfield–Minority Leader Lee Daniels and Democratic House Speaker Mike Madigan–thought it would be cute to "sunset" the Sunset Commission. So they did. I wish I could say that this was a "good government" move or that it was prompted by a desire to save taxpayers' funds. I can't say that, because I thought it was a scam by Daniels and Madigan to do away with commissions and grab increased patronage for themselves.

This created a huge problem because the Sunset Commission had less than one year left to rewrite the state's Public Utility Act concerning electricity and telecommunications–the act had been written back in the 1920s. Now with the commission gone, they didn't have anyone with any expertise on these issues. I'd been studying them in preparation for when they would be coming up before the commission. I knew something about them.

In legislation, knowledge is dangerous. Because I knew more than anyone else about the issues, lawmakers named me Chairman of a joint House-Senate committee to rewrite the act. But knowledge is also power, and if you can spend the time to learn about something, you'll be in a position to help make policy. So I worked at it and learned everything I could. I met with people to discuss regulation in the energy and telephone industry, went to seminars on these subjects, held hearings on them, and had lawyers and wonks answer whatever questions I had. In retrospect, I think I was chosen because everyone else thought that it was an impossible task, and it wouldn't get done. Nobody else wanted to have that failure on their hands. It was a "let Mikey try it" kind of thing.

On its face the challenge was daunting indeed. The last time anyone had tinkered with the Public Utility Act in Illinois was in the 1920s. Commonwealth Edison was put together and then guided on its way to becoming one of the largest energy companies in the United States. The original act made sure Commonwealth Edison would receive a guaranteed rate of return on investment.

Of the seven nuclear facilities that were under construction in Illinois in the early 1980s, Commonwealth Edison owned five. But there was a new public awareness that accidents could happen at nuclear facilities due to the Three Mile Island accident. So instead of costing the projected $400 to $500 million dollars to bring each plant on line, the price tag was spiraling up toward $5 *billion* dollars, and Commonwealth Edison didn't seem to care. It just wanted its guaranteed rate of return. The ratepayer—the Illinois consumer—would pay everything, and there was no mechanism in place to hold down costs.

Historically, electric utilities are required to maintain a reserve of between 8 and 10 percent. Commonwealth Edison's reserve margin was 42 percent. It was overbuilt, and its prices were very high. What we had to do was address the question of what a fair rate for consumers would be while maintaining electric services that were reliable. While I was struggling with this, federal Judge Harold Greene rendered a bombshell decision that required the breakup of the American Telephone & Telegraph Co. (AT&T) and revolutionized the phone industry. At the Illinois Bell office in Chicago, I remember, they were painting yellow lines down the middle of the floor. AT&T was on one side, Illinois Bell on the other.

Clearly, our system of regulating utilities had broken down and needed to be fixed. The bill that we got passed in Illinois soon became known as the hallmark piece of legislation for state efforts to deregulate the telecommunications industry. To me, it was further proof that you don't have to be a lawyer to get something done.

"Work doesn't feel so much like work if it's all you've ever known," *New Yorker* writer Jonathan Franzen pointed out in a profile of me in fall 2003. "If you're a legislator, simply being willing to read countless binders of complex and tedious policy materials can take you far. It can get you assigned to important committees."

That kind of work, and stress, can also impair your health. June 1985 was a strenuous time. I was still writing the Public Utility Act, and everything was coming together. I had two bills up—on telecom and electricity—and we were up very late at night trying to finish the appropriations process. I drove home to join Jean and the kids for Father's Day, and we cooked breakfast—ham, eggs, and potatoes—outside on the grill. I was standing by the fireplace cleaning out the big frying pan when, all of a sudden, bang! The next thing I knew, I was stretched out over the hood of a car in the driveway, and I couldn't get up, couldn't move at all. My back had gone out on me. I must have lain there for about twenty minutes.

It was Sunday, so we couldn't call a chiropractor. Then I remembered that a state senator, Doc Davidson, was a chiropractor and had a table on the third floor of the Capitol. Before I could get to see him, however, I felt pains in my chest, and I was sweating. The next thing I knew I was checked into the hospital. They did a chest x-ray and an EKG and said I was okay. I was still in so much pain that I couldn't sit in a chair; my back was hurting so much that I was kneeling on the floor. Finally, on Doc Davidson's third floor table in the Capitol, he pushed whatever he had to push back together again, and the pain was gone. Chiropractors didn't really need a lobbyist in the state capitol.

In the fall of 1985, Jean and I drove to Williamsburg, Virginia, for a conference on electric utility reform. We visited my aunt Doral Swan and her husband, Wade, in Bethesda, Maryland, and then drove to the Capitol. This was late November—between Thanksgiving and Christmas. We were sitting on the Republican side of the House, which was not in session, and I remember turning to Jean and saying, "You know, I'd really like to serve here someday."

"Oh, that would be nice," Jean replied. "I hope you get the chance."

As 1986 neared, I was in a good mood. For the first time since I'd entered politics five years before, no one had filed petitions to oppose me either in a GOP primary or in the general election. "I'm home free," I grinned. In January, when Governor Thompson led a state delegation to Asia, I accepted an invitation to accompany him. (My good friend Doris Karpiel came along as well.) The trip's purpose was trade: Mitsubishi was coming to Illinois and that would mean jobs, but I wanted to return to Japan to see some of the old friends I hadn't seen in nearly twenty years. When our official business was over, I went down to Osaka and spent time with them.

In Seoul, South Korea, we had to get up at four o'clock in the morning to watch Super Bowl XX on television (our Chicago Bears smashed the New England Patriots by a score of 46–10 in the Louisiana Superdome), but what I will always remember was the great sadness I felt upon hearing of two tragedies. One was public–the explosion of the spaceship *Challenger* one minute and thirteen seconds after it had lifted off from its launch pad in Florida. The second was more personal.

John Grotberg, the former state senator who had helped me get my start in politics, was completing his first term in Congress. He was sixty years old and had just been diagnosed with advanced cancer. He was out at the National Institutes of Health (NIH) in Bethesda, where he was receiving an experimental treatment. Something had gone wrong, and Grotberg had slipped into a coma there. Phyl Oldenberg, my old friend from Kendall County, had called to give me the news. "If you're ever going to run for Congress, you had better get ready," she said.

Grotberg had filed his petitions; he'd actually been renominated, and his people thought that if he was well enough to ride in the back of a convertible by the Fourth of July, they could run him for reelection that year. But he was on his deathbed, and the wanna-bes were testing the air. Dick Larsen, the Republican chairman for Kane County, and Dick Verbic, the mayor of Elgin, wanted to be the Congressman. So did a lawyer from West Chicago, Tom Johnson, who had lost narrowly to Grotberg in a primary just two years before.

Where did this leave me? At that point, I didn't know. In the course of discreet talks with Scott Palmer, we agreed that I shouldn't make any moves. To do so would be unseemly. Frankly,

I didn't want to make any moves. I wanted John to recover. Yet part of me was thinking that somebody has to be prepared. I talked to Jean about this, of course. She said she'd support whatever I decided to do.

Everything was in limbo until May 22, when Grotberg's family issued a statement. He wasn't resigning his seat in Congress, but he was resigning his nomination for a second term.

Going into the Aurora convention on June 22, on what turned out to be one of the warmest weekends in memory (what a time for the air-conditioning system to go on the fritz), it still looked like a four-way fight. At that convention, Kendall County was small, but a very solid block. In the end it came down to how hard we were willing to work. I must have telephoned five hundred precinct committeemen to line up those votes. When the convention was over, I walked off with the GOP nod.

Soon came the Fourth of July and our first parade. Democrat Mary Lou Kearns, the veteran Kane County coroner, had the help of the Democratic Congressional Campaign Committee. Its Midwest field director, a very young, very hard-edged Rahm Emanuel–now a Member of Congress from Chicago–was assigned to her campaign, while the media-savvy David Axelrod was running her press shop. The Democrats showed that they didn't know who they were dealing with when they charged that I was a captive of and beholden to special interest groups. Mary Lou didn't do much public speaking herself (she actually ducked out of a scheduled debate with me), but she didn't have to. She was very popular at home–she had been reelected coroner three times in a Republican county–and she had ample funds, union support, and friends in the media.

No matter what I said, the *Chicago Tribune* reporter would recycle the same piece almost every day about how this "evangelical" wrestling coach wanted to go to Congress. (Unspoken but implicit was the obvious question: Why would a *wrestling* coach think he could go to Congress? What business did a Christian believer have being in politics? It didn't seem to matter that I'd served in the legislature and had actual experience.)

Another issue my opponent raised was that I didn't actually live in the district. (When lawmakers had reapportioned in 1982, they had veered sixteen miles out of the way to cut our home out of the district.) Our home, across the Fox River, was eight hundred yards away, and the river was the line. So until we moved back across the river and into the parameters of the Fourteenth Congressional District, I remained the "evangelical" (that's a code word, too), carpetbagger wrestling coach who was running for Congress and depriving Mary Lou of the position that was rightfully hers.

In many respects, that campaign was an eye-opener for me. I had been a teacher for years; I was a National Education Association (NEA) member and so was Jean. So when I asked the union for its endorsement, I expected it to weigh the merits of my case. Yet all those teachers wanted to talk about was abortion, the ERA, and human rights in China. In their session with me, they never even mentioned educating kids. I knew far more about the issues than Kearns (who was reading her replies off a three-by-five card), but she won the NEA's endorsement. Actually, I don't think that endorsement made much difference—individual teachers from all over the district volunteered for me. After this incident, I never worried about that organization again.

When I was rewriting the Public Utility Act, I had worked with the United Brotherhood of Electrical Workers–they were pretty decent guys–so now that I was running for office, I asked for their support. Howard Cohen, a liberal operative from Chicago, interviewed me on their behalf. He was also the interviewer when I traveled to Chicago to do interviews with the conservation people, the environmentalists, and the Sierra Club. And when it came down to union issues for the union guys, Howard was across the desk once again. It was like Groundhog Day: "Howard, you're here again." I never did talk to the trial lawyers, but he probably would have been there, too.

By late August, my campaign was in trouble. People didn't want to tell me that, but I knew it was true. A lot of the Kane County Republicans were still resentful that tiny Kendall County had the congressional candidate, and a state central committee slot as well. My friend Dallas Ingemunson said they were even threatening to vote for Kearns. In mid-September, the race was still nip and tuck.

Then Kearns made an appearance before a group of students at Northern Illinois University. One student persisted with questions that seemed to rattle her. She didn't respond effectively. Finally, an aide led her away. She never recovered.

As we waited for returns on election night, Scott handed me two speeches. A win and a lose, he explained. By that time I was revved up and ready to go. "I'm not taking this lose speech," I told him, ripping it up and throwing it into the wastebasket. "We're not going to lose."

And we didn't.

CHAPTER FOUR

TIME TO GOVERN

If you can meet with Triumph and Disaster
And treat those two imposters just the same.
If you can talk with crowds and keep your virtue
Or walk with Kings—nor lose the common touch.
Yours is the earth and everything that's in it,
And, which is more, you'll be a Man, my son.
—RUDYARD KIPLING, "IF"

WHEN THE BALLOTS WERE COUNTED, I WON BY 6,995 VOTES, OR A margin of 52 to 48 percent. In my short speech that night, I thanked as many people by name as I could. Kendall County's volunteers had made the difference, I said, and I was going to be proud to represent them in Washington, D.C.

Jean was teaching at the Yorkville elementary school and had seniority, so we decided the best idea was for her to stay at home and raise the family in Illinois. If she needed something, my folks lived next door. Kendall County would be a far better place to raise the kids. And besides, it wasn't like I was scooting off to the moon. I'd be home every weekend just as I had been when I was serving in Springfield. Meanwhile, I found a one-bedroom apartment at Harbor Square in southwest Washington. Hubert Humphrey had lived in the same building when he served as Vice President, and realtors called it a prestige address.

After a year or two there, housing prices shot up about 50 percent, and in 1988 I thought I'd better buy. So I found a small townhouse over in Capitol Park. I hadn't liked living in an apartment—I felt like I was in a box—and this house had a front and back door, trees, shade, and a parking place. I bought it for $124,000 and I winced at the price. My aunt Doral and her husband had built their home in Bethesda in the late 1950s for $55,000, and I remember Mom, the penny pincher, exclaiming, "Fifty-five thousand dollars? You could buy a farm in Illinois for that. How could anyone spend that much on a house?" I determined that I would not tell her how much the townhouse had cost.

The Illinois delegation to Congress was strong, and we'd have Illinois meetings in a room on the second floor of the Capitol periodically. Bob Michel, who took me under his wing soon after I arrived, was the much-loved Minority Leader of the House. Unassuming and unfailingly polite, he led by quiet example. Not that we didn't have our attention-getters: Phil Crane, the veteran conservative from the Eighth District northwest of Chicago and one of the few Members of Congress then to have earned a Ph.D. (Newt Gingrich also had one from Tulane), had run for President in 1980. Lynn Martin, who was viewed as the rising star of the Republican Party, enlivened those meetings with her wit and unpredictability. Sitting over to the side was the hulking Henry Hyde, a respected World War II Navy vet, an attorney, and fierce abortion foe who'd spent eight years in Springfield before coming to Washington. Next to him sat John Porter, the moderate from the North Shore of Chicago who was later a "cardinal," as Chairman of an appropriations subcommittee. Then, of course, we had Ed Madigan, a moderate who went on a few years later to challenge Newt Gingrich in the race for Republican Whip—losing by just two votes—and wound up as Secretary of Agriculture. Harris Fawell, Jack Davis, and I were the rookies.

And those were just the Republicans. On the other side of the aisle were the Democrats. We had Dan Rostenkowski (Rosty), the larger-than-life Chairman of the House Ways and Means Committee who had been in Congress forever, it seemed. There was the old Italian guy, House Administration Committee Chairman Frank Annunzio, and there were also—among others—Dick Durbin, Marty Russo, Kenny Gray, and Bill Lipinski. Together, they carried an awful lot of prestige.

That first term, after everyone else would leave the Illinois meeting, I'd sit there and listen as Michel and Rosty talked about the good old days. The two of them, with Harold Collier, a Republican from Berwyn-Cicero, drove their station wagon back and forth to Illinois every weekend for about ten years. One would drive, the second would sleep, the third would ride shotgun. You really learn a lot about someone on such a road trip. And Rosty wasn't shy about his motives. When he got elected, old man Daley (Richard J. Daley, then mayor and the father of the current mayor of Chicago) said, "I want you in Congress, but you're going to be back in your ward every weekend." And he was.

Michel, who had first come to Congress in 1957 from the Eighteenth Congressional District (Peoria) of Illinois, was a giant of gentleness. I can't recall ever hearing him speak ill of someone or use a swear word. "Jimminy Christmas," "Jeepers Creepers," or even the mild "Gee Whiz" to express exasperation was as colorful as he got. Because he didn't view Democrats as adversaries, he just couldn't conceive of anyone bearing ill will toward him or other Republicans. Sure, there would be differences of opinion. But there was nothing personal about them, he believed, and besides, that's what negotiations should be all about.

By the time I arrived on Capitol Hill in 1987, Democrats had been in charge of the levers of power for more than thirty years, and they didn't want to share. Furious over what they perceived to be Reagan administration duplicity in the Iran-Contra affair, and frustrated by President Reagan's ability to go over the heads of the media and project his optimistic version of a "can-do" America, they determined to slow down—in the case of distinguished jurist Robert Bork, *savage*—the President's judicial nominations and grind his other initiatives to dust. Anything the President tried to pass was going to be dead on arrival and woe be unto any young Republican who got in the way.

In some important respects, the seniority system on Capitol Hill seemed like the caste system, with Republicans as untouchables. As a junior member of the minority, you rarely got a chance to speak on the floor or affect legislation. (Oh, sure, you could deliver a one-minute like anyone else, but you never got recognized or given time to say anything substantive.) You could try to amend a bill, but in order to do that, you'd have to go to the Rules Committee first and ask for a rule that allowed your amendment to be made in order. The odds of a Democratic committee making an important Republican amendment in order ranged between zero and none. It just didn't happen.

What you did get to do was go to committee meetings and listen to Democratic chairmen who'd been there forever expound on whatever they wanted to talk about and never even give you the chance to be recognized for a statement. And if they had anyone in their own ranks who balked at voting the party line, the leadership would change their locks, reassign their parking slot, or remove them from a committee. They played hardball then, and their margin—we had 180-odd votes and they had what seemed to be five thousand or more—was big enough to enforce those rules. (Years later, after he had served, a former Speaker conceded as much in a conversation with me. "Back in the old days, we would just change people's locks if they didn't want to vote our way," he said.)

In the words of one reporter for the *Washington Post*, we Republicans felt "shorted on staff, frozen out of decisions, denied information, and just plain ignored." Or, as Tip O'Neill was alleged to have said when he was Speaker, "Republicans are just going to have to get it through their heads that they are not going to write legislation." Still, we kept fighting the fight, pushing for less spending and smaller, smarter government. We kept talking about Republican principles even though no one seemed to be listening.

In my first and second terms, I was working on legislation to repeal the earnings test on Social Security. Seniors were having one dollar deducted from their Social Security checks for every two dollars they earned as income, and that was just plain wrong. People wanted to be productive. So why penalize them? This was also creating an underground economy. People were taking money under the table, and the federal government wasn't getting any taxes on that. Why make a criminal out of a senior who doesn't want to be committed to a rocking chair? We had chosen this to be our project for the 100th class, but we weren't making any headway. Finally, Bill Archer, a veteran Republican from Texas and Ranking Member of the Ways and Means Committee, said, "If you're going to make any progress at all, you have to go see Rostenkowski."

Rosty had a lot of seniority, so his office in the Rayburn House Office Building was one of the nicer ones on Capitol Hill. We walked in, and he was sitting in this big chair. The room was very dimly lit apart from a light shining on a huge portrait of Franklin Delano Roosevelt where, directly below, Rosty was sitting. We started explaining why getting rid of the earnings test would spur productivity, help seniors, and be a boon to the economy. He looked at us, turned in his chair and said, "See this portrait? Roosevelt passed Social Security so that everybody would have an entitlement, and I'm not about to change it." End of interview. That was it, the Word.

Victory took ten years, but with a lot of help from motel/hotel and senior citizens groups and the National Federation of Independent Business, we finally got our legislation passed. The lesson was clear: If you want to succeed in lawmaking or life, you have to remain focused and never, ever give up.

Initially, the GOP leadership appointed me to the House Transportation Committee as well as the Government Reform and Oversight Committee (GROC), which is where a lot of freshmen wind up. In my first few terms, GROC was a far more partisan place. Jack Brooks, a crusty old cigar-chomping Democrat from Texas, was using that committee to springboard investigations into almost everything the Reagan administration did, and he was ably assisted by two partisan Democrats from Oklahoma, Glenn English and the late Mike Synar. They were tough, ornery guys, so I grabbed onto my saddle and held on tight. Every time they tried to rip the administration apart, I did my best to come to its defense.

When I was not sitting in committee meetings or talking to colleagues or constituents in person or on the phone, I used to walk over to the House chamber, sit in the back row and watch what was going on. From the side of the back row, you could see everything. You could tell who was talking to whom, who was making deals, who was trying to get signatures on letters or bills, and who was signing up for bills. Watching carefully, you knew what was happening.

This used to drive my chief of staff, Scott Palmer, nuts. There he was trying to shore up my base and have me meet with every possible supporter or constituent who came through. He was making a lot of demands on my time—for my own good—and I was telling him, "I need to be on the House floor."

"*Nobody* needs to be on the House floor," he replied. "Why do you want to do that?"

The truth is I wanted to learn how the process worked and make friends at the same time. The second part was key. Establishing relationships was what it was all about. As I explained to Scott, "It's nice to know all the rules, but it's the people in the institution who count."

Some senior Democrats seemed to forget that simple lesson, much to my own advantage. Jack Brooks, for example, the unpleasant, crotchety veteran Chairman of the GROC, excelled at bringing pork to his Texas district. A case in point was the Super-Conducting Super Collider, a huge, multi-billion-dollar public works project that by 1988 almost every state—including

Texas and Illinois—was hoping to secure. One day in the House chamber, just as it looked as if the project was reaching a standstill, Brooks approached the desk, mumbling an amendment that he had in front of him. As soon as I heard what he was saying, I knew it was a scheme to free up additional funds for this Super Collider project and in the process afford a huge advantage to Texas in the competition for placement. I rose to object.

Well, I knew that Brooks's amendment couldn't become law without unanimous consent, and there I'd thrown down a challenge to my own committee chairman. "Screw the Chairman," I thought to myself. I knew I'd pay a price for that over the long term, but I still thought I'd done the right thing on principle.

Two or three days later, there was a vote on the House floor about something else. This was a GROC vs. the World kind of vote—not a Democrat vs. Republican thing—and I voted with the Chairman. My colleague, Jack Buechner, a Republican from Missouri, did not. Now Buechner and I are both big guys; some people say we look alike. The next thing I knew, Brooks was storming across the floor heading directly for me. I thought he had forgotten that I'd opposed his funding amendment a few days before. Obviously, I was wrong. He hadn't. He was going to get me, and he was coming my way now.

Brooks had a cigar in his mouth, and he was chomping on it furiously as he started to unload. Suddenly, it dawned on me that he was not talking about the Super Collider vote. He had mistaken me for Buechner, and he was going after me for the most recent vote.

"Mr. Chairman, Mr. Chairman." I grabbed him by the shoulders. "I'm Hastert, I'm with you."

He looked at me intently, waved the cigar stub, then said, "Oh yeah, you're okay."

I got out of there before he could remember anything else.

The fights we had in Washington were important, but I learned early in the game that it was even more important to put them in the proper perspective. It was Jean who was always my best sounding board. I remember calling her after we'd had this horrific struggle with the budget that was all over the network news. I told her about that, then asked, "What do you hear at home?"

"Well, there's a school board election," she said, "and the teachers"–Jean was still teaching then–"are worried about who's going to be on the board." As far as the budget problems in Washington were concerned, they just weren't on the radar screen for anybody in middle America.

Washington's chief conceit, as a *Chicago Tribune* reporter pointed out, is that because the work done there is important, the people who do that work must be important, too. Those people *do* make decisions that affect other people's lives, not only in our own country but around the world. But what people in Washington don't seem to understand is that folks outside the capital don't really pay that much attention to what we do in D.C. Oh, they might turn on a little television, spot a name in a headline, or even read part of a newspaper story; but what most real people are worried about today is their family, their job, their kids' schools, their next vacation, and making it through to the next paycheck.

I compare it to two ships passing in the night. The Washington politicians, lobbyists, and bureaucrats read the pundits in the *New York Times* and the *Washington Post* and listen to the talking heads on television while the rest of the country goes merrily on its way. When I'm home I spend time with friends who live in the real world, as opposed to the one in Washington. I may not be getting myself on television or have my face in the newspaper, but I much prefer to be in the hardware store or the grocery store talking to real folks. Jean says she can't send me out to buy a gallon of milk without it taking forty-five minutes or more.

From time to time, I'm introduced to some unsuspecting soul as "your Congressman." Soon it becomes quite apparent that they haven't the slightest idea of who I am, let alone what a Congressman does. Usually, they get the drift that it has something to do with government. They may complain about taxes or their neighbor's barking dog. There was a time when I was in the state legislature in Springfield, and a guy called me because dogs were barking all night. I told him there was an animal control officer to call, but he said I was the only one he could get a hold of. I still get those calls, and if it's out of my jurisdiction, instead of just telling the person to contact someone else, I'll have someone in authority call him or her back. It's always humbling for me to realize that there are real people out in the heartland living their lives, raising their families, and paying taxes, and they couldn't care less about Washington, D.C., or the people who work there.

Because both Scott and I felt sure that Mary Lou Kearns would challenge me again and because we really needed to build up the base, we returned to the district every weekend. (Actually, for my first six years in office, Scott spent much more time in Illinois than in Washington, D.C.) We scheduled town meetings—a few on Friday night, more on Saturday. We established mobile offices and did everything we could to increase recognition of my name.

When I first came to Congress, I was appalled by the deficit spending, and I figured everyone there in both parties was reading from the same playbook, a brown-and-white striped economics text by a guy named Samuelson, which I had used in college. His thesis was that the federal government *ought* to prime the pump and deficit-spend. For the past forty years, that's all Congress had done. Soon it dawned on me that these people actually believed in that. They believed that taxation helped grow a bigger government to do more things for more people more of the time. And that people needed government to do more things for them.

The counter to that, of course, was smaller government, less bureaucracy, fewer regulations, and a sense of economic freedom that said, "It's their money. Let people keep a little more of their own money in their own pockets. They'll spend it a lot better for themselves and their families than some bureaucrats in Washington." President Ronald Reagan had proved that to be true. Outside the GOP, however, I couldn't find too many people who agreed with him. I thought the country was headed for a financial train wreck. The liberals would blame that on Reagan, I knew, but they were the ones who still controlled spending on Capitol Hill.

Near the end of Reagan's second term, my rookie term in Congress, I was invited to accompany the President on Air Force One. What a great opportunity, I thought. But when we landed in Chicago and I hadn't even laid eyes on Reagan, I thought I had wasted my time. Then the President invited me to join him on his helicopter, Marine One. "Fly around Wrigley Field. I love the Cubs," he told the pilot. As the flight continued, he entertained me with stories about growing up in the Illinois district I represented, going to baseball games at the field as a kid, and of the years he spent as a radio announcer of Cubs games (based on telegraph reports he received in Des Moines from Wrigley Field). Returning to Washington aboard Air Force One, Reagan strolled back to find me and said how much he enjoyed our visit. And when he made his way back to his seat, I noticed that he didn't have any back pockets on his pants. When you're President of the United States, I guess you don't have to have back pockets on your pants.

Reagan served out his terms and was succeeded in 1989 by his Vice President, George H. W. Bush. During and after the first war in the Persian Gulf, people were tying yellow ribbons around trees at home, and patriotic feelings ran high. It was an exuberant time for Americans, and then, suddenly, we faced an economic downturn. Bush was focused on foreign policy; at least partly because of Dick Darman, who ran the Office of Management and Budget (OMB), he didn't seem to grasp economic reality here at home, and the Democrats delighted in setting traps for him. They issued an ultimatum. Senate Democrats said they wouldn't approve a budget unless Bush held an economic summit meeting and "put everything on the table."

"Okay," the President said, in effect, "we'll talk about everything." He didn't say he was going to raise taxes—although everyone sensed that was the bottom line. Then when he did, Democrats threw the "Read my lips" remarks he had made after his nomination in New Orleans a few years before back at him in such a skillful way that it really undercut his credibility. The combination of these things hurt him very much, and his approval ratings—once extraordinarily high—began reflecting that.

∾

In the first months of my second term, Bob Michel took me under his wing again. The soft-spoken, modest leader from Peoria was always giving me good advice, suggesting what to do and what not to do; whom to get involved with and whom to avoid. He had an opening on the House Rules Committee, and he wanted me to fill it. But there was a catch. Lynn Martin, also of Illinois, wanted to be on Rules. She was already on the House Armed Services Committee but said she was willing to sacrifice that for Rules. All of this tried Bob's patience.

"Lynn, you've only been there for two or three years," he pointed out. "How are you ever going to get any seniority if you keep jumping around? Why don't you stay where you are?"

"No, I don't want to do that," Lynn shot back.

She put on a pout, then engineered a deal that let Bob name her to Rules and put me on the Steering Committee—that's the committee that decides which Members serve where. Ironically, if Lynn had let Bob have his way, I would have been chair of Rules today, and I wouldn't be Speaker of the House. Rules is an important job, but being Speaker trumps it.

The game of musical chairs continued on Capitol Hill. Jack Kemp left the House of Representatives in 1988 to run, unsuccessfully, for President. Representative Trent Lott, tired of waiting for Bob Michel to retire, ran for the Senate that year and won. Early in 1989, President Bush nominated Republican Senator John Tower of Texas to serve as Secretary of Defense. When objections from Democrats—primarily from Senator Sam Nunn of Georgia, who was widely respected as an expert on defense—blocked that nomination, Tower withdrew, and Bush nominated Wyoming Representative Dick Cheney as his replacement.

Cheney, who had been chief of staff for President Gerald R. Ford, was serving as Republican Whip, the second highest position in the House minority, and his departure for the Pentagon in March

1989 triggered a race for his old job between Ed Madigan, a moderate, pro-choice representative from Illinois and Newt Gingrich, the former college history professor from Georgia who did not belong to the Bob Michel "Go along to get along" school.

Madigan, who had first come to the House in 1973 after eighteen years running the Yellow Lincoln Cab Company back home and serving in the state legislature in Springfield, was effective because he could work with Democrats, especially with Henry Waxman. He could cut deals and make them happen, and if you were in the minority, that's what you had to do to get anything done.

Many Republicans thought the race would be extremely close, and it was. Tom DeLay and I were Madigan guys and we were doing everything we could for him. The two candidates were tied with eighty-six votes each. The decision came down to one man on the last morning of the balloting. Larry Coughlin, a Representative from the Philadelphia Mainline, succumbed to pressure from fellow Pennsylvania Republican Bob Walker and changed his vote from Madigan to Gingrich after breakfast that day.

Gingrich was smart. He had put together three groups to help him win this thing. First there was the Conservative Opportunity Society (COS) that he had started himself. Second was the House Transportation Committee, on which he served, and finally he had put together an amalgam of northeastern liberals who weren't normally the sort to rally behind his flag. But Madigan had voted against the Clean Air Act, and acid rain was upsetting to northeasterners, so Gingrich turned that against Madigan and was able to woo moderates into his camp. Representatives Nancy Johnson of Connecticut, Steve Gunderson of Wisconsin, and Fred Upton of Michigan should have been Madigan people, but they jumped on Newt's bandwagon and that's how he won.

Some Republicans still thought Newt was such a loose cannon that he was sure to overstep his bounds. He kept pushing Michel, making no secret of the fact that he wanted Bob to step aside, even threatening him: "If you don't retire, I'm going to run against you."

I thought this was unseemly, so I had lunch with Newt and said, "You got to let this guy who's been here almost thirty-eight years finish with dignity. If you'll do that, I'll help you do whatever you want, but let's work together and not assert this power too quickly." To his credit, Newt agreed. Bob would retire but at a time of his choosing, and no one would move against him. He would go at the right time; there would be a smooth transition for everyone. Much later, Newt would tell me, "Hastert, I'll tell you why I've always trusted you: Because you never sold out Bob Michel."

Early in 1991, at the start of my third term, I won a seat on the Energy and Commerce Committee and went to see Madigan in an effort to get on the Telecommunications subcommittee.

"Well, you can't get on Telecom," he told me. "There are too many senior members on it already, but get on the Health Care subcommittee. I'm the Ranking Member there. I have this Waxman guy on the other side, and you can help me."

"Ed," I protested, "I've never done health care. I don't know much about it."

Madigan wasn't bothered at all. "That's okay. Get on there, and I'll do a little mentoring. I'll teach you the ropes." I joined the subcommittee.

In 1991 and 1992, reapportionment confronted us. For the past decade, Illinois had had twenty-two seats—fifteen Democrats and seven Republicans—in the U.S. House of Representatives. Due to redistricting, we were going to lose two of those seats. The question then became: Who would have to bow out?

Before that was decided, I filed a case in federal court arguing that the current redistricting scheme was flawed—I just didn't think there were twice as many Democrats as Republicans in the state, and it was my contention that legislators had reapportioned us in a very unfair way. A new map like the one we had designed would even the congressional representation at ten Democrats and ten Republicans and be much fairer. The court agreed with my argument.

This caused consternation among Democrats. This new map, readied for 1992, combined six Democratic districts into three, pitted Marty Russo and Bill Lipinski against each other; did the same thing to Glenn Poshard and Terry Bruce; and left Frank Annunzio (the old Italian guy who chaired the House Administration Committee) on the chopping block. "The only thing that counts up here is votes," the Democrat from Chicago once explained, in what was referred to on Capitol Hill as "the Annunzio Rule." "Everything else is bull–."

This felicity with words didn't save him when the crunch came. "Annunzio, time to retire," Rostenkowski said, and he did. But that was a Rosty move to save his own district.

Republicans were unsettled too. Madigan, having lost his race for Whip and hoping to protect his own Fifteenth Congressional District, was trying to convince Michel to resign. Madigan was a friend, but I thought Michel was far more important to keep around, so I went to Billy Pitts, Bob's floor guy, and said, "Pitts, think about this. It's in all our interests to have Michel stay. Madigan wants to cut this deal so that if Bob leaves, he can consolidate that district." Then I came to the clincher: "Don't you think Madigan would make a good Secretary of Agriculture?"

A light went on in Pitts's eyes. The present occupant of that Cabinet position, Clayton K. Yeutter, was stepping down after two years to become Chairman of the Republican National Committee. "We ought to push that," Pitts agreed.

Next morning I had breakfast with Newt Gingrich. "Madigan's around," I began. "He's trying to cut a deal so he can stay around. If he stays around, he'll probably be a political nemesis for you. I think one of the best things you could do is go to the White House and try to make Madigan the next Secretary of Agriculture."

Then I called Tom Ewing, an old friend from Illinois who had been my mentor in the state legislature. "Tom," I began, "get your money together. You have a chance to run for Congress." He and Madigan were the same age, and he thought he'd never get the chance to run while Madigan held that seat. Initially, he was hesitant, but he ran and came to Washington.

One of the weird things that you learn in orientation on Capitol Hill is that for protocol purposes, a Member of Congress is the equivalent of a two-star general. Somehow, this came up in conversation with Tom after he had arrived. "What do you know, Tom? You're a two-star general."

"I am?"

"Yeah." I winked at Scott, who was in my office, and asked, "Didn't they give you the hat?"

"No," Ewing said.

"Well," I replied. "Maybe that's because you missed the normal orientation. You came here on a special (election) so you didn't go through with the rest of your class. They'll give you a hat and a scarf, everything."

Ewing left. He had heard about surprises in Washington, D.C. He just didn't know how delicious this was going to be or who was going to do the tasting.

I turned to Scott and said, "Go get a hat. We'll send it over to him."

Scott trudged out to an Army surplus store and purchased the hat. Then he went looking for general's stars, but all he could find were these really big stars that looked like headlights. He brought them to me and I said, "Okay, now we have to write a note."

We wrote a pretty official looking letter that read, "Dear Congressman Ewing, Welcome to Congress. Here's your hat." Then we signed it, "Colonel Clinque."

None of us thought he was going to fall for it.

But days, weeks, months, even years went by, and we never heard a thing from him. From time to time I did get reports that he put his general's cap in the front window of his car when he drove over to play golf at Ft. McNair. That was so everybody would know he was a general. Finally, last fall, when asked about the cap in connection with this book, Ewing stammered, "But I never went out and tried to command any troops."

Tom was a very able and experienced legislator, and he shared my affection for Doris Karpiel, our former colleague in Springfield who was still a state senator. Normally, she complained that the only trip she ever got was to the coal mines of southern Illinois, but she had told us about going to Ireland with her family once. Now that Tom was in Congress and both of us had a chance to travel, we decided to send Doris postcards from an admirer she'd met over there named Biggy O'Toole.

"Gee, Doris," a typical card would begin. "How are you? Remember, we met in a bar in Ireland. The credit card you sent me is maxed out now. Would you send me another one? I'll get back to you someday, darling." And we sent those cards to her legislative office, so the girls in that office would see them first.

I never told her who was behind this, but I'm sure she knew. And she used to respond in kind.

"Dear Denny," she would begin. "We've been friends forever, but I'm bitterly disappointed. I read in the paper that you voted [this way or that] and I'll never forgive you for it."

During my first three terms, because Scott was spending so much time back home in Illinois, an experienced Washington hand named Peter Vroom ran our office on Capitol Hill. He was a good guy, but he didn't know the people back home. When he saw the Karpiel letter he kept it in his desk for weeks. "I just can't show it to Denny," he told Scott. "Isn't Doris a good friend of his? He's going to be devastated by the tone of this."

∽

Now with Ed Madigan gone to head the USDA, I had lost my mentor on the Health Care Subcommittee. If I was going to remain on that panel, I thought, I had better get involved in health care and write a bill.

Actually, I had an idea for a bill that would contain three pieces. Madigan's departure just meant that I'd have to write it myself. But as I was to discover, when you work on that legislation, you can become a player on health care almost overnight. In this business, knowledge is power, and if you spend the time to learn about something, you're in a position to help make policy.

Greg Busch, who had helped me rewrite the Public Utilities Act in Illinois and who had also helped me put together legislation for Medical Savings Accounts, helped me again. He's a solid professional, a clear thinker with health care experience. Two of my Republican colleagues in the House, Jay Rhodes of Arizona and Porter Goss of Florida, lent their efforts to the cause, and the measure we produced had three major components.

First was malpractice reform because the lack of such reform was driving up the costs of health care everywhere. Then we listed long-term care because Rhodes and Goss had large numbers of senior citizens in their districts in Arizona and Florida; and, finally, we had Medical Savings Accounts. MSAs, as we designed them, would let consumers continue to use private health insurance plans while encouraging them to set money aside to pay for deductibles and increased costs. Contributions to these individual MSAs and the interest they earned would be tax-free if the money was used for medical expenses within a one-year period. The key was if you didn't spend the savings account, you got to keep it and roll it over for the next year. In my view, MSAs were new and forward-thinking, and they eliminated many of the problems the present system had.

Chief among them was that no one knew—or even cared—what the costs for almost any procedure were going to be. If you needed an MRI, for example, the doctor said, "Just do it," and it was done if the insurance company was willing to pay for it. Even doctors didn't know how much was being charged. No one had any idea of the total cost of this. Meanwhile, the real cost of health care kept soaring.

In retrospect, our bill wasn't a bad way to start. Health care was an important domestic issue, a big issue, we told President

Bush and his White House team. This was late 1991 or early 1992; he was facing reelection and was being accused of not having a domestic vision. So health care was something we had to address. Even though we had what we considered a pretty good bill, we were still in the minority, so our chances of getting anything out of committee were remote. But we were coming up with ideas that the White House could use to counter whatever the Democrats said. Finally, the Bush administration caught on to the importance of our bill and doing something on the domestic agenda. We set up a huge press conference with the President in the Capitol's Rayburn Room. The room was packed with press. Great, I thought, but when it came time for Q and A, all the press focused on was a whimsical reference to the tabloid *Weekly World News*, which had just run a photograph of Bush with an alien from outer space. What a disappointment! The press didn't want a relevant domestic issue to be talked about in this campaign.

We lost the election in 1992 and bang, Bush was gone, and we had a new President. Bill and Hillary Clinton made it clear that their first priority was health care, and they drove their commitment home: "We're going to change health care as we know it in this country," they said. They were going to bring in some five hundred–odd experts from around the country, appoint them to the Health Care Task Force, and set them to hammering out a plan in the Old Executive Office Building (OEOB) next to the White House. Initially, I was envious of what they were doing there.

That's when Bob Michel appointed me to Hillary's Health Care Task Force—I think I was the only Republican—and Newt Gingrich wasn't happy about that. Gingrich, a rising star in the party and Michel's Whip, wanted that slot in the worst way, and he was very upset that Bob had given it to me. Newt, who was already giving speeches about this or that on the House floor all the time, was clearly going to be one of our future leaders, and I felt a bit dicey jumping him in this way. But I decided to do what Bob wanted done.

Even though I was the Republican point man on Hillary's task force, I was not invited to meetings at the White House, and I never went to the OEOB. The Clinton people said they'd send policy wonk Ira Magaziner, an economist-entrepreneur from Rhode Island, to my office once a week. We could tell him what our legislative parameters were, and he would let us know what they were doing. He should be able to show us a bill in March, he said.

But March became April; April became May; May became June; and the bill never appeared. I began to hear terms like "gatekeepers" with references to an alphabet soup of federal agencies, and it soon became apparent that everyone was going to be under the same type of health care and that this had become a vast, government-run health care system. Meanwhile, I kept working on and talking about Medical Savings Accounts. "Sounds good," Magaziner told me. "Tell Mrs. Clinton."

It was early fall, and John Kasich, a Republican from Ohio who was the Ranking Member on the House Budget Committee, announced that he had invited Mrs. Clinton to a dinner at his townhouse in Alexandria, Virginia. John, as best I could tell, didn't boast any expertise in health care. His committee didn't have jurisdiction here. He just upped and did it. He arranged for this dinner and invited me. Still, regardless of who put the session together or why, I was looking forward to hearing the First Lady's views.

For the better part of two hours, we talked about health care and asked questions. I was the last guy at the table and could see Mrs. Clinton was getting antsy because it was getting late, but I wanted to ask her about Medical Savings Accounts. Finally, I had my chance.

"Mrs. Clinton," I began, "I talked to Ira Magaziner about Medical Savings Accounts. He said he'd talk to you about them, that you were looking at them."

She simply replied that she had looked at them. I pressed her. "Well, what do you think?"

She said MSAs wouldn't be considered because if the money isn't spent on health care then the owner of the account gets to keep the money. And since she felt people are inherently greedy and can't be trusted to make decisions for themselves–they would not do the things necessary to take care of their kids, not get preventative medicine, and not get inoculations. So an account in which people get to keep their money wasn't a viable option. She felt the federal government would do better if we put people on a health care schedule.

That smacks of Big Brother, I thought, but I held my tongue while she continued.

She went on to say that she felt if money goes to individuals and they have control over it, then that is money the government doesn't have. People wouldn't spend their money as wisely as the federal government would.

As I listened to her, I was thinking this isn't about *policy*. This is about a difference in philosophy. Some people, and Mrs. Clinton is apparently among them, believe that government makes better decisions than people can make for themselves and that government will spend the people's money better than the people can for themselves. What she said convinced me that we couldn't work with these people and drove me to go in a different direction. Next day I told Bob Michel, "We need to go off on our own and write our own bill."

And that, of course, is what we did.

Representative Jim Cooper, a reform-minded Democrat from Tennessee (by way of Groton, Oxford, and Harvard), showed a willingness to compromise with Republicans, and that infuriated House Energy and Commerce Committee Chairman John D. Dingell. Nicknamed "The Truck," the balding, barrel-chested Dingell began his career as a House page in 1938, then won election himself from Michigan's Fifteenth Congressional District in 1955. That was almost fifty years ago. Today he's Dean of the House. I'm respectful of him, but he can be one tough customer if and when he wants to be. I saw just how tough he is when he and Cooper clashed.

Cooper was lead sponsor of something called the Managed Competition Act of 1993. Already, Cooper's plan was drawing bipartisan support. "They've got the big guns," Cooper told the *New York Times*, referring to backers of the Clinton plan. "I don't even have a pea-shooter in this debate. All I've got is a good bill."

Dingell didn't think so. During a subcommittee hearing that Waxman chaired on February 2, 1994, Big John began to vent: "You feel, I gather, that too many are getting too much [*sic*] benefits so you are going to make some of these benefits subject to tax by their employer so as to reduce the level of benefits to those who are deriving the best benefits."

That wasn't even remotely close to what Cooper had suggested, and the Tennessean sought to correct the record: "Perhaps
the Chairman was absent during the first part of the hearing in
which I stated clearly that we are adding a new $54 billion pro-
gram of tax subsidies for average Americans, so they can better
afford benefits."

Dingell: "Where is that coming from? The money is coming out
of the pockets of those who are getting a better level of benefits...."

Cooper: "As I stated in my testimony, the money comes from
trimming the corporate tax break."

Dingell didn't seem to like being reminded that he might want
to listen to or read the testimony before asking questions about it.
He zeroed in on Cooper again: "Does this bill give universal coverage or does it not?"

Cooper: "Our bill can achieve universal coverage by the President's timetable of 1998...."

Dingell: "You say it can. Can you make the bald statement
that it will?"

Cooper: "No one has a crystal ball, but I believe our bill has a
better chance than any other bill in Congress."

Dingell: "If I said it would not [achieve universal coverage],
would you deny that?"

Cooper: "No one has a crystal ball."

Dingell: "So you don't know whether it will achieve universal
coverage or not."

Finally, the hectoring stopped. Cooper tried to put a positive
spin on the heated exchange. "The Chairman [Dingell] and I disagree on the role of government," he observed. "The Chairman
has usually preferred larger government solutions to problems

than I perhaps do. That is not to fault the Chairman. You have your own views. I tend to be more of a new Democrat focusing on smaller government solutions."

"You're a young Democrat," Dingell snapped.

The Clinton health care plan was labyrinthine, Bob Michel said, and it was based on job-destroying mandates. For Bob that was pretty strong stuff. Everywhere you looked, it seemed obvious that support for the Clinton approach was eroding fast. Remember the Harry and Louise ads that we saw on TV almost every night? It's a cardinal rule of politics that when people start laughing at you—instead of just blasting you with critical attacks—you're in deep trouble indeed, and people were laughing at the Clinton plan now, holding it up to ridicule.

That emboldened Republicans of all stripes. Finally, we had a bill, and we were ready to move it. What we needed to know was: Would the committee hear that bill, give us a fair hearing and markup, and then help us get the bill out? That was a fair question because this bill sure didn't do what Dingell wanted it to do.

The truth is that Dingell preferred Mrs. Clinton's approach, but he had a problem: He didn't have the votes. Six Democrats had come over to our side and were backing a measure that Georgia Democrat Roy Rowland, a physician, was offering with Florida Republican Mike Bilirakis. Basically, Rowland-Bilirakis was beating the Clinton bill that Dingell and other Democrats still supported, and that posed huge problems for their leadership. Health care was their signature issue; did they dare jettison it now? Could they possibly accept a Republican alternative? Majority Leader Dick Gephardt had promised Roy Rowland a fair vote for his bill on the floor. It never happened, and Rowland, now retired, is still peeved that a promise wasn't kept. We'd have to wait a while for the answers on health care.

∽

During my first three or four terms in Congress, I kept a pretty regular schedule: I flew home Thursday night, worked the district over the weekend, and left for Washington again Tuesday morning. I didn't always want to fly back to Washington—I wanted to stay home, though I couldn't let that show. But it was hard to leave the simple comforts of home and family. Josh, our eldest son, wasn't into sports—music was his thing. He was also a great outdoorsman and the editor of his college paper. Ethan, who at 140 pounds wringing wet was much too thin to play center, but loved football, and in all those years I missed only one of his games. Jean really enjoyed gardening. I did that with her, and I tried to make myself as useful as possible.

I didn't always succeed. One time I was testing a new lawnmower outside on the big hill that overlooked the Fox River. Our two Labs, Max and Diamond, were watching me carefully, looking for some sign that I wanted to play. The mower steered by handles, and it started going down the hill. I couldn't stop it. Then it veered off to the deep part of the hill, moving faster now, and somehow I got it stopped just in time. Max and Diamond were prancing about, just yapping away, and I was half-hanging, half-teetering off that machine. That's when Jean, who had been watching this whole episode unfold, said, "I learned two things today—lawnmowers can fly and dogs can laugh."

In January 1994, Mom died a few months short of eighty. She had been battling cancer for almost a year. Dad, who was a year older than Mom, lived with us for almost five years after her death. He died in 1998, just before I became Speaker of the House. Jean and I had built a home for them next door to ours on the Fox River in Yorkville, and Mom loved it. She had never had a new home of her own, and she'd always wanted a place near the water. In the early years, when Jean was still teaching and the boys were young, Mom would babysit them two days a week. Talk about reliable babysitters. Whenever Jean and I wanted to take a trip, Mom and Dad were next door.

Back in Washington, Bill Clinton had presented us with the largest tax bill in American history. He had offered us a health care bill that nobody wanted–because nobody wanted the federal government making decisions for individuals about how they were going to get the health care they required. Then there was the battle over gays in the military and the dispatch of our Armed Forces to restore "democracy" in Haiti. We Republicans were talking in a positive way about what we wanted to do. Our poll numbers were moving up, and suddenly it began to occur to us that, as Newt Gingrich said, "We don't *have* to be a minority party."

I don't think Bob Michel believed that we'd ever be in the majority–that was one of his big shortcomings–but the younger leaders sure did. Gingrich, Dick Armey, a Republican from Texas, Bill Paxon from upstate New York, and Tom DeLay, another Republican from Texas, just weren't willing to roll over and play dead. They were envisioning taking control of Congress and even drawing up plans for something called the Contract with America.

When Bob announced his retirement, Newt was the heir apparent as Leader. This left open the Whip slot for the 104th Congress.

DeLay asked me to run his campaign for Republican House Whip in the summer of 1993. From that point I had been doing everything I could to help my colleague. Pennsylvania Representative Bob Walker (Newt Gingrich's candidate) and Florida Representative Bill McCollum were also in that race. They hadn't asked for my assistance and, besides, I really liked DeLay.

Born in Laredo on the Mexican border, he had grown up in Venezuela and then returned home to attend high school, before attending Baylor University and graduating from the University of Houston. Settling in Sugar Land, he started a pest control business and then ran for the state legislature in 1978. No Republican had ever represented Fort Bend County before, but that didn't stop Tom. There were a lot of rice farmers of Czech ancestry in the district at the time. Tom walked up to one guy wearing khakis and a big hat and asked for his vote.

"Are you a Republican or a Democrat?" the farmer asked.

"Republican," Tom said.

"Well," the farmer said. "I've never saw a Republican before. We don't elect Republicans around here."

But Tom won that race and came to Congress six years later. We got to know each other working on the Madigan campaign. He has a very high level of energy, I found, and he was a very street-smart politician. He was just savvy with this innate sense of what can and can't work in Congress and how you're going to accomplish things. I rely on his instincts. He can look at a situation and understand how our base is going to react, how the rest of the guys are going to think, and what the consequences are.

What you see with Tom is what you get—he doesn't have a hidden agenda. People make fun of him because he wears his black hair slicked down and because he was a bug exterminator in the Houston suburbs before he came to Congress. I don't care what you were if you have this gut feeling of how to get things done.

"Tom," I said, "you go out and talk to people, do the politics in the House, and I'll count the votes." So he did the schmoozing; I tied people down. Our strategy was to get as many people committed as soon as possible and try to bring them on delegation by delegation. One of the things we should do was surround Walker, I thought. He'd be able to carry Pennsylvania, his home state, but we ought to get New York, New Jersey, Delaware, Maryland, and Ohio—neutralize him with easterners and isolate him in his base.

Representative Dean Gallo, a good guy, helped me get the New Jersey delegation. Next we picked up New York, and Paxon helped us with that. Then we bagged Ohio with the help of some of the old-timers who were there, Ralph Regula and Mike Oxley. Finally, we got Illinois. I knew we were winning because I kept the tally, and I made sure that we had absolutely iron-clad commitments before we counted them.

We had eighty-odd already, more than half the number of Republicans in the House—and that wasn't counting new Members coming in—so our majority was building. And we still had time to spare. DeLay and I flew everywhere talking to House candidates, helping them and nailing down their support. We did it our own way; we weren't taking it from a textbook. This was the summer of 1994, and the Whip election wasn't until December. And there was another, very important election first.

I took every race seriously, my own especially, but ever since 1986 when I had had to go all out to defeat Mary Lou Kearns, the Democrats in the Fourteenth Congressional District hadn't thrown any formidable opponents against me. So wherever possible, I used my time and funds to help other Republicans. And what a positive, uplifting message we were able to hammer home in the Contract with America. Here were ten platform planks, common-sense ideas that when enacted into law would better the lives of average Americans. I thought they made sense, and people were looking for a change in Congress. When Newt Gingrich came up with the idea of having all incumbents–and all candidates–sign a pledge to support the Contract on the Capitol steps, I thought it was an outstanding move. Polls showed it resonating with voters in the heartland, and we stepped up the campaign.

In May 1994, we thought we had a chance to pick up fifteen seats. In June, it was twenty seats. In July, twenty-five. We needed thirty-odd seats to win a majority, and all of a sudden that didn't seem out of bounds to consider.

The Clinton administration tried to stop our advance by proposing a very expensive ($33.2 billion) crime bill. It made some liberals happy because it funded what we called "midnight basketball" and other efforts to keep at-risk kids off the streets at night, but it also included an assault rifle ban that the National Rifle Association (NRA) and some sportsmen's groups opposed.

House Speaker Tom Foley, a courtly, white-haired Democrat from Washington State and Gephardt, a Democrat from St. Louis, went to the White House and urged Clinton to separate the rifle ban from the crime bill. The President refused. By a vote of 225 to 210, the Democrats failed in their attempt to pass a rule in the House governing discussion and passage of the crime bill. A total of fifty-eight Democrats–including three committee Chairmen, seventeen subcommittee Chairmen, and a Chief Deputy Whip–voted against their own leadership, their own President. That told me the Democrats were in real trouble now. If you have a big majority, which they had, you should never lose a procedural vote like that. As political analyst William Schneider told the *Los Angeles Times*, Clinton's defeat was likely to reinforce the growing perception that he was "a weak and ineffectual leader who cannot deliver on his promises."

For Democrats, the news just kept getting worse. Foley himself was facing a stiff challenge in his Spokane district from Republican George Nethercutt, and he was somehow enmeshed in a court case in which he seemed to be suing his own constituents. That didn't bode well for him.

In the closing days of that campaign, I was campaigning in freshman Republican Pete Hoekstra's district in western Michigan. I remember hearing on the television in my motel room that Foley had just announced that Congress wouldn't be considering health care. As far as he was concerned, health care as an issue was dead for the rest of that year.

I was ecstatic. We won. We beat them, at least for the time being; they couldn't move their bill. That was a big deal, a sign that we were on the cusp of revolutionary change. All of a sudden we were back; in fact, we were surging ahead.

On election night I was home in my district, and I watched the returns on television at the Williamsburg Inn in Yorkville with local supporters. For a while, I couldn't believe what was unfolding before me. No House Speaker had lost a bid for reelection since during the Civil War, but Tom Foley was trailing Republican George Nethercutt and seemed in real trouble now. Some of the seasoned pillars of the old order were tumbling to defeat. Among them:

- Dan Rostenkowski, then Chairman of the House Ways and Means Committee, forced out after thirty-six years by a young Republican long shot nobody had even heard of before.
- Neal Smith of Iowa, then Chairman of the Appropriations Subcommittee on Commerce, Justice, and State, gone after thirty-six years.
- Jack Brooks of Texas, then Chairman of the House Judiciary Committee, an institution unto himself, leaving after forty-two years.

As the night progressed, it was becoming clear that Republicans had won a huge victory. We picked up fifty-two seats and captured the majority for the first time in forty years. Bill Clinton was in trouble. If he'd been a candidate that year, he wouldn't have been reelected.

With everyone watching the television screens, there were cheers and whistles and shouts and high-fives and a lot of people slapping each other on the back.

I smiled. "Now we have to govern."

Chapter Five

NEWT AND THE CONTRACT

*I predict future happiness for Americans
if they can prevent the government
from wasting the labors of the people
under the pretense of taking care of them.*
—Thomas Jefferson to Thomas Cooper, 1802

Now that Republicans had the majority, Newt was going to be Speaker; no one doubted that. Dick Armey of Texas would become his number two as Majority Leader, and Tom DeLay—yes, we won that race—would serve as Whip. Conference Chairman John Boehner of Ohio and Campaign Chairman Bill Paxon of western New York would join him. When Tom named me Chief Deputy Whip, Newt included me in the leadership. I remember sitting there at the leadership table, and Newt said, "Well, from now on, the six of us are going to make all the decisions."

Armey wasn't sure I should be at the table. He looked at Newt and said, "What do you mean 'the six of us'?"

Newt did not retreat. "The guys who are here are going to be here," he said. "All six of us," he reaffirmed.

Newt was the leader of our revolution. He had stormed up San Juan Hill and brought the rest of us along—some kicking and screaming—and it didn't matter to us then that he was a polarizing force or that Democrats hated him. Of course they hated him. He had brought down Wright; he had beaten Foley and caused them to lose control of an institution that they had controlled for forty years. He was an adversary in the toughest sense of the word because even before he was in the leadership, he was taking them on. He was just a scourge of the Democrats.

Newt was always a "bigger picture" guy. He had an incredible ability to organize and direct and encourage and inspire people to do things that were helpful in creating a Republican majority. He was one of the few people who really had a vision, who was able to articulate his goal and then achieve it. As an optimist, he thought that he would always eventually win, that there would never be a situation where he might lose. One question he never asked was, "What's the exit strategy?"

He was a blur of activity. He wrote two books while he was in office. People followed him around taking pictures all the time. They were documenting everything he did. He traveled a lot; he was either teaching, talking to health care groups, or going out on a dig looking for Indian remains. He kept a life-sized replica of a dinosaur skull in his office–Tyrannosaurus Rex.

Newt needed to be involved. When he formed a task force, he liked to have his fingers in its activities. He was a brilliant guy, but he was also a wonk. He liked to be messing around with policy. (He could sit and listen and finally say, "These are the seven principles we need to follow; these need to be our parameters on the budget issue.") He wanted to help form policy, and he was frustrated by all the committees on Capitol Hill, with their overlapping and conflicting timetables, jurisdictions, and goals. I sat at his leadership table for four years, and I was always somewhat in awe

of his huge intellect, his ability to articulate, and his seemingly
endless energy. He had a lot of talent. At one point he declared
that he was going to change the universe. He was even talking
about running for President.

House Majority Leader Dick Armey, elected without opposition as Newt's number-two-man, was a blunt-spoken economics
professor originally from Cando (pronounced "can do"), North
Dakota, who first came to Washington in 1985 representing the
Twenty-sixth Congressional District of Texas (Dallas-Ft. Worth). In
every election since he arrived, he had pulled about 72 percent of
the vote.

Initially, party leaders viewed Dick as a very presumptuous,
pushy junior Member who liked to wear cowboy boots. He was
against farm subsidies, and he wanted to close down excess military establishments. For a Texan, those positions seemed heretical.
He had written books on economics, and he used his own textbook
as he talked. He was very focused and hardheaded on what he
wanted to do. He didn't have a good relationship with Tom
DeLay—there was always a little Texas push and shove separating
the two—and Bob Michel wouldn't put him on the Rules Committee. That upset Dick, and there just wasn't good blood between
them. (Michel resented the fact that Armey had opposed President
Bush's 1990 tax increase. "Mr. President," Armey had warned him,
"if you raise taxes, you will be a one-term President.") I remember
sidling up to him one day early in my career and saying, "Dick, we
ought to create an Illinois-Texas alliance so we can work together
and not against each other all the time. You're not going to get on
the Rules Committee," I told him, "but I think there is something
we can get you on."

We went to Michel about that, and Bob put him on the Joint Economic Committee. For an economist with a Ph.D., that was a great fit, and it was something Dick loved to do. Later, before becoming House Majority Leader, Dick served as Conference Chair for Newt. Even when you're in the minority, that job–keeping the Conference in line–required a lot of work, and Newt began to realize how capable Dick was. Newt relied on him to manage the legislative affairs of the House, as well as measures relating to taxes, because he sensed, correctly, that Armey was interested in that sort of sausage-making and could do the job well.

Now we had the majority; the Democrats and the media expected us to fail. "They can't run this place; they don't know how," was the constant refrain. The truth is that since the last time we had a majority in 1954 only one Republican, Missouri's Bill Emerson, had ever stood on the House floor–and he stood there as a page. We had been in the wilderness so long that nobody remembered anything about being in the leadership. We didn't know where the special back rooms were; we didn't even know where the *keys* to those rooms were. Scattered about the Capitol were lots of hidden rooms/hideaways that we didn't even know existed. Everything that could tell us how the House should be run was in chaos. In fact, the books were in such bad shape that an auditing firm could not even perform an audit.

Some of the abuses we were determined to correct were obvious. Take the House Resources Committee, for example. When Democrats were in charge, it had seventy-two staffers–and only eighteen were Republicans. This four to one ratio extended throughout the House, and during the fall campaign we vowed that we would cut committees and their staffs. We even included that in our preface to the Contract with America.

On the first day of the new session, we passed a number of reforms that fundamentally changed the way the House works. We eliminated three standing committees, twenty-eight Legislative Service Organizations, and one-third of the committee staff—the first time since 1947 that such a step had been taken—saving over $35 million in the process. And that wasn't all. We placed term limits on committee chairmen, effectively ending the ability of someone like Rostenkowski to block legislation indefinitely. We ended proxy voting so that Members of Congress had to be present to cast a vote in committee, and we passed a law to require Congress to live under the same rules that apply to every other citizen and business in this country.

Not only did we have this huge burden of running the House untutored, but we also had promised to move the Contract and get it done in the first one hundred days. Newt, of course, was the intellectual force behind all this, the conceptualizer. Armey was the scheduler. DeLay and I had to deliver the votes. All this high thinking and high-stakes politics would end in failure if we didn't produce the votes to make it happen.

We had, we hoped, figured out how to get the committees to act and pass the legislation we proposed. Armey had lined up these measures and put them into a queue, as if they were on an assembly line. He had constructed a very elaborate matrix so we knew where everything was in every committee and subcommittee along the way for the first one hundred days, and it was designed so that the moment something veered off track, we would know about it immediately. Newt marveled at that. "How did you know how to do that?" he asked Dick.

He was just applying a principle he had learned as a kid on a power line construction crew in North Dakota, Armey replied.

Armey had been taught how to put one job ahead of the other, how to take the crew that finishes one task and leapfrog it forward to tackle the next. Armey had never forgotten that lesson. Then the focus turned to me.

If you're in the majority, you can't bring a piece of legislation to the floor unless you know you have the votes to pass it. You need to know ahead of time, and those commitments need to be ironclad. As Chief Deputy Whip, my job was to line up those votes every day, sometimes three or four times a day. That took a lot of effort. I got to know all the secret telephone numbers; I got to talk to my colleagues' wives, husbands, and children because I was trying—at all hours—to find them. I had some help, of course. At any given time, about fifty-five deputy or assistant whips reported back to us.

And bang, bang, bang, bang—we were moving an amazing amount of legislation. There was a balanced budget amendment and a bill to give the President line-item veto power to squash any appropriation he didn't want. There was a measure to convert welfare programs into block grants to the states, another to add a tax credit of $500 per child and ease the "marriage penalty" for couples who filed joint income tax returns; there was a popular proposal to reduce unfunded federal mandates, another to cut back on federal paperwork, and on and on and on. A lot of this legislation was coming out of the Energy and Commerce Committee; some originated in Judiciary. In those first three months we learned how to run a majority. That was our baptism by fire.

With an energy and determination I had seldom seen in my eight years on Capitol Hill, Members pushed themselves and stayed up until two, three, four in the morning to complete the Contract with America in that first one hundred days. Actually, it took us just ninety-three days. Excepting term limits, the House passed just about everything in the Contract except those items deemed to be constitutional issues or those that required a two-thirds vote. In the process I gained new insights into my colleagues' leadership skills and character.

The Contract had a lot of moving parts and was very complex. We were moving so much legislation so fast that the public had a hard time digesting it. They didn't know the legislation, how it affected them, or why it was necessary. I had argued from the moment we took the majority that Newt ought to hire a PR team. But he had his own organization. And every one of the other leaders—Armey, DeLay, and Boehner—had his own press shop and nobody wanted a centralized team. Nobody focused on getting the team message out; there was, in fact, no team message.

Newt was impulsive. Representative Robert Livingston, a Republican from New Orleans, had written the defense plank of the Contract with America and he had told Newt that he was prepared to cut the federal budget. So Newt named him Chairman of House Appropriations and jumped him over five other Members who were senior to him. Some Members began to complain that Newt thrived on chaos. He was drifting away from the committee system, which he apparently felt was a threat to him, and he appointed task forces to do what committees were supposed to do.

One of Newt's favorite sayings was "promises made, promises kept," but Newt tended to over-promise. He would convince members and staff that they should press on because we were doing historic things; he would almost whip you into a frenzy of belief about what lay ahead. But then, just when you were ready to strap on your sword and head out to meet the Philistines, he would just not be there. You would feel let down. Pretty soon a lot of people were unhappy with him.

I had a preview of this in the wake of the Contract with America. In retrospect, during those first few months, we accomplished some remarkable things—victories for the American people that never would have happened under the old regime. The turnaround was incredible. Yet at the leadership meetings—and they tended to drone on forever now—Members' staffs would be throwing grenades on everyone else's back porch. Press leaks were rampant. There was always a leak by one person or another, and it was truly palace politics at its worst.

At the end of March or the start of April, I told my staff that I was going home. "Put me on a train where I'm not near anyone," I said. I just wanted to be by myself for at least twenty-four hours. I just wanted to sit in that compartment and look out the window. And that's what I did.

One of the things I was thinking about at that time was how very long it takes to succeed on Capitol Hill. Term limits was an idea that many Republicans applauded, and one of the first things we did when we gained the majority was put term limits on our chairmen. The reason was obvious. Guys like Rostenkowski and Dingell had been chairmen for thirty years, and we didn't want that to happen again. But we didn't put term limits on Democrats. If they regained control, we said, they could do what they wanted to do.

The point is that succeeding here takes time. Some Members come to Congress and term-limit themselves. After six or eight years, they're gone and they wonder why they never got anything done. You are limiting the time it takes to make any real change in policy. It took me nine years to end the earnings limit on Social Security with the help of Senators Jim Bunning and John McCain. Medical Savings Accounts (now called Health Savings Accounts) took twelve years. People who term limit themselves are never here long enough to sit on the right committees to do the things they say they want to get done.

I just mentioned "the right committees." I don't mean to imply that some are better than others. You can use any committee or subcommittee of Congress to engineer the changes that you want to make. You don't have to sit on Ways and Means to do legislation that's important. Even when Rostenkowski was there, I was leading the fight to wipe out the earnings test for Social Security. That had all the markings of a Ways and Means issue, but I never got close to Ways and Means. Instead, I did it on my own with three or four members of our class. We took it outside the proscribed parameters because it was a big issue—one that millions of people could understand.

After I'd served in Congress for two or three terms, I surrendered my seat on GROC to pursue new opportunities on Energy and Commerce. That's when I began to get involved in all the health care policy. Soon we took the majority, and I became Chief Deputy Whip. No one in that job had ever sat at the leadership table before, and Newt sure gave me a lot of responsibility. Then Newt asked me to return to GROC to help Bill Clinger, the Pennsylvania Republican who was chairing it. He needed someone who knew how to count votes, and I said I'd do that. Soon I'd be into the drug issue, the census issue, and many others that were timely as well.

While all this was going on, the Democrats were trying to discredit Newt by filing ethics charges against him. David Bonior, the Democratic Whip, who probably felt cheated out of his opportunity to succeed Foley as Speaker, eventually hired lawyers to go through every file, every financial disclosure, and every bank statement that Newt had ever received.

"Be careful of making too many rules," I always say. "It's like setting mousetraps. You tip-toe through them, you set something off." You could say the same thing about forming too many groups.

And that, of course, is what happened. Newt had five or six different organizations, and a lot of them were staffed with the same people. So what the Democrats did was say, "Look, you're paying this guy here, but he's really on your political staff." Or, "He's on your think tank staff, so it's a conflict of interest." And that's what the ethics charges were. Soon there were eighty-five charges against him.

Meanwhile, we had new concerns. First was a test of wills over the federal budget. We were all trying to reform Medicare and balance the budget, and we asked the President to sign the budget that included our reforms. In past years, Democrats had done that to Republican Presidents all the time. During the Reagan and Bush administrations, while the Democrats still controlled Congress, they'd stick a huge omnibus bill in front of the President and say, in effect, "Sign it or shut the government down."

Newt really believed that our Medicare reforms would save the budget, and he kept saying we should try to get the bill signed. Well, Clinton wouldn't sign it so long as it contained those reforms. He and Hillary and their people had lost their own health care initiative, and they were pretty resistant to any other changes—especially from Republicans.

In mid-November, in the midst of this stalemate that had partially shut down the government, news came that Prime Minister Yitzhak Rabin had been assassinated in Israel. The White House announced that Clinton would lead a U.S. delegation to the funeral. Newt and Bob Dole, a Republican from Kansas who was the Senate Majority Leader, would accompany him on Air Force One. I remember Newt telling me, "I'm flying all the way to Israel and back so I'm sure I'm going to get a chance to sit down and talk with President Clinton and maybe we can work this thing out."

Once the leaders had reached Israel, White House press secretary Mike McCurry announced that Clinton would discuss the budget crisis with Republicans on the long flight home. But no such conversations occurred. Clinton never did talk to Newt or give him any time. According to what I heard, he played hearts with a *New York Times* reporter all the way back. Then Newt uttered some remark about how Clinton "made us go out the back door and not even be close to him." This is all it took to give the press and the Democrats fodder for great demagoguery.

The headline over the story in the New York *Daily News* was, "Cry Baby. Newt's Tantrum: He closed down the government because Clinton made him sit at back of plane." That mirrored coverage elsewhere, and Newt's response played into his critics' hands. He told reporters that he felt he'd been snubbed by the President—"You just wonder, where is their sense of manners?"—and that, as a result, he was determined not to retreat on the budget impasse.

Gleefully, the White House released photographs of Clinton speaking with Gingrich aboard Air Force One. In mock humility, the President himself chimed in with, "If it would get the government open, I'd be glad to tell him I'm sorry," and Representative Luis V. Gutierrez, a Democrat from Chicago, took to the floor to explain that he had taken a recent flight. He had asked for an aisle seat, he said, but had been given a window seat instead. "The pilot never came back to say hello. I, as a Member of Congress, had to walk out with all the rest of the passengers. So I drafted a bill to shut down government until the airline apologizes to me."

When I was a wrestling coach, we'd take kids out west to the mountains of Colorado. First thing they'd want to do was roll the rocks down the mountains. That was a no-no. You didn't roll rocks in the mountains because once you did, you never knew what the consequences were going to be.

In politics, especially in Congress, the same rule applies. You don't want to roll rocks because you don't know—you can't know—the unintended consequences. Well, words are the rocks of politics. You need to think through the consequences of what you're going to say before you say it because once you get that rock rolling, you just can't stop it. Newt had a hard time remembering that.

While this was going on, we were trying to refocus public attention on Clinton's refusal to give us a timetable for balancing the federal budget. John Kasich, House Budget Chairman, was our party's negotiator on this. While home for Thanksgiving I was watching television and there was Kasich coming back from the White House with his hands up in the air, the classic signal for victory. He was mouthing, "We won. We beat them."

But I said to myself, "It ain't done yet." And it wasn't. Kasich kept goading Newt into being tough. "Don't give in," he said. So

Newt played that role. There wasn't any compromise. After Kasich's victory dance, the White House got its back up. "We can play this game, too," they said. Eventually, we reached agreement on the budget, and some 750,000 federal employees went back to work. It took us almost six months to recover from that. We had been on a roll with the Contract, and even though most of us thought Clinton was really responsible, we got blamed for shutting down the government.

During the fall campaign in 1996, labor unions spent something like $8 million on television ads that morphed the faces of freshmen Republicans into the visage of a glowering Newt. Both *Time* and *Newsweek* pursued him relentlessly, calling him "Scrooge" or "The Gingrich Who Stole Christmas" and asking "How mean will Gingrich's America be to the poor?" (This is the same *Time* magazine that had named him "Man of the Year" less than two years earlier.) His approval ratings bounced between 30 and 35 percent, and voter discontent reflected itself at the polls. In November, Clinton won reelection handily over Republican challenger Bob Dole, and although we kept our majority in the House, our margin was slashed to nine votes.

The immediate question for us was whether Newt could survive as Speaker. The harsh tone of the campaign had affected him and demoralized his allies. As Representative Susan Molinari, a New York Republican from Staten Island (who was married to western New York Republican Bill Paxon) has observed, "By Christmas 1996, he was under self-imposed House arrest." Along with Paxon, Armey, DeLay, and Boehner, I did everything I could to offer him support. Between sessions, the Republican Conference voted to reelect him as Speaker. Before he could take office, the full House would have to ratify that tally when the new Congress met in January. It seemed sure to happen.

Then, on New Year's Eve Day, December 31, in what looked like some sort of plea-bargaining deal, Newt acknowledged that his response to the Ethics Committee contained misleading information (he blamed that on his lawyer, and he may have been right). Still, what seemed to be an admission of guilt—after years of denials—depressed Republicans who just wanted Newt and his troubles to be behind us now. (Eventually, he was given a formal reprimand and slapped with a $300,000 cost assessment.) On January 7, 1997, we reelected Newt as Speaker by a vote of 216 to 205, which was much closer than it appears, and he reacted by saying, "To whatever degree, in any way, that I have brought controversy or inappropriate attention to the House, I apologize. I feel humbled." This wasn't over yet.

∾

My committee assignments continued to challenge me.

Ten months earlier, in March 1996, the House Republican Health Care Task Force, which I chaired, unveiled a measure to boost the accessibility and affordability of health insurance and help the nation's forty million or so uninsured receive coverage at last. House Minority Leader Dick Gephardt blasted our proposal as a "special interest smorgasbord" filled with "divisive provisions that would doom its chances of becoming law," and the Clintons, still smarting over the defeat of their health care initiative eighteen months before, didn't seem interested in advancing it.

The Senate, at the time, was working on its own health care bill that Kansas Republican Nancy Kassebaum had authored. Her measure had attracted some bipartisan support, but most people seemed to think that our approach went further. One potential stumbling block in the Senate to health care reform was Massachusetts Democrat Edward M. Kennedy. He lashed out against Medical Savings Accounts, calling them "another give-away to the rich," which simply wasn't true. The back-and-forth escalated to the point where White House Press Secretary Mike McCurry said Clinton was not ideologically opposed to MSAs. "He just needs to test the concept, and see if it works," McCurry said. Well, at that point, fifteen states had enacted MSA-type laws covering 68.2 million people. They had found that MSAs work. This was an issue that I'd have to bang on, and bang on, and bang on again.

Early in 1995, New Hampshire Republican Bill Zeliff, a GROC member, took over as chairman of what is now called the Subcommittee on National Security, Emerging Threats, and International Relations. The staff director and chief counsel of that panel was a young man named Robert (Bobby) Charles, a Dartmouth alumnus with a graduate degree in economics who was passionate in his belief that stamping out the scourge of illegal drugs was his life's work. When Zeliff asked what he thought the subcommittee's focus should be, Charles didn't hesitate: "Start with the drug war. It affects every district. More importantly, it has impact world-wide."

Zeliff heeded that advice. On March 9, 1995, Nancy Reagan testified before the subcommittee. As Bobby expressed it to me, "Her presence sent a signal; we're taking this issue seriously again."

It was about time. Between 1985 and 1992, under the Reagan and Bush administrations, the nation had seen a 78 percent drop in the monthly use of cocaine (from 5.8 million to 3 million users), and marijuana use had fallen 61 percent—from 22 million down to

8.5 million—this according to a report our committee published in
1996. As Bobby put it, "Education at home, effective programs
abroad." That was the formula.

But it was unraveling. The new administration just didn't seem
to think that drugs constituted a threat, and they saw no link
between the drug war and domestic or international terrorism. No
sooner had Clinton assumed office in 1993 than he slashed the
Office of National Drug Control Policy (ONDCP, otherwise
known as the drug czar) from 146 positions to twenty-five. At the
same time he cut its budget from $102 million to less than $6 million. The General Accounting Office, a nonpartisan group, provided grim corroboration of the disturbing trend: "Funding for
drug interdiction declined from about $1 billion in fiscal year 1992
to $569 million in fiscal year 1995. While a reduction in the inter-
diction effort was envisioned in the [administration's] new cocaine
strategy, the strategy also contemplated an increase in host country funding that never materialized." Even Charlie Rangel, the
New York Democrat, conceded on television, "I never thought I'd
miss Nancy Reagan. There can't be a rating [on the Clinton drug
policy] where there hasn't been a performance."

Meanwhile, Donna Shalala, Clinton's Secretary of the Department of Health and Human Services, endorsed a federal giveaway
of needles to heroin addicts. I thought that was lunacy. And drug
"legalization," touted by some as being "compassionate," was
sheer lunacy, too.

The results of the Clinton administration's lack of seriousness
on this issue were totally predictable. The DAWN, or Drug Abuse
Warning Network, a survey of hospital emergency rooms nation-
wide, had recorded a surging number of cocaine and heroin

emergency incidents in 1995, and Bobby worried that the trend was worsening. As he put it to me, "Most kids are still drug-free, but no child goes unapproached in modern America."

I didn't need to read any formal reports. I'd been a school-teacher myself for sixteen years—my wife was still a teacher—and I'd watched as drugs invaded our street corners and tougher neighborhoods. Aurora, Illinois, where I was born, was reporting drive-by shootings now. Drive-by shootings! *In Aurora!* That's the town where we used to go to the Oberweis Dairy for ice cream on Sunday nights. I wondered: What was happening to America?

Parents weren't supposed to have to bury their children, but drugs were making that happen now. We were losing 16,000 kids a year to drug overdoses and a total of 40,000 to drugs and drug violence. If we lost that many in some adventure overseas, people would be marching in the streets. These escalating losses consti-tuted a threat to our national security, to the security of our Andean allies, Peru, Bolivia, and Colombia—already, drug traffickers had murdered nearly 2,000 Colombian National Police officers and executed an additional 3,200 women and children for "non-cooperation"—and a threat to the health of our nation's youth. We were supposed to be waging a "drug war," and we had a "drug czar." But he had no power or authority so no one was in charge. The President didn't seem to care or take this seriously, and federal agencies kept blaming each other for mistakes. We had to find some way to break through the layer of indifference out there.

Everyone made fun of Nancy Reagan when she started her "Just Say No" campaign. But whether you liked it or not, there was a real decline in drug use among kids during that time. National leaders were showing a real intolerance to drug use. Alternately, after Clinton's famous statement that he had smoked marijuana but didn't inhale, drug usage among kids went up—now that national leaders were showing a tolerance toward drugs.

Over an eighteen-month period beginning in January 1997, when I took over the subcommittee, we held sixteen hearings dealing with every aspect of the drug danger confronting America. At that point there were some fifty-three different federal agencies involved in the drug war. We brought representatives from many of them to testify before us, asked them to explain where they were going and why, then tried to suggest how they might coordinate with others doing the same thing. We wrote and passed legislation—the Drug-Free Communities Act of 1997 (with the help of Representative Rob Portman, a Republican from Ohio), the Drug Law Reauthorization Act, and the Speed Trafficking Act, and we called public attention to our activities.

I kept coming back to the fact that we had all these alphabet soup agencies involved in the same fight. I had been saying for years that the only way to deal with problems at the border was to have one agency in charge. Nobody agreed—not the Immigration and Naturalization Service (INS), which was part of the Justice Department, nor U.S. Customs nor the Border Patrol. Each was out to preserve its own function and prestige. But that didn't change the fact that 70 percent of the illegal drugs pouring into this country were crossing our southwest border with Mexico.

We needed one agency, I said, because we had as many as ten agencies—INS, Customs, Border Patrol, the FBI, the military—overlapping each other on the border, and they didn't share assets, intelligence, or personnel. Union contracts limited what each could and couldn't do. The INS people, for example, could check passports, but they couldn't open the trunk of a car. Customs could check cars, but not passports. Because we couldn't function in a unified way, we had no border security at all. All the drug smugglers would have to do was sit on a bridge with binoculars and watch to see what lanes the INS and Customs inspectors were working that day.

Even before I took over as Chairman of the subcommittee, I'd been following what was going on in Central and South America. (Actually, my interest stemmed from the time I had spent in Colombia and Venezuela in the late 1960s, and it had never diminished.) I couldn't speak Spanish well, but I understood a lot of what others were saying. I admired the culture (Hispanics account for some 20 percent of my district now), respected the strong sense of values, and just felt an attraction to the region. You had to keep your eyes open all the time, and that was brought home to me on one of the first trips I made in 1991, as a junior member of Congress.

Our helicopter had lifted off from Tegucigalpa, the capital of Honduras, and we were on our way to visit Enrique Bermudez, a Contra general in Nicaragua. This was a Vietnam-era "Huey" held together by baling wire, and the pilot said he was from "Rhodesia."

"Hey, mate," he kept addressing us.

We were looking out the sides of this chopper. It was smoky and hazy because they were burning the forest below. I could see the ground through these little holes in the metal floor. All of a sudden it occurred to me: They were *bullet* holes. What else in this ancient chopper had those bullets penetrated?

"What are these, bullet holes?" I asked.

"Yeah, mate, bullet holes," was the pilot's reply. Well, we landed safely and talked to Bermudez about observing human rights. He was shot to death a month afterward.

Fast forward now to April 1996. Our subcommittee had requisitioned a Boeing 707, the former Air Force One on which Vice President Lyndon B. Johnson had been sworn in as President of the United States shortly after the assassination of President John F. Kennedy in 1963. We had stopped to refuel in Panama and had just taken off for Bogotá when we received a warning message from the State Department's diplomatic security detail: Some twenty-two people had just been killed by terrorists in Colombia's capital. Police stations there had been threatened or bombed, and twelve sticks of dynamite had just been pulled from under the building that housed Colombia's Supreme Court.

For us, Bogotá was less than an hour away. "We have a security issue," Bobby was telling me (and here I'm relying on an unpublished manuscript he wrote about our travels together to jog my memory). "We need to make a decision. Diplomatic security understands the threat. They're going to leave the decision to you."

Thanks a lot, State Department, I was tempted to say. But I held my tongue. We had not been planning to spend the night in Bogotá, and the Colombians had really been counting on this visit. General Rosso Jose Serrano, the chief of the Colombian National Police and the man widely credited with the dismantling of the Cali cocaine cartel, and Prosecutor General Alfonso Sarmiento Valdivieso were brave, incorruptible public servants who put their necks on the line every day. We had been scheduled to meet with them. If we turned back now, that would send a signal about U.S. resolve.

Bobby wanted a decision. I cleared my throat. "Well, we're halfway there already, aren't we, Bobby?" I asked.

Our stay in Bogotá was short, uneventful, but very productive, and a few days later we were in Santa Cruz, Bolivia. This was the jumping off point for our trip to the Chapare, a vast, undeveloped region the size of Connecticut that produces half the world's supply of coca. Our Boeing 707 was too big for the tiny airfield that was our destination in the Chapare, so at sunrise one morning we boarded an old C-130 military cargo plane that was designed to land on a short jungle strip. Initially, the Bolivian pilots seemed to be debating what to do about the ceiling of fog that was overhead at about 1,000 feet. Did it extend throughout the region? Was it at ground level in the Chapare? Someone pointed out that there was no radar in that part of Bolivia.

Its four engines at full power, the plane rolled down the runway, slowly gathering speed until, suddenly, we were airborne. The flight was supposed to be short—no more than half an hour— and some Drug Enforcement Administration people were waiting to meet us there. Our mission that day was to get deep into the Chapare, watch the physical destruction of a clandestine coca base lab, ask some pointed questions of officials there, and then be on our way.

But we had to find our destination—a base camp codenamed UMOPAR—first. And our C-130, its engines sounding like coffee grinders now, just kept droning ahead. The half hour became a full hour, then an hour and a half. In a C-130 they give you earplugs to keep out the roar and strap you into canvas seats along both sides of the fuselage. The cabin itself soon begins to smell of gas; as the flight continues, it starts to reek of gas. My friend Bill Zeliff was strapped in tight with me. We sat on a bench-like seat in the cockpit directly behind the pilot and co-pilot; we looked over their shoulders, and as the plane descended toward the little dirt strip that was our destination, we could hear them say, "There's a lot of clouds. We can't see down there."

We dropped down one more time, and the pilots couldn't find anything so they pulled up right away and made a circle again looking for a hole in the clouds to come to this dirt strip. We went through the drill a third time, and the chief pilot said, "If we don't make it this time, we're pulling out."

Hearing that, I didn't feel reassured. But the plane hit the ground hard; we finally made it—me with my heart in my mouth.

These adventures in the jungles might have made for tall stories in the cloakroom, but they actually had a legislative purpose that most people didn't see or appreciate. No sooner had we reached home again than we began writing reports, the first of which was sixty pages or so and was completed within days of our return from the Chapare. It detailed the deep cuts the Clinton administration had made in our anti-drug programs, highlighted the worrisome link between drug producers and terrorist organizations around the world, and stressed what opportunities we had to turn the situation around. That would mean increased aid for countries like Colombia that were struggling for their own survival, as well as a renewed emphasis on interdiction as a strategy to prevent drug traffickers from unloading their poisons here.

As House Speaker, Newt Gingrich had plenty of things to worry about. He grasped the importance of what we were trying to do right away and gave us his full support. After Zeliff and I had met with him privately, Newt began a push to persuade House appropriators to accept new drug war asset priorities. He had his staff hand-deliver letters to each of the five major appropriators explaining our dollar figure needs and urging that they be met. Newt was human after all. I could fault him occasionally for not staying focused, but I could never say—indeed, I would *never* say— that he didn't treat the drug war with the seriousness it deserved. He did, and he never wavered once.

From time to time people would ask, "Did I want to move up and become Speaker someday?"

I shook my head. I watched Newt. He was taking flaming arrows all the time, and I didn't relish that. I was still Chief Deputy Whip. I was coordinating all our health care legislation. Since Zeliff was leaving the Congress to run for Governor, I had his National Security Subcommittee chairmanship to assume, and Newt had also asked me to carry his portfolio on the 2000 Census. That count was coming up fast; decisions had to be made soon.

In Congress, I found out, almost nothing is new. So many of these issues, if you've been here ten, twelve, or fourteen years, you've dealt with them one way or another before. In 1991, I was in my third term, and we were trying to agree on how best to determine an accurate count from the 1990 Census. What the Democrats wanted to do was use statistical analysis to determine the size of those districts that were in dispute instead of actually counting them. That, to me, was a great opportunity for political mischief. With statistical analysis, you could overcount the cities, undercount the suburbs, and who would ever know? I invited the assistant director of the Bureau of Labor Statistics to come before our subcommittee and explain why statistical analysis was a good idea. She was making her pitch about how much more accurate her way was than the old way of counting when I tried to puncture that balloon: "You know," I began, "if I put a stack of $10 bills in front of you and said, 'Statistically, this is $10,000; it's so many inches high and weighs so many ounces.' Would you count it?"

She hesitated. "Yes, I guess I'd count it," she said.

"That's exactly my point. Nobody's going to take anything for granted. You ought to count. The Constitution says you ought to count and do it every ten years. Our forefathers knew something."

But the issue wasn't settled. Here we were again in June 1996 having the same debate. We put $4 billion into the Census to make sure we got an accurate count. This time it was before the full Committee on Government Reform and Oversight, which Bill Clinger chaired. This time the Clinton administration witness was Everett M. Ehrlich, Undersecretary of Commerce for Economic Affairs. From the Q and A, you can see that nothing, really, had changed:

Hastert: "You said that the result of this [statistical analysis] would be zero undercount. Is that correct? Did you say zero undercount?"

Ehrlich: "That is the goal of the program, yes."

Hastert: "Zero undercount means..."

Ehrlich: "Complete accuracy."

Hastert: "So it is not an overcount."

Ehrlich: "Absolutely."

Hastert: "So there is no tolerance for anybody, if the population was 260 million and 3 people, you would not have 260 million and 2 people. How are you sure of that?"

Ehrlich: "Through the use of statistical methods."

Here we go again. I've heard this song before, I thought.

Hastert: "Statistical is a best guess, right?"

Ehrlich: "Well..."

Hastert: "I mean, it is not accounting. Let me ask you a question. If you went to the bank and got $1,000 in one-dollar bills, [would] you just take that, put it in a pocket, and walk away, or would you count it?"

Ehrlich: "I am not sure."

Hastert: "You are not sure? You would take that count on faith?"

Ehrlich: "Well, if it was a bank that I did business with, yes."

I could tell that he was tiring of this exchange. I pressed forward again.

Hastert: "What?"

Ehrlich: "Yes, I would count it, Congressman."

Hastert: "You would count it. Because you are afraid that there might be an undercount. Right?"

Ehrlich: "Right."

Hastert: "So 'to get an accurate answer,' people must count one by one?"

Ehrlich: "Right."

Every American, it seems to me, has a constitutional right to be counted, not "sampled" or guessed. The Census is too important to American taxpayers for federal bureaucrats to adopt statistical analysis or some other cavalier approach. Our Founding Fathers recognized the importance of the Census, and that's why it was the first function of government spelled out in the Constitution. Today its importance hasn't diminished at all. The Census is, after all, a linchpin in factoring how many tax dollars are returned to the states and local communities for schools, roads, and other programs. It also determines how representational lines are drawn for school boards, town councils, all the way up to congressional districts. So, yes, I have a personal stake in making sure the job is done right.

Just for the sake of argument, take away these constitutional and/or historic justifications for counting people in the old, traditional way and apply the common sense rule. The Census Bureau itself had tested statistical guessing in 1995 and concluded that it didn't work (that's assuming you don't accept an error rate of plus or minus 35 percent at the basic census-block level, which would surely violate the fundamental principle of "one person, one vote"). So why was the Clinton administration so insistent in putting this method in place?

They said it was the best way to correct undercounts of poor and minority Americans. You had to give them credit. They were determined to find advantage anywhere they could, and they were very persistent about it. Eventually, the U.S. Supreme Court ruled that the Census Bureau couldn't use "statistical sampling" in counting the U.S. population in 2000 and the 5–4 decision, written by Associate Justice Sandra Day O'Connor, handed the GOP a big victory. But I fought in those trenches for years, and it was tough slogging all the way.

The Clinton-Gore White House also pushed for something called "Citizenship USA." This was supposed to be a pristine, politics-free immigration program run by the Justice Department's Immigration and Naturalization Service (INS) that would open the doors to U.S. citizenship for qualified applicants. It didn't take us long to hear allegations that it had been used as a political tool to open the floodgates for thousands of illegal immigrants—many of them convicted felons—simply to register more Democrats before the 1996 vote.

In December 1996, Attorney General Janet Reno rejected a Republican request that she appoint an independent counsel to investigate. So in January 1997, our national security subcommittee began looking at that. The INS had processed some 1.3 million applicants through "Citizenship USA," we discovered, and 1.1 million had become citizens. What we wanted to know was what role Vice President Gore and several of his top aides had played in orchestrating that. I wrote Gore directly and asked. I wanted to interview those aides myself, I said. A Gore spokeswoman replied that his lawyers were working with the subcommittee to try to come up with a response.

To me, the issue wasn't complex. You didn't need a team of lawyers to figure it out. If normal procedures had been followed and routine safety checks observed, the successful naturalization of more than one million new citizens should be cause for celebration. We are, after all, a nation of immigrants. But if INS officials had winked at widespread cheating on citizenship tests and just waved applicants through without the mandated FBI background checks, that would be something else entirely.

And we had plenty of warning signs. Consider:

- Between August 1995 and September 1996, the INS began a massive drive to create 1.3 million new citizens eligible to vote in 1996. This was four times the number of applicants ever processed in a single year before.
- INS officials acknowledged their failure to conduct background checks on at least 180,000 of the total, and of the applicants who were given citizenship, it turned out that nearly 72,000 had criminal records studded with convictions for such offenses as rape,

murder, and the sexual assault of a child—people who would have otherwise never been let in.

- The INS insisted its efforts were nonpartisan, yet in Chicago and, presumably, other cities, it licensed Democratic officials and political activists to conduct "outreach" with government funds.

- INS headquarters, according to sources and records in our possession, had authorized the agency's largest regional offices to relax their rules for hiring temporary employees and then increased their budgets by 20 percent.

- Finally, we had copies of some two dozen e-mail messages from Gore's office to officials at the INS urging them to "move forward, move faster, reach the goal, reach the number." This correspondence stopped on September 30, 1996. Maybe this was a coincidence, but that was the last day people could register to vote in Illinois, New York, California, Florida, New Jersey, Texas, Arizona, and New Mexico.

Reno wouldn't talk, and Doris Meissner, the head of the INS who reported to her, kept insisting that her agency had done nothing wrong. The Justice Department official to whom Reno had passed the buck, Assistant Attorney General Stephen Colgate, at least recognized that he had a problem. It is a "national disaster," he said.

As those who know me are aware, I am not a sermonizer and I don't give lectures on morality—or on anything else, for that matter. But I do believe deeply in—and feel very strongly about—the institutions most paramount in our lives today, whether those

institutions be marriage and the family or integrity in government. At a subcommittee hearing, I called my colleagues' attention to what was troubling me—"acts of shocking indifference and
incompetence by an agency of the American government."

This "involves the gift and privilege of U.S. citizenship," I
went on, "something almost as precious as life and liberty itself.
The naturalization process has long been sacred to Americans,
and rightly so. Those among us who have friends and relatives
who were naturalized or who were ourselves naturalized, know
the sanctity of this gift.

"Citizenship is something that every naturalized citizen is
proud of, and so are their families and friends. When the process
is tainted by misdeeds of this order, it cheapens the process and
endangers the honor of every one of us. It also inflicts a wound
upon our identity as a nation. Let me say this as clearly as I can.
We are a nation that does value good moral character, does value
the behavior of law-abiding citizens, and has long taken pride in
our naturalization process and in ourselves as a nation of immigrants. It is therefore with profound concern but also with great
sadness that we have to confront this problem publicly."

To this day we have no idea about the background of some of
those people. Some 72,000 we do know were felons and perhaps
terrorists.

࿋

From time to time, people I meet on my travels say they envy my
spending so much time in Washington, D.C., with the John F.
Kennedy Center for the Performing Arts and all the other theaters
and museums there. And they ask if I've seen this or that show or

cultural event. I don't want to tell them how one-tracked my life there really is. I've never considered Washington home because I never get off Capitol Hill. I'm up at the Hill at seven-thirty or eight in the morning, and I go straight home at eight or nine at night. Washington is not a comfortable town for me, and I think that is good for my constituents. Yorkville is my home. If I've been home for two or three days and Jean has me working in our yard, I'm really reluctant to go back to Washington.

Back in 1977, a House committee study found that members worked eleven-hour days and spent only thirty-three minutes "at such contemplative tasks as reading, thinking, or writing." I haven't checked recently, but I'm sure the breakdown is even worse today.

In the middle to late 1990s, I was still Chief Deputy Whip. I was also running the Subcommittee on National Security and attending leadership meetings that droned on until all hours of the night. I was carrying Newt's portfolios on the INS, Census Bureau, and health care reform. In addition I had to referee fights between Republican committee chairmen—one from the Midwest, the other from New York—who were behaving like alley cats. The pressure would build up on me so much every two or three months that I'd be stretched to my absolute limits. I'd close my office door and say, "God, this is *too much* for me. *Help me.*" Sam Lancaster and Scott Palmer would see it coming every time. The way to pull out of these every now-and-then dives would be to let them handle, at least for a while, the less important burdens while I focused on one thing at a time.

That's what I was doing—concentrating fully on the matter at hand—that Thursday night in July 1997, when I first got word of an anti-Newt revolt. We had an appropriations package on the floor, and the debate was about an Interior Department bill. The coal guys wanted money for coal gasification, and the logging interests wanted to fend off an amendment that would eliminate road funds for fire protection. There were amendments to knock both pieces out of the appropriations process, and I was trying to get both sides to cooperate so they could persevere. As Chief Deputy Whip, I was doing my job—whipping—and I thought that before I got too far into this I had better check with DeLay. I wanted to make sure he knew what I was doing so we didn't get our signals crossed. I was looking for him because I was trying to broker a deal.

But I couldn't find him anywhere. I called his office.

"Oh, he's busy," one of his aides said.

"Well, I need to talk to him," I replied. He's my friend. I share an office with him. I want to talk to him, and his aide says only that he's "busy?" What is going on?

Then I discovered that DeLay was having dinner with Bill Paxon in Paxon's hideaway office on the first floor of the Capitol. I walked down there and knocked on the door. They were friends of mine, eating Italian food, so I expected a welcome of some sort. What I got was ice. They stopped talking and stared.

"I hate to interrupt you guys," I began, looking at DeLay, "but Tom, I just wanted to let you know what I'm doing."

"Yeah, yeah, okay, fine," he said.

I left. I didn't know what to think. Clearly, they had been talking about something they didn't want me to hear. Okay, that was their right.

We were done on the House floor about ten o'clock that night. I got a call from Paxon's office: Come on over.

I did. Armey was there with Paxon and DeLay. "What's going on?" I asked.

"This is hush-hush," I was told. Some younger Members, most of them sophomores (former pro football player Steve Largent and obstetrician Tom Coburn, both from Oklahoma, and Lindsey Graham from South Carolina), and staunch conservatives wanted to depose Newt so badly that they were planning to use a parliamentary maneuver called "a motion to vacate the chair." If that motion attracted a simple majority of House votes, they could use it to boot Newt.

"Wow," I said. "That's a problem. What would be the consequences? Can we handle that?"

Paxon, Armey, and DeLay were batting ideas back and forth. Could the Speakership be saved? If Newt left, who would succeed him as Speaker? Who would become Majority Leader? Whip? Both Paxon and DeLay seemed to think that this was inevitable, that it couldn't be stopped, that Newt was going to be tossed, that what they had to worry about was getting the House back up on its feet and running again.

Armey was very reluctant. He wasn't sure he should even be talking to them.

Armey's chief of staff, Kerry Knott, knew what his boss was discussing, and he was having fits. He kept pulling Armey out of the discussion; the others kept pulling him back in. I was very uncomfortable. Finally, I said to all of them, "I don't know what's going to happen, but I think we ought to sit down in the morning and talk to Newt about this, let him know what's going on before we decide anything."

It was now well after midnight. While we had been talking, DeLay had gone over to Lindsey Graham's office and met with the rebels about their demands. We had been presuming all along that should Newt have to leave, Armey would take his place. Now DeLay returned and said, "We have a problem. They don't want Armey as Speaker." They preferred Paxon instead.

Armey wasn't happy with that result. So he left the room. The rest of us called it a night. But the suggestion I had made earlier was still on the table; we needed to talk to Newt about this thing.

At that point, just two and a half years after becoming Speaker, Newt was floundering. I was weary. Working for him was like being a graduate assistant to the professor who never slept.

Conservatives were angry with him. All of a sudden they didn't want him to come into their districts anymore. They felt he gave away too much to the Democrats and ignored GOP principles. Newt kowtowed to them because they had made him Speaker. He gave them good committees—all of a sudden he had committees to give away, which Republicans hadn't had for some forty years, and they had demands that no other group had ever made. They expected more out of Newt.

He had far-reaching visions, but something always got in the way of those visions. He would have good ideas; he was just amazing with good ideas. The problem was he would have three good ideas a day. He'd give me the job of following through on at least one of them. I'd still be working on this one idea that was, say, two weeks old when all of a sudden he'd change course. Whoever had talked to him last, he'd go off in that direction, and there was no consistency.

You'd have a leadership meeting–and he had a lot of them–
and he would decide we were going to do such and such. Next day
he'd be on some Sunday television show saying something com-
pletely different. We were all running out of patience and time
covering for what he said. He was off on a different track. You
never knew where you were going with him. And it wasn't just
small things; it would be major things as well. In May 1997, for
example, Newt declared the GOP willing to separate tax cuts from
other items in a balanced budget deal that we were negotiating
with Bill Clinton. That was news to us and represented a huge
change in policy in less than twenty-four hours. (Eventually, Newt
had to retreat; Armey split with him publicly and said he couldn't
support any budget deal that didn't contain tax cuts.)

The press would pick up on this and say, "Discord in Republican ranks," and members would feel trapped. Reporters would
come up to them with microphones and ask, "What do you think
about Newt?" and they'd say, "The Speaker sandbagged me."

Peter T. King, a Republican from Long Island, an Independent
who writes books and has worked tirelessly for a peaceful resolution to the strife in Northern Ireland, commented one day that
Newt is "roadkill on the highway of American politics." It's pretty
damning, I thought, when someone from the middle of your ranks
says that.

On Friday morning we had our meeting in the Speaker's office
on the second floor of the Capitol. "I am not going to vacate the
chair," Newt said. "I am not going to do this. We'll just change
their minds."

"I'm with you, Newt," Armey chimed in. "We'll fight this
thing. You're our leader, you're our Speaker. We'll do it." What

none of us knew then was that just before this meeting had begun, Armey had gone to Newt and briefed him on what had happened the night before.

I sat in on that meeting and didn't say much. I was sitting in all of these meetings and not saying much. I wasn't in on this thing from the beginning. The following Tuesday, at a leadership dinner, the principals met again: Newt, Armey, DeLay, Paxon, (GOP Leadership Chair John Boehner of Ohio may have been there as well.) I spoke for the group when I addressed the Speaker and said, "We're going to work this thing out. But Newt, you have got to be more accountable. You have to tell us what you're going to do, what we're going to do."

Paxon drove the point home: "If you're going to make a decision, you have to run it by us so we know what the heck is going on."

I doubt that any Speaker had ever faced such demands before. Newt wasn't happy with that, but he agreed to it.

For the last several days, ugly rumors had been spreading on Capitol Hill about Paxon. Paxon blamed Armey for these rumors. We were called to a meeting in the office of Arne Christianson, Newt's chief of staff, and all of a sudden there was this altercation, almost a fistfight, between Armey and Paxon over Paxon's belief that Armey was trying to do him in by spreading rumors to the press. The situation was really nasty. What happened next had nothing to do with the rumors, although many people thought it did. It showed the real division that had developed in the leadership. Paxon, the former Chairman of the National Republican Congressional Committee, had been in on the discussions about replacing Newt. Paxon was the only one who had been appointed–by Newt–to the leadership. The others had been elected. Instead of confronting Paxon directly himself, within hours of the altercation, Newt sent his chief of staff, Christianson, to tell Paxon to resign his chairmanship. He did.

I was aware that much of this stuff was going on, but I wasn't a plotter. I figured that if Newt or Armey ever moved up or out, then DeLay would move up, and I'd probably run for Whip. Now I didn't know what to think. I remember walking back to my office as Chief Deputy Whip and clearing out my desk. All of this maneuvering made me very uncomfortable.

Toward the end of July, there was a nearly three-hour meeting of the Republican Conference in a cramped room in the basement of the Capitol. All our Members were asking, "What in the world is the leadership doing? Can't they get along?" It was kind of a "Come to Jesus" meeting, you know.

Paxon stood up and said, "If you want a head, you've got mine on a tray."

DeLay had met with the leaders in Paxon's hideaway. Worse, he had told the rebels that he might vote with them to vacate the chair. Now he volunteered: "I really did some things I shouldn't have done."

Armey said, "I really didn't do anything wrong."

The conservatives were just after Armey then. They were livid. Lindsey Graham bolted from his seat and started going after him until someone grabbed him and sat him down again. Graham wouldn't forget. Neither would anyone else. Newt had held onto his job although his tenure had peaked–you can't give your Members whiplash on a daily basis and survive very long as leader—and the backbiting was becoming a huge problem with our leadership.

Paxon was going to challenge Armey for the Majority Leader's spot. He was rounding up votes and was set to go. That's when things got very ugly. One day Paxon was counting votes; the next day he had just dropped out of the race, deciding not to run. He would have been the natural candidate to replace Newt, but he got into this fight with Armey. Vicious rumors were swirling around, and Bill just didn't have the stomach for it.

The timing of the blowup couldn't have been worse for us. Here we were on the verge of a big win in the budget fight—we were about to produce an agreement to balance the budget over the next five years while making some tax cuts permanent—only to have ... this. It complicated our negotiations with the Clinton White House and also, frankly, raised anew the question of how long we could govern effectively with a margin of just nine votes.

Conservatives especially were complaining that Clinton was besting us in the public relations wars, taking credit for welfare reform that he had vetoed twice while making it appear that we opposed dispatching desperately needed aid to victims of severe flooding in North Dakota and the upper Midwest. Clinton was always outmaneuvering us; he was even stealing our lines—"The era of big government is over"—and getting away with it.

Newt didn't want to step down as Speaker; that was not his preference. One of the things he wanted to do was make sure that we stayed together as this homogenous group and kept the leadership intact. I remember having dinner with Newt, Armey, Boehner, DeLay, and California Republican Chris Cox, and Newt was saying, "Listen, I don't want any of you guys running against each other. I don't want any challenges out there."

Over the next few weeks and months, Newt tried to absorb the lessons of the aborted coup. He withdrew from the isolation and self-pity he had wallowed in after his painful brush with the ethics committee. He took charge and asserted his authority (against rebellious chairmen) when he had to in order to protect the leadership's credibility. At the same time, he became more focused. He listened again to individual Members' concerns and complaints, and he actually *heard* what friends and advisers were telling him. Even some of his critics allowed that he was finally beginning to act as Speaker of the whole House.

We'd seen new Newts before. We'd have to wait and see how long this one would last.

Denny (far right) and his cousins hanging on the back of the truck, circa 1946.

The luxury of a horse-tank swimming pool, circa 1949.

Coaching with Bob Williams at Yorkville High School, circa 1966.

Teaching at Yorkville High School, circa 1966.

Emil Punter/Photovision

With Jean during my first run for Congress—no gray hair!

Long before you become Speaker, you have to spend a lot of time doing your homework in committee.

A consummate storyteller and one of my heroes, President Ronald Reagan let me join him on a trip to Illinois on Air Force One. One of the best parts of this trip was the Marine One flyby of Wrigley Field so that the President could get a glimpse of his Chicago Cubs.

I was honored to be a part of the Congressional Gold Medal ceremony for Rosa Parks, a true inspiration to us all.

I had the incredible opportunity in January 2001 to meet His Holiness Pope John Paul II.

U.S. House Office of Photography

It was a great experience for me to join Senator Robert Byrd and President George W. Bush to present a Congressional Gold Medal to former First Lady Nancy Reagan. She then accepted a medal for her husband, former President Ronald Reagan.

U.S. House Office of Photography

Here I join then Republican Conference Chairman J.C. Watts at a rally highlighting Republican accomplishments. J.C. was always a leader and someone I consider a good friend and partner.

In September 2002, to commemorate the one-year anniversary of the attacks of September 11, 2001, Congress went to New York for a special Joint Meeting in New York City. Here I place a flag in the Wreath of Remembrance near the site of the tragedy.

My childhood friend Tom Jarman and I enjoy a break from campaigning while in Maine in September 2002.

Vice President Dick Cheney and I greet British Prime Minister Tony Blair during a Joint Meeting of Congress.

The Library of Congress's Congressional Research Service hosted a Speaker's symposium that brought former leaders to the Hill for an incredible day. Here (clockwise from bottom left) former Speaker Newt Gingrich, former Speaker Tom Foley, former Speaker Jim Wright, and former Republican Minority Leader Bob Michel join me to reminisce. As the current Speaker, I get to put my feet up!

Courtesy of Meet the Press./Getty Images

An appearance on *Meet the Press*.

Adam Punter/Photovision

Jean, Josh, Ethan, our dogs, Diamond and Homer, and I around one of my favorite trucks.

Chapter Six

IMPEACHMENT, SCANDAL, AND SPEAKER OF THE HOUSE

*We demand of our rulers such qualities as
"vision," "dynamism," "creativity" and the like...
We should demand qualities much rarer,
and much more beneficial—virtue, knowledge,
diligence and skill. "Vision" is for sale... everywhere.
But give me a man who will do a day's work
for a day's pay... and has learned his job.*
—C.S. Lewis, "The Poison of Subjectivism"

For Republicans, 1998 was a tough year in Congress. We passed a lot of legislation, but we just couldn't get our message out. Every time you turned on the TV, there was something about Bill Clinton and Monica whatever-her-name-was. Back home, people were getting sick of it. And they would ask, "What are you guys doing in Washington?"

The drug war and health care measures took up much of my time. Newt had given me the okay to form the Speaker's Task Force on a Drug-Free America, and that lent his imprimatur and clout to our activities. One year earlier, over the Memorial Day weekend in 1997, subcommittee members and staff had journeyed to Colombia. Bobby Charles likes to say, "When you travel with Hastert, you're up at 5:00 AM, and you're out."

Our schedule that long weekend was full. We were going deep into territory controlled by the Marxist rebels (the Revolutionary Armed Forces of Colombia or FARC) to witness the destruction of a cocaine-processing lab. I wanted to talk to people on the front lines of this war to find out what they needed in terms of help from us. We learned a lot on that short trip. One memory falls into a category that I want to label, "Do Not Repeat." We were in a helicopter looking at the coca fields when we got word that we had better get out of there pronto because the FARC was in the area. Our helicopter shot straight up into the tops of these trees. It sounded like a string of firecrackers exploding and sure enough, the tops of some of those trees shot out across the sky. Our helicopter shuddered, wobbled and for a few long seconds couldn't seem to decide whether to continue on its way or plummet to the earth below. Finally, it recovered, and we landed safely. Bobby came up to me. "That was pretty scary," he said. "You know you just took off the tops of a couple of trees."

In July 1998, Andres Pastrana, the President-elect of Colombia, and the son of a former President, announced that he had a plan to end the war in his country that had raged on for more than thirty years. I met with him both in Colombia and during his visits to Capitol Hill. In one particular meeting, he laid out big maps on the table in my office in Washington. As he gestured to the maps, he told me how he planned to designate a small chunk of Colombia—roughly the size of Switzerland—as a demilitarized zone in which the rebels could travel through without fear of arrest.

Once he invited the rebels to the peace table, he said, negotiations would start and the conflict would end.

When he had finished his presentation, I asked, "What's your Plan B?"

Unfortunately, he had no Plan B. Pastrana made a good-faith effort, but he didn't seem to understand that the rebels, who were pocketing hundreds of millions of dollars in drug money every year, were never going to come to the table unless you pressured them.

On the other hand, General Rosso Jose Serrano, the Colombian national police chief, clearly understood that, and together we worked to more than triple our anti-drug assistance (mostly in the form of helicopters and planes) to Colombia from $87 million in 1998 to $287 million the next year. What's more, this represented only one part of a hemisphere-wide drug interdiction package totaling $690 million.

I had seen firsthand the harm drugs bring to children, so this was a national security issue for me; I couldn't understand why my colleagues on the other side of the aisle—who opposed aiding Colombia—couldn't see it the same way. I was moving legislation leading to Plan Colombia when the Nancy Pelosi wing of the Democratic party launched a total assault. I couldn't comprehend their motives. Didn't they want us to stop the drug trade in Colombia and hence the flow of cocaine to the U.S.? Nevertheless, I was determined that 1998 would be the year that we started to turn this battle around.

Meanwhile, we had other battles, and Newt had asked me to put together and follow through on something we called the Patients' Bill of Rights, which was formally known as the Patient Protection Act. What we tried to do was give people choices in health care where they had the power to choose their doctor in a cost-effective way. If health care was going to be accessible, it had to be affordable. This measure's bottom line was that Americans would continue having access to affordable, high-quality health care.

Medical Savings Accounts were very close to my heart—I'd been struggling to win passage of them for years—but I knew that none of this was going to happen without a fight. So I spent nearly three months in early morning meetings in my first floor office in the Capitol with Bill Thomas, a brilliant but prickly California Republican, on one side of the table and Charlie Norwood, D.D.S., a Republican from Georgia, on the other. Sue Kelly, a Republican from Westchester County, New York; Kay Granger, a Republican from Texas; and Missouri Republican Representative (now Senator) Jim Talent added to the mix.

We had a lot of different opinions and one of the reasons for that was different personalities. Thomas and Norwood just didn't like each other. And now it was my job to find some compromise.

Working on that bill was just like pulling teeth. While Thomas was making his points, unrelenting in his belief that his approach was best, Norwood was flirting with the Democrats, expressing his interest in a "bipartisan" measure that would have threatened health care providers with even greater legal liability than they faced at that time. As if they didn't have their hands full already fighting off constant trial lawyer assaults.

Charlie Norwood, in my opinion, always wanted to do the right thing. He thought that HMOs were too forceful, too impinging on the medical community and that doctors and dentists were being forced into becoming creatures of the HMO instead of making their decisions on the basis of what was best for their patients' care. A lot of times, Charlie could tell you, I had to kick him under the table to keep his mouth shut so we didn't have fist-fights over the top of the table.

Eventually we got everyone at that table to agree on the same document and, on July 24, we passed the Patients' Bill of Rights (the Patient Protection Act) by a vote of 216 to 210. For us, that was a huge victory.

At about two o'clock I was talking about the bill in the press room on the third floor of the Capitol. My staff went on ahead and as I was walking out, a wire service reporter stopped me to ask some follow-up questions for about three minutes. Then I walked across Statuary Hall to descend the winding stairs toward my office, where Jean was waiting for me. She had come to town that Thursday—she didn't do that very often—because we were planning to go to New Hampshire for the weekend.

Just then, I heard a sound like someone was kicking trash cans down the steps: "Bang, bang, bang, bang," with an echo. A policeman, one of Newt's security guys, was standing near the entrance to the Speaker's office, and I said, "What in the world is going on?"

"Get back, get back," he said. "There's been a shooting downstairs and we don't know if there's one or two of them. One's down, but we don't know if there's another guy in here or not."

Turning back to the House chamber, I heard someone say, "Go downstairs. Underneath the chamber, it's safe there. We think there's a gunman down, another gunman loose."

Suddenly, it hit me: *My wife's in my office. And there's a shooting down there.*

I pushed into the Whip's office and found my staff. Jean was under the table, and they had put the couch up against the door, barricading it. Jean was scared to death. What a way to say "Welcome to Washington."

The gunman, Russell Weston, was shot down in the hallway. If I hadn't stopped and talked to the wire reporter, I would have walked down the spiral staircase to the Whip's office and been right in the middle of the shooting. As it was, the carnage was terrible enough; Capitol Police officers Jacob Chestnut and John Gibson, both of whom I saw almost daily, respected, and considered friends, died from their wounds. And now I know what people mean when they say, "There, but for the grace of God go I."

～

Though we were all shaken by the incident, there was work that had to be done. All during the summer and fall of 1998, impeachment was the huge, lumbering "thing" we all knew was there but wanted to ignore. But we couldn't ignore it because it was growing right before our eyes. On October 8, by a vote of 258 to 176, House members agreed to begin impeachment proceedings against Clinton.

"The President betrayed his wife. He did not betray the country," Florida Democrat Robert Wexler insisted. "God help this nation if we fail to recognize the difference."

Illinois Republican Henry Hyde, Chairman of the House Judiciary Committee, said the hearings would not begin until after Election Day, which was November 3. His committee would review the evidence and then decide whether to present the articles of impeachment to the entire House. "We're pulled by many competing forces, but mostly we're moved by our consciences," he said. "We must listen to that still, small voice that whispers in our ear, 'Duty, duty, duty.'"

Partisan rancor, always present here, became more pronounced and nasty again. Democrats kept insisting this was just about sex and rallied behind their President. Republicans pointed out that Clinton had lied under oath, and the impeachment machinery gathered strength in the House. Gingrich, DeLay, and Hyde were its proponents, along with Representative Bob Barr, a conservative Republican from Georgia, and several members of the House Judiciary Committee. Those who supported it certainly weren't coming from the fringe; they truly believed it was the right thing to do.

The leadership team would have long talks around the table in the Dinosaur Room—so named because it contained the T-Rex dinosaur head—lasting into the night. One night I asked Gingrich, "Are you sure we're doing the right thing?" He didn't answer the question directly.

I don't know how many Members of Congress went to the room in the Ford House Office Building (the former FBI fingerprint center) where they kept the exhibits, closed the door, reviewed the evidence, and read the transcripts. I read part of it.

From what I knew and had been told, there wasn't any question that Clinton was guilty as charged. So I decided to vote for all the articles of impeachment. I kept thinking about the time 131 years ago after the Civil War when the House had impeached President Andrew Johnson. Although the Senate refused to convict him, the House action weakened the Office of the President—strengthening the role of Congress—and that really did change the course of American history. It was a huge step for us to be taking now, unsure of what the ultimate conclusion would be.

It was tricky at that point to make Clinton a sympathetic person, and I am sure there wasn't much sympathy for him. But I sensed that the American people were sick of hearing about illicit sex, sick of having to protect the kids from what was on television, and sick of hearing Monica Lewinsky's name. They just wanted it to go away. I'd go back to my district, and my constituents would ask, "What in hell are you people doing in Washington? All I ever see is this stuff." And I knew all too well what "stuff" they were talking about. I feared they'd start to think all of us were bums.

Maybe they thought that already.

The November 3, 1998, election was a disappointment for us. Newt had been predicting a large pickup for the Republicans. In actuality, we lost five seats, and that pulled our margin down to a razor-thin five votes.

Everyone, it seemed, blamed Newt. Look at some of our Members. Newt had empowered Pete Hoekstra, a conservative Republican from western Michigan, given him opportunities, and Pete was against him now. The same with moderate Republicans Fred Upton of Michigan, Mike Castle of Delaware, and Jim Leach of Iowa. At that point I don't think that Don Manzullo, a Republican from Rockford, Illinois, would have voted for him. Bob Livingston, a veteran Republican from Louisiana who was Chairman of the Appropriations Committee, had been toying with the idea of retirement earlier that year. Newt had been instrumental in convincing him to stay in Congress. Now he was so miffed at Newt that he had decided to challenge him.

As Chief Deputy Whip, my job was to do the count before we went to conference to elect our officers, and I was saying to Newt, "You can get nominated, but I don't think you can get elected by the whole House."

There were conference calls where everyone else was telling him what he had to do. I called Newt right back after such a call to say, "I see twelve to eighteen Members who aren't going to support you."

"Well, we'll make them support me," Newt replied. "We'll bind them in the Conference"

"You can try, but you're not going to bind these people," I said. "No matter what you do, you're not going to make them vote the way they don't want to vote."

"What should I do?"

"Do what you have to do."

There was a long pause. Then Newt said, "I'll get back to you."

This was Thursday, November 5, after Tuesday's election. He never did get back to me, but the next afternoon, Friday, November 6, he announced from his home in Georgia that he wasn't going to run again for Speaker of the House. It was a personal humiliation for him, but the fact is he stepped down when he found he didn't have the votes.

Armey, the Majority Leader, was next in line, and he seemed the logical choice to replace Newt. But Livingston, who, as Chairman of Appropriations, headed up what we called the College of

Cardinals, jumped in immediately instead. A prodigious fund-raiser who had served in Congress since 1977, he had been lining up people and urging them not to vote for Newt. I wasn't privy to this, but I think he also confronted Newt and said, "If you don't step down, I'm going to challenge you."

That's when people started asking me to get involved in the leadership fight or, at least, to think about running for Majority Leader. Two friends, Mike Castle from Delaware and Tom Ewing, my fellow practical jokester from back home in Illinois, approached me and said, "We're going to put your name in nomination whether you want it there or not."

I tried to talk them out of it. I had pledged to support Armey's reelection bid, and I could not go back on my word unless released by him. Besides, I wasn't sure I even wanted the Major-ity Leader's job with all that extra traveling. As I'd said to Jean just the other night, "I'm happy with my life just the way it is." This was a week or ten days after my uncle's death, and I was home in the district for a couple of days because Dad, who was living with us and was in his eighties, was not doing well. Congress was not in session. I didn't want to leave Illinois, but I made an appoint-ment to see Armey and flew to Washington. It wasn't that I wanted his job, just that I felt I owed it to Castle, Ewing, and others who supported me to see where things stood.

Armey's situation was precarious. Some were set to challenge him. He had two real challenges in Steve Largent and Jennifer Dunn. It was also unprecedented that a sitting Majority Leader be challenged for his job. I considered him a friend; I had offered him my support, and here I was seeking permission to be released from that pledge.

The conversation was awkward, uncomfortable. "Dick, there are some people who want to put my name in nomination for Majority Leader," I said. "I've given you my commitment and I'm asking you to release me from that commitment."

"Well, what if I don't release you?"

"If you don't release me, then I won't run," I said. "I gave you my word."

Armey stared at me. "I'm not going to release you," he said.

Everything happens for a reason, I thought. Maybe it wasn't my time or maybe I wasn't supposed to do this. Anyway, Dad had just died. Jean had called me right before my meeting with Dick and I had to go home and bury him.

Days later, when the conference met to elect Newt's successor as Speaker of the House, Livingston won without challenge. Then the balloting for Majority Leader began. Although I had said I was going to vote for Armey, Castle and Ewing still put my name in nomination. I didn't say a thing; I thought I'd let the chips fall where they may. And here came a surprise. On the first ballot, Armey had one hundred votes, but that wasn't enough to win. Largent had fifty-eight, Jennifer Dunn forty-five, and eighteen voted for me. Armey led the second ballot by twenty-six over Largent and fifty over Dunn, but he still didn't have enough to retain his position. That's when Dunn dropped out. Armey needed a third round, which he won by thirty-two votes, to hold onto his job. He wasn't operating from a position of strength.

Newt had played such a big role in my life—personally as well as professionally—that it took me a while to adjust to the fact that he was going to be gone. Under Newt, I'd sat at the leadership table, I'd served as Chief Deputy Whip, been point man on drugs and the Census, and done almost all the health care legislation. With Newt, I always knew where I stood in the pecking order. With Livingston, I simply had no idea. I wasn't close to him and he had his own cadre of supporters. I thought I might not have the ability to do the things I had done before.

∾

When you bury your dad, it's not like checking off some "to do" item on the daily calendar. The sadness burrows deep and stays with you, has a lasting effect on you, and it takes a while before the happy memories can return. When I was growing up, I'd pop off about this or that, and Dad would reply, "Well, that's one way to look at it," meaning that there was another side and I'd better go find and listen to it. I thought back to the times when I was coaching, and he would always say, "Why don't you get a real job?" I think he was proud that I was in Congress; I know Mom was, but it was hard for him to say. And I wondered if I'd told him enough, if he knew how very proud I was of him. I was home for that service, of course, and for Thanksgiving, and then I flew over to Japan for a few days as part of the Japanese Diet–U.S. Congress exchange.

While I was gone, Livingston was trying to set up shop, put people in place, and hire staff. He listed who he wanted to serve on key committees and who he did not. Newt, to his credit, was pitching in to help. He knew the chips were down for the institution of the House Speakership, and he wanted to make sure Bob put it together right.

About a week before Christmas, Armey and I went to a leadership meeting that Livingston had organized in the Library of

Congress. I was just back from Japan, exhausted and suffering from jet lag, and boy, this meeting was disorganized.

We had sat through four years of these meetings with Newt, and Bob had never been to any of them. He and his people still had no idea what they had to do to run this place. He was getting his feet wet and showing himself to be naïve. Saying "We're going to do something" was one thing. Getting people to buy into it was something else. He had named his deputy speakers; no one had ever had deputy speakers before. No one was sure how roles were defined or what they were going to do.

Someone pointed and said, "those five guys there" were the "judges," his assistant leaders, and I was wondering, "Every decision is going to have to be run through *these* guys?"

Armey and I looked at each other after hearing a few more statements, and we just rolled our eyes. I was starting to think, "Maybe I don't want to be in this leadership," and at that point I wrote Scott Palmer a short note.

"I'm quitting," it said.

Scott said he would do anything for me—except help me quit. We agreed to discuss it again after I'd had some rest.

Even then one thing seemed clear: My whole world had changed. There was a new Livingston world. Either I'd get used to it, or I'd leave.

I didn't go out and test the waters; but Paxon had just landed a good job in the private sector, and I talked to him about it. Then I learned there was an opening for president of a financial services group, an association of big banks. Maybe this is a good time for me to leave this place, I thought. I called and made an appointment to talk to a headhunter on Sunday, December 20.

The impeachment bill was still moving forward in the House, and a vote on it was scheduled for Saturday, December 19. I remember getting up that morning, six days before Christmas, and feeling that nobody else was in Washington–they were already home with Christmas trees and Christmas cookies while we were staying here to vote on this thing. The American people very much appeared to want it to go away, but we were actually going to vote on it on the floor of the House that day.

Tom DeLay gave me a quick heads-up that morning that something else was afoot: A sex magazine "publisher" named Larry Flynt had been trying to dig up dirt on Republicans; he had placed an ad in the *Washington Post* offering a million bucks to anyone who could prove that Members of Congress had been unfaithful. Rumors were swirling around that Livingston may have some problems with allegations of extramarital affairs. We had already nominated him to succeed Newt. He was due to be elected the first week in January.

What triggered the alarm were remarks Livingston himself had made to the leadership during a meeting in the Capitol a day or two before. Something along the lines of, "I'm running for Speaker not for sainthood. I may have had a few indiscretions in my life."

"Hang tight," DeLay told me. "I think we're going to hear more. There's a big problem here."

A Democratic Congresswoman from California was completing her anti-impeachment remarks during the unusual Saturday session that December 19 when Hyde, the impeachment floor manager, recognized Livingston and gave him two minutes to speak.

I was sitting in the back row of the House by the exit and the elevators on the Republican side. That back row seat is where I usually worked because as Chief Deputy Whip, I was always telling Members what our position was when they came into the chamber to vote on amendments.

Livingston began in a rambling, roundabout way by discussing Saddam Hussein's Iraq, then regretting the "enmity and hostility" that "has been bred in the Halls of Congress for the last months and years." Soon he cut to the chase and addressed President Clinton directly: "Sir, you have done great damage to the nation over this past year... You have the power to terminate that damage and heal the wounds that you have created. You, sir, may resign your post..."

Representative Maxine Waters, a Democrat from California, had risen to her feet, her supporters beside her. "No, no, no," they shouted. "You resign, you resign."

Livingston raised his right hand. He wasn't finished yet.

"... and I can only challenge you in such fashion if I am willing to heed my own words... I must set the example that I hope President Clinton will follow. I will not stand for Speaker of the House."

People were dumbstruck. You could have heard a pin drop on the floor of the House. Even before Livingston finished his remarks, one of our floor assistants came out to find me and said, "The Speaker wants to talk to you. He's on the phone in the cloakroom now."

"Hey, you're the only guy who can pull this conference back together again," Newt said. "Nobody else can do it. You're going to have to be Speaker."

Boom, I had this thing in my lap. I knew the situation was serious. I took a deep breath. "Well, I'm going to have to think about
it," I said.

The idea that I might be Livingston's replacement had never
occurred to me, and I wasn't exactly thrilled by it. Sure, I'd had a
heads-up that morning that there was a problem for Livingston. But
nobody started coming to me until Livingston made his announce-
ment. First, it was Newt. Then it was everybody saying, "You've got
to be Speaker."

Although Paxon was retiring from Congress, he was still there
that day and he came up to me and said, "You're going to have to
run." DeLay said much the same thing.

All these guys were pushing me to make the decision so I said,
"Wait a minute. I have to call my wife, let her know what's going
on, and give myself a minute to think about this."

I thought Jean would say no. It is not her thing. She doesn't
like to be in the public eye, and she would not be comfortable with
it. Besides, she didn't like politicians all that much. She thought I
spent too much time doing this anyway. So I stepped into Armey's
second-floor office in the Capitol and called her.

"Jean, what are you doing?" I asked. This was the first day of
her Christmas vacation from school, so I expected her to say,
"Well, I've trimmed the tree," or "I was baking cookies," or "I was
doing Christmas things." Instead, she said, "I'm watching TV."

"So you know what's going on?"

"Yes."

"They want me to be Speaker."

There was no response. Finally, she said, "You've got to do
what you think is right."

What I didn't know until later was that Paxon had called her a few minutes before to give her a heads up. He is relentless—push, push, push—that's just how he is and he had given her this bum rush on "how great it is that Denny's going to be Speaker and how much we need you to support him now."

But she didn't give me a way out.

I called Tom Jarman and said, "You won't believe what's happening out here."

"Yeah, I've been watching some of it," he said.

"So do you believe it? What do you think?"

He wouldn't give me a way out either.

Don Manzullo approached me on the floor. "You're the next Speaker," he said, his face six inches from mine. "Can you withstand the scrutiny?"

I told him I could, adding, "I need to pray about this."

"You'd better pray quick," Manzullo said.

At that point, I needed some time by myself. I stepped into Room H-219 in the Capitol, and they left me alone for a while. I looked up and said, "Why me, Lord?"

Hours later, Newt addressed the Republican Conference. "Denny is the guy who can pull people together, and I support him," he said. Once Newt did that, it was over.

As I was sitting in my office making calls, the House sergeant at arms came by to tell me my security detail would be there to take me home whenever I was ready to go. My security detail. It struck me then how my life had really taken a turn.

CHAPTER SEVEN

THE RINGMASTER'S RULES

The reward of a thing well done is to have done it.
—RALPH WALDO EMERSON

I STILL HAD MY INTERVIEW SET UP WITH THE HEADHUNTER THE next day, December 20, to talk about the job of president of a financial services group. I called to say, "I think something else has come up."

"Yes, I guess so," the man responded.

Although we had all been caught up in internal House politics, it is important to note that while concerning itself with who its next Speaker was going to be, the House had also, significantly, voted to impeach the President on two counts (perjury and obstruction of justice) that Saturday and would be sending those articles over to the Senate soon. (We didn't whip that vote; Members voted their consciences.)

Meanwhile, we had home affairs to attend to as well. Jean's aunt had died down in Macoupin County in southwestern Illinois. The funeral was going to be held Tuesday. That Sunday afternoon, December 20, we were going to fly back to Illinois. Christmas was around the corner, and I hadn't done anything. Usually, in preparation for Christmas, we stuff baskets and give them to friends. I hadn't even done that.

The flight to Chicago was full. When we landed at O'Hare, my security man, Jim Belka, was with me. We stepped out of the chute. I looked up, and there must have been twenty or thirty TV cameras, just banks of cameras and lights. And I was asking myself, "Who the heck is on this plane, Michael Jordan or Brad Pitt?"

Then it dawned on me. All of a sudden, I'm news. Walking down O'Hare's long corridors, these guys were backing up in front of me, almost tripping over each other, and they all had microphones in my face. I asked Mike Stokke, my deputy chief of staff and political go-to guy, "Is it going to be like this everywhere I go?"

The press was asking similar questions about me and pointing out what seemed to them to be obvious shortcomings. "The soft-spoken former schoolteacher has little hands-on experience in the cutthroat rough-and-tumble world of national party leadership battles," Don Lambro pointed out in the *Washington Times,* "especially the kind of political combat that the House has been embroiled in over the past year."

The *New York Times* was even more skeptical: "He comes to the job of Speaker as one of the most untested leaders in memory, a no-name congressman new to the battles of top-tier politics and he confronts one of the most sharply divided, least forgiving Congresses in years."

A "no-name congressman?" Where did they get that?

The *Times* continued: "Mr. Hastert did not work his way up to Speaker through the ranks of the top leadership. He was never a majority leader or a whip or a conference chairman. He doesn't even have a leadership political action committee yet, which is an invaluable tool to raise money and build support...."

No PAC yet? Oh, perish the thought. I had plenty of concerns. Frankly, the *New York Times* wasn't one of them. The 106th Congress was set to begin in less than two weeks, and there was so very much to do.

At five o'clock Monday morning, the phone started to ring–we lived like everyone else and had a listed number–and it was the unrelenting press. Five hours later, by ten o'clock that morning, the old numbers were gone, and we had three private lines coming into the house. A security phone was being installed. All of a sudden three security guys we'd never seen before were standing in our kitchen. They said they were checking exits and doors. We'd never locked those doors, so we didn't have keys, and that seemed to drive them crazy. Then we turned on the television and there were the press people interviewing our neighbors. And it was four days before Christmas. I think that's the point where Jean winced and said, "My God, what's *happened* to us here? Our life will never be the same."

All of a sudden, I didn't have any free time. One of the things I used to relish about going home is visiting my good friend Loren Miller's auto body shop and having coffee with the guys. Now they said I had to have three guards accompany me. I began to learn: Whatever you do, you're escorted. They know where I am and what I am doing at all times. I had to accept it; I wasn't able to change it.

I was keeping an eye on the calendar. My fifty-seventh birthday was January 2, and I was due to be sworn in–as just the second Republican Speaker of the House since Joe Martin in 1947–on

January 6, 1999. We had to be ready to run the place. We had to have the people we needed where they needed to be. We had to hire staff–experts on everything from appropriations to parliamentary procedure–and we sought help from other offices on Capitol Hill and the private sector. We had to find the right people to work the floor for us and handle the problems we'd face. As Chief Deputy Whip, I had twenty people on my staff. Now as Speaker, I would need a lot more.

Scott Palmer spent those weeks in Washington–he didn't even take off on Christmas Day. My stalwart friend Dan Mattoon pitched in to help, and we were on the phone several times every day trying to put everything together. We even hired former Reagan speechwriter Peter Hanaford to write a speech. Piece by piece, things started to come together.

A few other memories from that December blur:

I received a congratulatory call from the Republican Governor of Texas. "Hey, Speak, how ya doing?" George W. Bush began. I'd been a junior Member of Congress when his dad served in the White House. I'd liked and admired his dad, and I told him so. The Governor of Texas didn't know me; this was an awfully nice thing for him to do.

New Year's Eve brought a howling blizzard to northern Illinois. My security guys, who were used to Newt's mild Georgian winters, seemed to be having a hard time with snowfall ranging from eighteen to twenty-two inches.

Jay Keller, one of my wrestlers when I was coaching at Yorkville High School, was a successful businessman now, married with kids, and he was coaching the youngest, smallest wrestlers in town. I think their weight class started at thirty-five pounds. And he was sponsoring the first annual Denny Hastert Open Tournament.

Ten days earlier, he had called to say, "Coach, you're bombing Iraq, impeaching a President; there's a lot going on and just for scheduling purposes we wanted to know: Are you going to be able to make it to the tournament?"

"Jay, I'll be there," I said.

On Wednesday, December 30, with everyone battening down for the blizzard to come, Jay asked me again: "Hey, Coach, or should I call you Mr. Speaker? Are you going to be able to make it Sunday?"

"It's my birthday, Jay, but I'll be there."

And I was, arriving about noon. They had a birthday cake waiting. Jay was standing there in the gym with three or four kindergartners or first graders in their wrestling uniforms, and he kept saying, "Boys, do you know how lucky we are?"

"Yeah, yeah, Coach, we know."

"Do you know who this is?"

"Yeah, yeah, Coach, we know."

Jay tried one more time. "Do you know how lucky we are to have Speaker Hastert here? Do you know who this is?"

"I know who he is," one of the kids replied. "He's my gym teacher's husband."

Every time I see Jay, I ask him to remind me of what that little guy said that day. It helps put everything in perspective for me.

∽

Customarily, a new Speaker gives his remarks from the Speaker's chair, but as soon as I received the gavel from Minority Leader

Dick Gephardt on January 6, 1999, I handed it back to him so I could go to the floor. I was breaking tradition, I told Members and their guests, "because my legislative home is here on the floor with you, and so is my heart."

"This is not a job I sought," I continued, "but it is one I embrace with determination and enthusiasm." I thanked Newt and told him that the institution had been "forever transformed" by his presence and that "all Americans would benefit from the changes he had engineered." Then I introduced myself to people beyond the Fourteenth Congressional District of Illinois and pleaded for a return to comity.

"In the turbulent days behind us," I said, "debate on the merits often gave way to personal attacks. Some have felt slighted, insulted, or ignored. That is wrong, and that will change. Solutions to problems cannot be found in a pool of bitterness," I pointed out. "They can be found in an environment in which we trust one another's word; where we generate heat and passion but where we recognize that each Member is equally important for our overall mission of improving the life of the American people. In short, I believe all of us, regardless of party, can respect one another even as we fiercely disagree."

I introduced Jean and our sons Josh and Ethan. I thanked two special Illinois friends, Governor-elect George Ryan and Rich Daley, the Democratic mayor of Chicago, who were in the visitors' gallery, and I asked them to stand.

Then I reached back to my coaching career to establish the framework for what I wanted to accomplish. "A good coach knows when to step back and let others shine in the spotlight," I said. "A good coach doesn't rely on only a few star players. Everyone has something to offer. You never get to the finals without a well-rounded team. Above all, a coach worth his salt will instill in his team a sense of fair play, camaraderie, respect for the game and respect for the opposition. Without those, victory is hollow, and defeat represents opportunities lost. I've found this to be true around here, too."

This was not going to be a "do-nothing" Congress, not if I had anything to do with it, I vowed. "To my Republican colleagues, I say it is time to put forward the major elements of our legislative program. We will succeed or fail depending upon how sensible a program we offer.

"To my Democratic colleagues, I say: I will meet you halfway, maybe more so on occasion, but cooperation is a two-way street and I expect you to meet me halfway, too ... stalemate is not an option; solutions are."

"There is a culture here in Washington that has grown unchallenged for too long," I pointed out. "It combines three notions. One is that government has a prior claim to the earnings of all Americans, as if they worked for the government and not the other way around. Another notion is that a government program, once begun, will never end. The third notion is that every program must grow with each passing year. Well, to borrow a musical line, 'It ain't necessarily so.' At least it won't be as long as I'm around here and have anything to say about it. We must measure every dollar we spend by this criterion: Is it really necessary?" I paused and looked up. "As a classroom teacher and coach, I learned the value of brevity. I learned that it is work, not talk, that wins championships."

Between mid-November and December 19, Livingston, as Speaker-designate, had made leadership decisions and placed

people on committees. They were his appointments and they were
ready to go. I let most of them stand because replacing them with
my own selections at that point would have caused more trouble
than it was worth.

Washington being Washington, (in the immortal words of
former Pentagon spokeswoman Victoria Clarke, "Only people
from Washington have to start their sentences by saying, 'Honestly...'") my seeming acceptance of the "status quo" caused
some people to start calling me the "Accidental Speaker," as if
they expected me to be a caretaker who would relinquish the
reins as soon as the next likely candidate for the job came along.
I didn't worry about that. A strong performance, I knew, could
change perceptions overnight. But we had big-ticket legislation
we needed to pass, and, because we needed Democratic votes to
succeed, I hoped we could do something to make the House a
less partisan place.

Tempers were hot and flaring on both sides of the aisle. We
looked like a bunch of kindergarten kids who couldn't get along.
No wonder our approval rating was only 26 percent. Furthermore,
according to various polls and media reports, Americans trusted
Democrats more than Republicans to solve the nation's ills. The
New York Times was even suggesting that "House Republicans have
actually lost touch with ordinary Americans, or rather are captive
to a base that is itself out of touch with ordinary Americans." Well,
so much for the *New York Times.*

One of the things I wanted to do as Speaker that first year was
establish a friendly relationship with Gephardt, my counterpart
from across the aisle. I walked over to his office to see him one day.
I thought that effort would signify I was willing to meet him more

than halfway. It was early 1999, and I knew Gephardt had been toying with the idea of running for President. When I walked into his office, somewhat to my surprise, I noticed a sign stuck over in the corner of his office that said "Gephardt for President" with a line drawn through the word "President" and the word "Speaker" in its place. His intentions had become clear to me. It was harder than it should have been. Every time we'd try to negotiate with him, he would say, "I think I can do that, but let me check with my people." He'd never give you an answer directly; he always had to go back and check with his troops. The first few times that happened, invariably, even before calling me with his reply, he'd be out in front of the television cameras holding a press conference to blast me and the Republican leadership for some alleged failure on our part. That didn't exactly solidify our relationship.

The Democrats kept saying that because I was an "Accidental Speaker," that I was bound to fail. Specifically, they said I could never pass a budget resolution or a supplemental request. I decided to pull their string. Shortly after I became Speaker, President Clinton sent up an emergency spending bill which he called a supplemental budget request and challenged Congress to pass it as soon as possible. Because we saw this as a potential budget-buster, we insisted that the non-defense-related items in it (totaling about $1.2 billion) be offset by spending cuts somewhere else. To indicate how seriously I viewed this exercise, I convinced the House Appropriations Committee to do the offsets. I was on the floor before and during the vote, grabbing Members by the arm, asking for their help and telling them how much a win would mean to me. Conservatives were upset that we hadn't cut enough, but when I brought the warring factions

his committee. He held so many chits in his pockets and was so powerful that his attempt to take transportation spending off the budget in 1997 failed by only two votes. People just buckled under him because he used pressure to get his way, but I thought it was important for me as a new Speaker, especially in front of the other chairmen, to stand up to him. "Bud, I didn't take you off [the committee]," I began, "but I'll tell you this: I'm not going to put you on either."

Not long after I took over as Speaker, I appeared on CNN and tried to explain how I differed from Newt and to sum up my leadership style. Maybe I should have said that I intended to work through the regular order and rely on committee chairmen instead of loosely structured task forces to accomplish things, but I thought that might sound like typical Washington gobbledygook, so I tried to put it in terms people could understand.

"Newt was a visionary," I said. "He was articulate. He had his own ideas, and he was on television a lot. My job is to make sure that we can put the right people in the spotlight to get the job done. That's part of going back to my old coaching career where we made stars out of a lot of people, but I was never in the spotlight much myself. That's how I see the job."

Stripped to its essentials, my job is to run the House and make sure we hold the House. So I have two functions. One is governmental, the other political. The governmental function is to run the House, move the legislation through, make sure the chairmen and the committees are all operating smoothly. It reminds me of duties of running any other large institution, such as a school. The other function is political. I have to recruit the best possible candidates for Congress and make sure they have the financial and other resources they need to run or, if they're already in Congress, to make sure they have enough to stave off potential challengers. That's the part of my job that keeps me on the road so much. I'm just not very good at blowing smoke. I pretty much say what I think, what my view is, and run a no-nonsense operation.

Also in my portfolio is the task of developing the junior leadership and evaluating talent. We have a lot of good, smart, and, in some cases, brilliant people. John Boehner and Mike Oxley, for example, are outstanding committee chairmen. They fit the Ohio mold. There's a lot of power in the Ohio delegation. Deborah Pryce and Rob Portman are very talented as well. I think that delegation is one of the most powerful in the House.

As Speaker, I'm Chairman of the Republican Steering Committee, which makes the committee assignments to the Members. Prior to Newt Gingrich's tenure as Speaker, committee assignments were voted on by members of the leadership and by Members chosen to represent regions of the United States. The regional votes had the strongest say in who would become chairman. Newt changed the rules when the Republicans gained control in 1994 so that leadership would have more clout in the committee than the various regions. The Speaker's vote is weighed more heavily—he gets five votes—and each regional representative gets one vote. In my first Steering Committee meeting as Chairman we interviewed Members for committee chairmen due to the six-year term limit rule—another reform of the Class of '94.

Although there were efforts to eliminate the term limit at our organizational conference, those efforts were soundly defeated by the rank and file. Several major committees had vacancies for chairman, including Ways and Means, Appropriations, Financial Services, Energy and Commerce, Education and the Workforce, and Budget. Selecting the new chairs turned out to be one of the best experiences for me as Speaker but also a very difficult one.

I had decided we would conduct the interviews of the chairman candidates in December and then vote in early January after the new Congress convened. It was very rewarding to see several very worthy and talented Members seeking the various chairs. Budget was contested by Nick Smith (MI), John Sununu (NH), Saxby Chambliss (GA), and Jim Nussle (IA). Tom Petri (WI), John Boehner (OH), and Pete Hoekstra (MI) were all candidates for the Education and the Workforce Committee. After each interview you thought that was the best one, only to be outdone by the next. We were all tremendously impressed and realized the meeting in January was going to be difficult.

On the morning of January 4, 2001, the Steering Committee met to decide Energy and Commerce, Budget, and Ways and Means. After we made the selections we took a lunch break while I called the winners and losers. I had more hard calls to make than good calls—which seems to be the way it goes around here. But I was thinking then and in the days that followed of ways to soften the blow to those that didn't make it. Jim Nussle, a talented reformer who was in and out of Gingrich's inner circle, won the race for Budget Chairman in a very close contest. Saxby Chambliss, a solid and experienced legislator, didn't make it, but I appointed him to the House Intelligence Committee. He used that perch to launch a successful run for the U.S. Senate. I made John Sununu, one of the smartest members of the House, vice chairman of the Budget Committee. He too ran successfully for the Senate. Saxby and John were losses to us but real bonuses for the Senate.

When we reconvened in the afternoon one of the Members asked to be recognized. I was anxious to get on with a very full agenda but recognized him. He said he just wanted to say that he thought the interview process had been terrific. He expected that I would come in with a slate of people I wanted as chairmen. Instead, I went into the meeting wanting to hear what everybody had to say and then let the group decide as the group should. We actually had long discussions about the candidates, and I didn't try to impose my will.

As disappointed as many of the unsuccessful chairmen candidates were, they all thought they had received a fair hearing and fair consideration. That helped ease the disappointment. I continued to help as much as I could as well.

∾

Perhaps I came at running the House with a different attitude than Newt. No surprise there, for we clearly had different life experiences. Newt had a whole spectrum of things he wanted to do, an accordion file full of ideas. I tried to listen more and say, "Let's take three or four things and just do them well." Doing a few things well is much better than doing twenty-five things halfway.

Another difference between the two of us: Newt was never able to negotiate with Clinton successfully. For better or worse—and I think it was because he saw that I wasn't posturing and that I really wanted to get things done—I was able to succeed where Newt just simply could not. I remember one time when we were working very late on the budget in Washington. At two o'clock that morning, I reached Clinton on his cell phone as he was riding in a limousine toward an airport in Turkey. "The budget needs a haircut," I said, "an across the board cut of two percent."

He was not in agreement. We negotiated back and forth and eventually reached an agreement we could both live with. It was less than I wanted, but we had made a deal, and it would save the taxpayers about $1.5 billion, which was not small change.

I learned a lesson a long time ago, the first year I was coaching, when I tried to be just like my high school coach. That didn't work well because I'm not Ken Pickerill; I'm Denny Hastert, and I had to do things my way, which I could do best.

One of my strengths is listening to people and bringing them together. I had ideas about where I wanted to take the Conference, but I didn't try to force the agenda. You want to listen to where people are and try to build that consensus. When I took over as Speaker, we had the smallest margin ever—just five votes. There was very little room for mistakes, and you couldn't get too far off track one way or the other. I knew we had to bring people together before we could get anything done. And I also knew I couldn't bring a bill to the floor unless I had the votes to pass it.

As Chief Deputy Whip, my job had been to go out and find out where people were on issues. DeLay was very good at counting votes and having a sense of where the votes were. Sometimes we went to the floor and weren't quite sure if we had the votes. We thought—hoped, actually—that the momentum would carry us. We had less room for error now. Part of my job, the media kept saying, was to take Republican Members to the woodshed when they misbehaved. (And, occasionally, they did misbehave.) But the image that conjures up is negative. As Speaker, you listen to their concerns and sometimes those concerns are pretty legitimate. You can tweak a bill or change an issue slightly to help them sell it back home.

With a five-vote margin, I didn't have any disciplinary options available. I couldn't punish people; I couldn't knock them off committees or take away their chairmanships—as the Democrats had done when they were in control and had almost one hundred more votes than we did—because I knew I'd need those people for another vote the next day (or even the same day). We couldn't give someone a bridge or a new fire engine; we didn't have a lot of things in our bag to give away.

That gave me the same frustrations—and exhilarations—that I used to have as a coach. Coaches know that winning is a necessity for keeping their jobs. Same way here. And I also knew that if one or more of my Members defected, I could be in trouble.

People often ask me how I boned up for this job. Reading is not my strong point. Growing up, I was a slow reader—I still have a hard time reading—but my comprehension was good and my grades reflected that. In our office the basic rule is: "If you can say it, don't write it down. If you can nod your head, don't say it."

I'm not comfortable with computers, but I have fifty of them in my office. I work a lot with Senate Majority Leader Bill Frist, a Republican from Tennessee, and he is always on his BlackBerry communicating with someone. I can't do that. I need to be focused on what's going on in the room and who's saying what to whom. I base most of my knowledge on listening to people. I get a lot of briefings and have good people working for me. Some say I have an incredible memory or recall for exactly what happened when and who said what to whom. I *do* listen pretty diligently, more than a lot of people listen, and I do pick up facts that way.

I don't want to leave the impression that I dislike books or avoid them whenever possible. It's just that reading them takes me longer than it should. When I became Speaker, Barry Jackson, who was then on John Boehner's staff, sent two books over to me. One was a biography of former Speaker Joe Cannon, "Czar" Cannon, a Republican from Illinois who presided over the House from 1903 to 1911.

Cannon never had much help. When he became Speaker, he called in this reporter from one of the Chicago newspapers and said, "I want you to be my chief of staff."

"I'm a newspaper guy," the reporter replied. "I can't do this."

Cannon called on the man's publisher, who gave the okay. Then Cannon called in the reporter again and said, "You're my man."

"But I told you, I can't," the reporter stammered.

"Here's your publisher," Cannon said and handed him the phone.

That reporter served as Cannon's chief of staff for eight years.

The second book Barry sent me was an anthology of different Speakers. Most were Democrats who had labored in the fields for years. They kept climbing up the ladder, making it all the way to Majority Leader and then, finally, winning election as Speaker. Then, after a year or two, they died. It happened over and over again. Not much future to this job, I thought.

Those books made me reflect on where I was. There is so much history right here in this storied place. I didn't want to be walking so fast that I'd stride right by it. Even before I became a Member of Congress, I used to take my kids through the Capitol building when we came to Washington on our way to or from wrestling camp. There was—and is—such a majesty to this place.

You can talk about it, but to really understand it you have to feel and see it yourself. I just thought it was so important for my kids to see this, be here, have a sense of what this is all about.

People from my district come here as tourists. They want to walk through and see what this place has. Some are wide-eyed when they recognize people they've read about or seen on television. Others have an interest in the history. I like taking them through the rotunda of the dimly lit Capitol at night when there's no one else around and you're enveloped in the quietness. You walk to the center of that floor, and you know that the bodies of Lincoln, Reagan, and other great Americans have lain there in state. It's almost a quasi-religious experience.

Or if you walk in there early in the morning–or in the early evening in the summertime (after 4:30, most of the tourists are out)–there are shafts of sunlight streaming down into that spectacular place. That whole edifice embodies so many ideas. The whole essence of democracy–where people act for and represent other people–lives and breathes right here.

It was an experiment that some people thought might work, and they did it by the seat of their pants. They drew up, first of all, the Declaration of Independence, and then–when they found out that those separate states couldn't work together very well–they drew up the Constitution for us to govern ourselves. It's a Constitution that's stood up for more than two centuries now.

Every time I walk through Statuary Hall, I look over to a spot where Abraham Lincoln sat. Elected to Congress in 1846 at the age of thirty-seven, this gaunt former railroad lawyer and outspoken opponent of the Mexican-American War spent only one term here, yet his early ideas emanated through the time he served. Lincoln acted in good conscience in voting against the war. He got out way ahead of his constituents; it lost him the renomination for a second term. It makes you understand anew how frail the relationship is between you and your constituents. Lincoln was the first real hero in the GOP and the first official who supported Republican principles. Our shared Illinois connection is a great nexus for me.

When I took over as Speaker, I got a hold of the museum that owned the dinosaur head Newt placed in his office and asked them to take it back. I wanted that room to become my Lincoln Room and to contain some Lincoln memorabilia. Lincoln is a much better symbol for our party than a dinosaur—so I added a Lincoln bust, a reproduction portrait of Lincoln and his Cabinet writing the Emancipation Proclamation, and some Lincoln pictures on loan from various museums.

∾

As Speaker, I discovered, there are unlimited demands on my time. Just fulfilling the requests would take a triple schedule, twenty-four hours a day, seven days a week. Speaker here, Speaker there, cutting this ribbon, doing that.

Staff—and I pride myself in the fact that our staff has more longevity than anyone else here—knows I can't do that, so they ration my time very carefully. Any Member of Congress who wants to see me will see me. But if it's about scheduling issues or problems with a chairman, I push those meetings off to DeLay. That's his world.

The *Chicago Tribune* once said that I had an "uncanny knack for being in the right place at the right time." That may be true, but it's nothing I ever planned. In life you play the cards you're dealt. I've accepted the fact that if this is what the Lord wants me to do, then I'm going to do the best job I can with it. A lot of things have happened that I can't explain, and I can't say I ever planned to do any of this. The last thing in my mind going to work that fateful day, December 19, 1998, was becoming Speaker of the House. But it happened.

People are always asking how I feel about being third in the line of succession to be President. I'm not sure that office would be a good thing to have to step into, but that's what the constitutional responsibility is. I try to live up to that and stay apprised of what the issues are. I get briefed by the CIA once a week, usually Thursday morning, for about an hour and a half. They give me a general overview, and then in the last twenty minutes they hit seven or eight different hot spots. I go to sleep at night mulling over a lot of problems.

In my travels around the U.S., people often ask what's the toughest job I ever had. I used to say it was teaching sixteen-year-old kids the basics of economics. Now I say it was teaching economics to some Members of Congress. What's the best way to prepare to become Speaker? Try driving a school bus, as I used to do. You've got to (1) keep the bus on the road, (2) keep your eye on the kids in the rear-view mirror, and (3) watch your back.

From time to time, people ask how I'd describe this job. I've heard it compared to "herding cats," but I like to say the Speaker's job is like being a ringmaster of the circus. He has to keep things moving, make sure the acts appear on time, and that everything is in order. But the Speaker is not the trapeze artist or lion tamer himself. One of the things you learn is to let the committee chairmen, the people who are experts, do their work. In that sense, being Speaker is like being a coach. It doesn't matter which sport. A coach's responsibility is to bring people on and make them part of the team. The coaches who have the most success put their best and most talented people out front to achieve and everyone else comes together to work. A talented coach isn't always in the headlines.

Not everyone understood or appreciated the similarities. Representative Marge Roukema, a moderate Republican from New Jersey who had been a high school teacher earlier in her career, had a problem with my approach: "Well, all you ever do is sound like a coach all the time," she said. "You give us these footballs..." and her voice trailed off.

"Marge, you have to realize that I am what I am, and I'm not going to change," I replied. "What I'm constantly saying is we've got to pull together and work as a team."

On a day-to-day basis, most of my work in Washington is done in two average-sized rooms inside the Speaker's office suite, and it amounts to sitting down and trying to get people to come together. Even when people are in conflict, they want to find a resolution. If you let people talk themselves out, you can eventually persuade them to reach a compromise. I have a lot of patience. I don't have a personal agenda that I'm trying to push myself, so I listen to all sides that want to come in and talk. I give them an opportunity to make their case and, if they have a good case, they do. And then, when we're finished, I don't go out and blab to the press. In this business, I have found, things aren't done until they're done and to go out and say, "We're going to do this or that" builds up people's expectations and often leads to disappointment.

Our Members, I knew, wanted their leaders to be doing their jobs and not getting into controversial situations that they, the Members, would have to explain to the people back home. That would embarrass them—it was, at least in part, what Newt's downfall was all about, and I resolved to keep my eye on the ball.

There were just two other pieces of advice I wanted to share with them in those early days. The first had to do with the importance of keeping your word. If you're going to make a pledge, you're going to keep it. That's your word. It's the currency here, and if you can't cash that check, well, you're nothing. That's especially true for the leadership. If people don't trust you, if they're just not sure you're going to do what you said you were going to do, then you can't do anything on Capitol Hill. What makes it really tough to keep your word is that sometimes you get in situations where you have to change your position or you have to compromise. So you learn that you don't give your word if there's a chance you can't keep it. I think Members appreciate that, too.

The second piece of advice involved keeping an even temper in the face of adversity. Every now and then, something unexpected happens or someone says some crazy thing; I get upset and my left leg starts bouncing up and down, but that lasts for only about two minutes and then I'm back to speed. Actually, I think I'm pretty even-tempered, and there's a good reason for that. When you lose your temper, someone else is controlling your behavior, and if they know they can get to you, they're going to get to you all the time. They wind up being in control instead of you being in control. So you don't give them that satisfaction.

Enough advice for a while. Soon after I became Speaker, I said, "All that people back home see in Washington is Congressmen pointing fingers at each other, blaming each other. We need to get to work as a Congress and pass something so people will know that Congress can still function." After talking to our Members at a February retreat in Colonial Williamsburg, Virginia, we agreed there were four things we needed to do that fit under the slogan of "Securing America's Future." We should:

(1) Be fiscally responsible and balance the budget. Take the surplus we had and make sure it goes to reduce the size of the debt.

(2) Make sure every child has the opportunity to receive a good education.

(3) Support our men and women in the military, pay them decently, and make sure they have the training and equipment they need.

(4) Take steps to preserve Social Security and Medicare for senior citizens.

All of this, of course, was part of our overall effort to make government smaller and smarter, and one way to do that was to give money back to the people who earned it in the first place. That meant a tax cut; we could decide the details later.

Some in the other party opposed that idea. But they *always* opposed tax relief. I remember when Senator Dick Durbin, a Democrat from Springfield, Illinois, who had been a trial lawyer and then served seven terms in the House before running for the other chamber in 1996, was opposing a tax cut that was up for consideration in the House. "We can't afford to give this money away to people," he said. "This is a big giveaway, this tax package."

It was late at night; few Members were in the chamber when all of a sudden someone stood up in the gallery and shouted, "What do you mean, the government is giving away that money? That's *our* money."

They dragged him out of the gallery, of course, but that statement summed up the situation well, and Durbin's attitude was what we were trying to change.

CHAPTER EIGHT

INTO THE LION'S DEN

Question not, but live and labor
Till yon goal be won
Helping every feeble neighbor,
Seeking help from none;
Life is mostly froth and bubble,
Two things stand like stone,
Kindness in another's troubles,
Courage in your own.

—ADAM LINDSAY GORDON, "YE WEARIE WAYFARER"

ON FEBRUARY 12, 1999, FIVE WEEKS AFTER I BECAME SPEAKER OF the House, the Senate did what we expected them to do. We did not agree, but the Senate failed to convict President Clinton of the charges of perjury and obstruction of justice in his impeachment trial. Finally, *that* was over, and we could focus on other things. I was down at the White House doing business with Clinton on legislation he was trying to get passed—initiatives on matters like urban renewal and how best to deal with hot spots in the Balkans like Kosovo. This was the first meeting congressional leaders had had with him since July 1997, and the President was pretty focused on what he was trying to do.

In my view, the Lewinsky episode not only marred his legacy—besides the dubious one he earned as being the first elected President ever to be impeached—but it also impaired his ability to gain the political support he needed to move other issues as well. That's because in the last two years of his White House term, Lewinsky was all the press wanted to talk about. It would be ironic if his ultimate legacy were to be "husband of the first woman President." That could happen, too.

Soon after the First Session of the 106th Congress began, I reserved the first bill (House Resolution 1 or H.R. 1) for legislation that President Clinton had vowed to send up to strengthen Social Security. I wanted him, and the nation, to know that we stood ready to work with him in achieving that goal. And the convivial spirit of my remarks applied to Democrats in Congress as well.

In April 1999, the House passed a budget on time. That doesn't sound like much, but it was just the second time since 1976 that Congress had lived up to its statutory requirement that one be produced before April 15. And we didn't just come up with a budget; we produced a *balanced* budget that locked away 100 percent of the surplus for Social Security and Medicare and paid down $450 billion more on the national debt than President Clinton had suggested. That budget also opened the door to fair and responsible tax relief.

I let some conservative Democrats—"Blue Dogs," we call them—offer a budget proposal, and we convinced fourteen of them to support the Republican rule that set the terms and parameters for the upcoming budget debate. Many Democrats had complained that under Newt, the minority didn't participate in the process. I made sure that we found Democratic cosponsors for six of the first ten bills on our agenda that session.

The U.S. was having trouble in the Balkans again. We were bombing Serb positions in Yugoslavia. Democrats in the House offered a resolution to support the air war. It failed on a tie vote. Although I supported the measure, I didn't try to push colleagues one way or the other on what I acknowledged was going to be a "vote of conscience." If I had to do it again, I would have signaled my support for it early in the roll call vote. But hindsight is always 20-20 and this gave Democrats a chance to take their shots. "The Republican leadership has shown an amazing lack of leadership," Gephardt accused. "The extreme right wing remains in control of that party." I was getting tired of listening to him.

I winced, however, when I spotted the headlines in my home-town paper, the *Aurora Beacon-News*: "Dems: Hastert Fails to Lead on Kosovo" and "The Honeymoon Might Be Over for New House Speaker."

Early in June I gathered my troops and tried to stiffen their spines and buttress their morale. "I wish I could make all of you happy all of the time," I began. "But, my friends, you cannot be happy all the time. Some days you have to give your leadership the benefit of the doubt and just follow. That is the difference between a majority mentality and a minority mentality.

"We need to show some courage...our goal is to show the American people which party is for a smaller government, which party wants to strengthen Social Security, and which party wants to return the surpluses to the taxpayer...Ben Franklin talked about hanging together or hanging separately....I need you to stand together, to move forward together, to not just cry out for leadership but be willing to follow it." What I didn't say—I thought my message was already clear—that was if they didn't follow their leaders, we'd risk losing control of the House for lack of a Republican record on which to campaign.

Then the *Chicago Tribune* weighed in with a Bruce Dold piece entitled, "Why Is Hastert Rolling Over and Playing Dead?" It just served to show that the critics were going to attack anyway, so some days you probably shouldn't even try to get out of bed.

"Hastert's elevation," it began, "was a chance to bring some common sense back to a party that had treated the power it gained in the 1994 election like schoolboys with their first bottle of muscatel." I knew where this was going, and I was correct. "[Hastert] has justified all the suspicions whispered back in December that he was a nice guy, but he wasn't wily or rascally or mean enough to lead the House of Representatives. The title of Speaker was loaned to him, but the job has stayed firmly in the Southern pipeline now ruled by Whip Tom, The Hammer, DeLay...."

"While Hastert makes all the right symbolic moves, he has lost any pretense that he leads the Republicans in the House.... Few expect to see Hastert as Speaker after the election. Few even expect he will be the Republican Minority Leader. He will be out. DeLay will be in, plotting to become Speaker in 2002."

You read or hear about that stuff, and there's nothing you can say or do. So you just move on. The crown jewel of our agenda that year, 1999, was a $792 billion tax cut, and I knew my credibility rested on passing it. At that moment, it wasn't even close. I didn't have the votes. I went to Ray LaHood, the Republican who had replaced Bob Michel in the "Peoria" seat. "We've been friends for twenty years," I reminded him. "My Speakership is on the line. Our majority is on the line. Please, I *need* your vote."

I got it. I approached other Members the same way, one after another and we won that battle by a vote of 223 to 208. The moment our count crested at 218, the magical number here, Connecticut's Chris Shays led the applause: "Coach, Coach, Coach." It was nice to be called "coach" again.

"I hope that now somebody will finally write that Denny Hastert is Speaker of the House," Majority Whip Tom DeLay told reporters. He was always scotching reports that named him as the man who was actually in charge. "After today you can't write anything different. This was Denny Hastert's bill."

I felt good about that win and about our prospects for a successful session. But challenges, I was to discover, came in oddly shaped packages. They didn't always appear dangerous at first.

A few months after I became Speaker, House chaplain Dr. James Ford, a Lutheran minister, came to me and said he wanted to retire after serving for more than twenty years. He graciously volunteered to stay on for as long as we needed to find a replacement and bring him along. I wondered what was the best way to replace the chaplain. There was no lesson plan for that. Eventually, I decided to appoint a bipartisan group of eighteen Members—nine on each side. I named Virginia Republican Tom Bliley, and Dick Gephardt named North Dakota Democrat Earl Pomeroy, to co-chair the panel and take a close look at applicants. "Give me three names without prejudice," I asked. "I'll take them to Armey and Gephardt and we'll make a decision."

That panel considered fifty applicants. Soon it became clear that inasmuch as 1999 was the 2000th anniversary of the Roman Catholic Church, some Members thought we ought to name a

Catholic chaplain, our first. I felt very strongly that just as the chaplain position should never be closed to anyone based on his or her religious affiliation, it shouldn't be awarded to someone based on that affiliation either. Finding the best person for the job should be the only criterion.

Of those applicants selected for interviews, three were Catholic priests. One was a local parish priest on Capitol Hill, another was affiliated with Georgetown University, and the third was affiliated with Marquette University.

The priest from Marquette University, Tim O'Brien, was among the finalists forwarded by the committee. O'Brien had run a Washington intern program and had many contacts on Capitol Hill, both among staff and Members.

Another finalist was Dr. Chuck Wright, a retired Presbyterian minister who had long been associated with the National Prayer Breakfast in Washington, D.C. The final candidate was Dr. Robert Dvorak from the Evangelical Covenant Church.

Bliley gave me a ranked list, and that got my dander up. "I don't want a ranked list," I said. "I want a list of names without prejudice, and that's what I told you." So he gave me a second list with the same people on it.

In his interview with Armey, Gephardt, and me, O'Brien did not make a favorable impression. Perhaps it was because he was nervous or because it was our first interview. When asked why he wanted the job, O'Brien mentioned that he just liked to be around Congress, that he had written a lot about Congress, and that it would be a good thing to continue to write about Congress.

That set off red flags for me. This guy is going to be chaplain and continue with his writing?

Furthermore, I was looking for a minister and counselor for the Members and staff, not necessarily an academic who spent years studying Congress. Of the finalists, Wright, in our view, possessed the best interpersonal and counseling skills. We were way overdue in deciding this matter, but every time I tried to arrange a meeting with Gephardt, he was either busy or off somewhere. Finally, after talking to Majority Leader Dick Armey, I reached Gephardt on the phone. "Dick and I like Chuck Wright," I began. "What do you think?"

"I like the guy from the Covenant denomination," Gephardt replied. "I'll check with my people."

That's what he always said. He seldom made a decision by himself. Soon he got back to us and said, "My people think the right guy is the priest."

Faced with a split decision, we opted to go with Wright since two of us supported the same candidate. Wright accepted and said he was looking forward to serving Members and their families "with a caring, sensitive heart." Gephardt, Armey, and I then issued a joint press release announcing the decision.

I called the other two candidates personally to give them the bad news. Dr. Dvorak was disappointed but very gracious. The call with Dr. O'Brien didn't go as well. I think he had been led to believe the job was his and that the final round of interviews was a mere formality. If that was the case, no one ever told me. He wasn't just disappointed, he seemed stunned by the news. I guess I would too if people had told me the job was going to be mine. What happened next stunned me.

Mike Stokke, my deputy chief of staff and a Catholic, was at his home parish in Bloomington, Illinois, that weekend for a building dedication. His bishop, John Meyers (now the archbishop of Newark), had known me for a long time—we had played football against one another in high school. The bishop knew Mike worked for me, so he pulled him aside and said, "Hey, what's the deal on this thing?"

"Why, what have you heard?" Mike asked.

"Well, the bishops were all meeting on Friday. We got this phone call about how this anti-Catholic stuff was going on in the House, and it was being led by Denny Hastert."

The bishop had stood up for me, he told Mike, but then he thought he'd better find out what was happening. That's why he was asking. Mike said, "Well, you know, I haven't really followed it either." He knew what we were doing although he hadn't been part of the process himself. Still, it was clear to him that if somebody was calling into the meeting of the Conference of Catholic Bishops to tell them about the bigotry of Denny Hastert and Dick Armey, this was not good news.

"We have a real problem," Mike told me when he got back to town. I knew he was right. Then the ugliness started popping up here as the bigot-mongers started doing their thing. "It's too soon to say that it stinks of anti-Catholic bigotry, but it sure smells," noted *Roll Call*, one of the newspapers of Capitol Hill. "Republicans have done themselves no good among Catholic voters."

"The House chaplains have all been Protestants, and they'll continue to be so," thanks to Hastert and Armey, "who have rejected the first Catholic priest to have a real shot at the job"—that from columnist Dennis Byrne in the *Chicago Sun-Times*. Commentators Mark Shields and John McLaughlin, both loudmouths on television, raised their eyebrows and voices at what they clearly perceived to be "intolerance," and soon it developed that O'Brien, a former communications director for the Catholic League for Religious and Civil Rights in New York City, and a man who seemed to know all the right buttons to push, was feeding those fires himself. "I do believe that if I were not a Catholic priest, I would be the House chaplain," he said.

Some people told me, "This will blow over," but it never did. It got worse and worse. Clearly, it was a Democratic strategy to paint us as anti-Catholic. That just made no sense. A large percentage of the Republican Conference—and of my congressional district as well—was Catholic. Why would I do, or countenance the doing of, anything that might offend them?

Tony Hall, a Democrat from Ohio and a former Peace Corps volunteer who was widely respected in the House for his work on worldwide hunger, had nominated Wright. "Tony," I said, "you guys are killing us."

"Oh, I know, it's not right," he agreed.

Chuck Wright had spent time trying to break down the walls of apartheid in South Africa, and he'd worked very hard to seek better understanding between blacks and whites at home. Because I believed him to be a good and decent man, I asked Gephardt to allow him to meet with the Democratic caucus. Tony Hall made the same request. The answer was no.

This thing was mushrooming out of control. I asked Mike for his suggestions on how to deal with this, and he said, "Call your friend the cardinal."

I didn't know Chicago's cardinal, Francis George, that well. But we'd met several times and I both respected him and considered him a friend.

When the cardinal came on the line, I told him the story, explained it from my point of view, and said that I wasn't anti-Catholic, that I'd be happy with a priest but I had reservations about one of the candidates we'd seen.

"Well, if you want my help finding someone good," the cardinal replied, "I'll be happy to send you some names." About a week later, he called me in Washington. He had several people in mind, and he wanted me to send some staffers to Chicago to interview them. So with only Scott Palmer and me being aware of what was going on, Mike and my counsel Ted Van Der Meid flew to Chicago and interviewed the priests. They narrowed the list to two. Then I flew to Chicago one night very quietly to interview them myself and make a decision.

I had told Tony Hall what I thought was going to happen and asked him if he thought Wright might withdraw his name. Wright was still chaplain-designate. Through no fault of his own, this thing was affecting his reputation. Finally, on March 22, he said, in effect, "enough." In a letter to me withdrawing his name, he said he didn't want to serve in a divided House. I felt awful about that. I felt awful about the whole thing. Dick Armey's son, a convert to Catholicism, had even been verbally abused, reportedly over his dad's "anti-Catholic" views.

Over and over again, I reviewed the facts as I knew them and tried to pinpoint where the problem had begun. Before me, every Speaker had made the choice of the House chaplain arbitrarily, and no one had questioned it. I had sought to open up the process and–BAM! Well, it was long past time to put an end to this.

On the afternoon of March 23, 2000, things had gotten very ugly. People were trying to stir things up. I rose on a question of personal privilege and stepped to the well of the House chamber, the same spot where I'd made my first remarks as Speaker more than a year before. I outlined the steps I had taken in an attempt to be fair and said I'd consulted with Armey and Gephardt twice before I'd made the final decision. Both had signed off on the choice of Dr. Wright, I said. "I thought we had reached consensus."

Then I described how I found out that that was wrong. "I can only conclude that those who accuse me of anti-Catholic bigotry either do not know me or are maliciously seeking political advantage ... political maneuvering on this issue may have catastrophic unintended consequences, like children playing with matches.

"My friends, in all my years in the Congress, I have never seen a more cynical and destructive political campaign. That such a campaign should be waged in connection with the selection of the House chaplain brings shame on this House ... As Speaker of the whole House, I will act to stop those who want to persist in this unseemly political game. I will not allow this House to be torn apart."

Then I shifted gears and announced my choice: Daniel Coughlin, the bishop's vicar whom I had interviewed in Chicago myself. "Father Coughlin," I continued, "is the vicar of the Archdiocese of Chicago and comes with the highest recommendations from a man of God for whom I have great respect, my good friend, Cardinal George of Chicago ... I believe Daniel Coughlin will bring to the House a caring and healing heart. Let us embrace our new chaplain, put this episode behind us, and move forward to do the people's business," I said.

That took Gephardt by surprise, and it also seemed to astound Jerry Kleczka, the Wisconsin Democrat who had been pushing O'Brien and who was just going bananas on the floor. Anna Eshoo and Earl Pomeroy were stunned. Charlie Johnson, who served in the House parliamentarian office for forty years—ten of those as House parliamentarian—was quoted as saying in his forty years on Capitol Hill he had "never heard the House floor so quiet."

Father Coughlin and I stepped into a press conference near my office in the Capitol, and the first question, addressed to the priest, was: "Don't you know you're walking into a lion's den with all this controversy going on?"

The priest smiled and replied, "You know, my first name is Daniel." And that was the end of it.

Gephardt never said anything later about the charges of anti-Catholicism that had been leveled against me. That was not his style. But after that, I never expected much from him.

∾

Going into the 2000 election at the end of my first term as Speaker, I could say that this second session of the 106th Congress had actually accomplished a good bit. We had passed a prescription drugs bill, taken care of the chaplain episode—which the other party had used to sandbag me—and passed a round of tax cuts. We had also stopped a raid on the Social Security surplus, put the nation on course to retire our national debt, and enacted the first reform of campaign finance laws in more than twenty-five years. Yet everyone said we were vulnerable, and I had to agree. We had a narrow margin, just six seats, and we had to defend a presidential candidate, George W. Bush, who in the campaign's last days was running for his life.

The Bush campaign invited me to St. Louis to watch one of the Bush-Gore debates on the campus of Washington University. Bush was talking about health care. Gore came up and confronted him, got right in his face, and I asked myself, "What in the world is Gore trying to do?"

People were saying, "He's doing it to show his manliness." Nonsense. Gore looked like an idiot doing that, and it was the dumbest thing I ever saw. Then Gore tried to reinvent himself, and I was wondering what he was trying to reinvent. First, he was suave and sophisticated. Then, all of a sudden, he got up and kissed his wife in front of everybody. That kiss lasted a very long time. He had to have been coached. But who was he appealing to? Then he changed his clothing style in the middle of the campaign and became this casual guy. Al Gore might have been a better candidate if he had spent more time getting to know the real Al Gore.

As Speaker, I had more contact with Clinton than with Gore. For some discussions on hotspots like Kosovo or Iraq, the Clinton administration would invite the House-Senate leadership to briefings at the White House. Gore would be in the room for five minutes. Then he'd leave, so we didn't have much contact with him at all.

The only other brush I had with him was not a pleasant experience. Back in December 1997, before I became Speaker of the House, Gore led the U.S. delegation to the UN Convention on Climate Change in Kyoto, Japan. Negotiators from some one hundred and fifty nations were scheduled to debate global warming and how to reduce the air pollution that causes it. Because some of the discussions were sure to intersect with issues I'd worked on while serving on the House Energy and Commerce Committee, Newt had asked me to attend and keep an eye on things.

Initially, I thought the U.S. was holding its own and we seemed poised to leave the conference with a positive result. Then Gore arrived. Representative Henry Waxman, the liberal Democrat from California, got him off in one corner and was in his ear for about ten minutes. Then Gore, as the head of our delegation, caved on everything. In just ten minutes he sold out America to advance radical environmental policy. Third World countries could do whatever they wanted to the environment. The European Union (EU) had to be considered as one entity instead of, at that point, fifteen individual states. The only countries facing any penalties were the U.S. and Japan. Everyone else got off free. After that experience watching Gore, I was thinking, "I don't need to work with this guy."

At this point in the 2000 election campaign, I didn't know George W. Bush that well. Still, I liked him a lot. He struck me as a good listener—someone who was willing to argue the issues back and forth yet who was very decisive at the same time. He wasn't the sort to make up his mind one day and then come back and change it the next. He didn't try to please by saying, "Oh, yeah, we'll do that," and then not do it. (Bill Clinton would say, "Well, that's important, you know." And then he'd go do something else.) Bush struck me as pretty straightforward, the sort of guy who would tell you what he thinks and then go do it.

And the issues he wanted to push—education, tax cuts, a strong national defense, and the strengthening of Medicare and Social Security—were the same ones I had helped focus our Conference on two years before. So our values and ideas were in sync. I sensed that he wanted to push the envelope. His attitude seemed to be, "Well, if I get this job, I'm going to make a difference." He wasn't doing this just to get a job and hold onto it.

As for Cheney, I'd known him in the House before he moved over to become Secretary of Defense in 1989. He had considered running for President, briefly, the year before, and I would have supported him if he hadn't backed out on account of persistent problems with his heart. Earlier, Cheney had been a super chief of staff to President Gerald R. Ford. Don Rumsfeld, who had once been a Member of Congress from Illinois, had brought him into the fold, and when Rumsfeld left to go to the Pentagon, he became heir apparent. That was an incredible job for a kid—he was just thirty-five—and he tells the story about how he first came to Washington and worked for the late Bill Steiger, a very bright Republican representative from Wisconsin. He'd never been in the city before.

I'd say he did pretty well. One thing you have to understand about Cheney is that he's not a talker. He's the consummate listener—he'll always beam a welcome with a half-grin but never with much more. Then he'll just sit there, blue eyes looking out over the tops of his glasses, his gray-haired, balding head resting on two fingers pressed against his cheek while he listens to complaints, proposals, or even negotiations for long periods of time. Finally, when he's heard enough, he'll say, "Okay, why don't we try it this way?" Usually, that carries the day.

His passion is fly-fishing. Mine is just fishing. Being a flatlander from Illinois, I've never fly-fished much at all. But, a few years back, there we were fishing together on the Snake River in Wyoming. I was standing up toward the bow of the boat trying to look respectable by not tangling up my line. But it was hard to look respectable there. We were accompanied down that river—there were boats ahead of us and behind us and mounted horses with riders on each side of us. I was thinking that no self-respecting trout would come within three miles of this entourage. Dick never said a word. He just fished all day.

Now he and Bush were on the campaign trail, and they were fishing for votes. The November 2000 election, as everyone knows, was one of the closest, most controversial in American history. I was watching returns come in on television at Walter Payton's Roundhouse Restaurant in Aurora. I thought we'd retain the House, but I wasn't sure about the next occupant of 1600 Pennsylvania Avenue, and I remember saying before I went to bed that night that I was prepared to work with whoever was going to be our President for the next four years.

When I woke up the next morning, the new parameters were becoming clear. Republicans had won the House (221 to 212 with two independents), and the Senate was a squeaker whose final makeup was too early to predict. The White House was still up for grabs.

Personally, I felt a great sense of relief about our party's retaining control of the House. The first few months in this job had been like drinking water from a fire hose, but overall in my first two years as Speaker of the House, I thought I had grown. Our Members had responded well to all sorts of challenges. Our Conference had stuck together, and we had accomplished the things we said we were going to do.

Another hopeful sign was a phone call I had just received from Dick Gephardt. He wanted us to work together more productively in the next session, he said. As he told a reporter later, "That's my goal and I'm going to see if we can get that done." I wondered why he felt he had to notify the AP.

Unfortunately, the next few weeks were ugly. The Bush-Gore presidential race depended on who won Florida, and that contest remained too close to call. For a while the scene there, the one we saw nightly on television, resembled a tragicomedy, soap opera, or farce. The ballots and voting machines in that state seemed to lack uniformity, terms like "hanging chads" entered the nation's vocabulary, and the allegations people were hurling back and forth on television were just scurrilous. Democrats charged that we had illegally purged thousands of African Americans from the voter registration rolls. That was simply false. Then we pointed out that Democrats were trying to find ways not to count the absentee ballots from our servicemen and women overseas, and we had evidence to back up that claim.

Florida was a melodrama, a roller coaster. But even before the nation had its decision, Bush was exhibiting a winner's confidence. Late in November, he asked me to join Senate Republican Leader Trent Lott (since that chamber was deadlocked at fifty for each party then, we couldn't designate him Majority Leader yet) at his ranch in Crawford, Texas. Then he widened that invitation to include members of our senior staffs. Trent and I had a good professional relationship. I got along fine with him, but our personal relationship wasn't that strong.

Right after I became Speaker, he flashed me that one-sided grin, slapped me on the back and said, "Oh, we're going to make a great team. You're like one of those Big Ten fullbacks. You just pound the line, three yards and a cloud of dust every time. That's how you play football up there. Now I see myself as a Southeast Conference wide receiver. I like to catch that long pass."

I thought I had been in Congress for a long time, but Trent had been elected to the House in 1972, and he'd served on Capitol Hill ever since. He was—and is—a man of fixed habits. He went home and ate supper at 5:30 every afternoon. What I found interesting about his being in politics was that he was never a good listener. He was a good talker. You'd go into a meeting with him, and he wouldn't listen to what you had to say.

But his heart was in the right place. He wanted to get the right thing done, and on occasion we worked together very effectively.

We were on our way to Crawford to see Bush to discuss his agenda. Scott Palmer was wearing a trench coat. Lott started making fun of it. "It's not Western," he said. Lott himself was wearing a plaid shirt, denim jacket, and jeans. He was sporting a cowboy hat with a big turkey feather in it and looked like he might have been one of the original Three Musketeers. "Nice hat," I deadpanned. "Are you going to wear it?"

"Oh, yeah," he replied, smiling tightly. "You don't know Western, do you? You don't know Texas." He was right. I really didn't know Texas.

We pulled up in front of the old ranch house where Bush had lived while he was still Texas Governor. Bush stepped out to welcome us. He took one look at Lott and said, "Where did you get that hat?"

Our meeting in front of a crackling fire lasted for more than three hours; we listened as Bush laid out his agenda and explained his priorities. The agenda contained a familiar list: education reform, tax cuts, offering seniors prescription drug coverage, bolstering the military, and fixing both Social Security and Medicare–all of the issues he had discussed during the campaign. Now we were several steps closer to having a chance to actually implement it; we were focusing on timing and proper order now.

A few days later, I was at my district office in Batavia, Illinois, preparing for a visit to a nearby General Mills facility. Ted Van Der Meid, my staff counsel in Washington, and Randy Evans, my outside counsel from Atlanta who's an expert on election law, had come along to brief me in the car about a future possibility that had once seemed remote–that of my becoming Acting President of the United States. As Ted explained it, "Well, if this electoral battle is not resolved by January 20, you will become President. By default, it will go to you."

What was I supposed to say? I really didn't want to be President, temporary or permanent. And Jean, who wasn't thrilled with my present job, would not be happy with this. My staff had tried to talk to me about it before I went to Crawford, but I just didn't want to hear it or even consider it. Now I realized I needed to be briefed on this. Things could happen that would impact me. If we had to take over, we needed to know the breadth and scope of what we had to do.

The Constitution itself was clear. "If, by reason of death, resignation, removal from office, inability or *failure to qualify* [emphasis added], there is neither a President nor Vice President to discharge the powers and duties of the office of President, then the Speaker of the House of Representatives shall, *upon his resignation as Speaker and as a Representative in Congress* [emphasis added], act as President." For how long? Again, that esteemed document spelled it out: "Only until a President or Vice President qualifies...."

As our conversation continued, I learned some fascinating trivia. For example: you don't have to be a Member of Congress to be Speaker of the House; you don't even have to be an elected official. You can't be Acting President and a Member of Congress at the same time. But you can resign your seat in the House, step down from your Speakership, become Acting President for however long a period of time, and then resign that post to reclaim your Speakership.

Under the succession laws, the proscribed sequence after the President and Vice President was: first, the Speaker of the House; next, the President Pro Tempore of the Senate (in late 2000 it was ninety-seven-year-old Strom Thurmond, Republican of South Carolina), and then to the members of the President's Cabinet, the Secretaries of State, Defense, and Treasury, etc.

The way the statute is written, the Speaker has an opt-out provision. He can just say no to the office or, if he can't be found, the office passes to the Senate President Pro Tempore. If he accepts it, he becomes President. If he allows it to pass onto the Secretary of State, then either the Speaker or the President Pro Tempore can reclaim it. That's the anomaly in the law, which was originally written—not concisely at all—back in 1947. Congress may want to take another run at that.

The opt-out provision might have seemed attractive, but I understood that it wasn't really an option because if you had a constitutional crisis and you were Speaker, you couldn't pass it up. You had to accept it, and then, when you did, you had to know what the consequences were going to be.

The recount in Florida was still continuing, and we decided that I couldn't comment on or become involved in any way with that because I could be perceived as having an interest in how that turned out. And that would appear to be self-serving indeed.

What I remember about those briefings in early December in both Illinois and Washington, D.C., was that Ted and Randy kept laying out different scenarios, then saying, "In this situation, you would become Acting President."

I kept asking, "How likely is this?" or "What are the chances that this will happen?" Then I added, "If it is unlikely, I don't want to go down that path."

Randy replied that everything depended on what the U.S. Supreme Court decided to do. Right now it was considering a Florida Supreme Court decision, welcomed by Gore supporters, that the recount in selected Florida counties should continue. The Bush people had appealed that to the U.S. Supreme Court. Randy said he expected that court to vote 5–4 in favor of the Bush position. If the court decision went the other way, however, the Bush people would probably demand a recount of other counties in Florida. Those recounts, and he seemed sure that request would be granted, would surely stretch out beyond January 20. Stripped to its essentials, what that meant for me was: If the court sided with Gore, I would become Acting President. When Scott was briefed, he grabbed Randy and said, "If Denny becomes President, you're fired." He wasn't kidding. We had all ended up in our jobs in a roundabout way. Scott was not interested in winding up as White House chief of staff, temporary or not.

For years I had taught my civics students about the structure of government and presidential line of succession. Of course, I never imagined that I would be in this position. Here I was, living this moment of history, and here was this possibility–coming to me. I was third in line. It was a sobering realization.

And that wasn't all we had to worry about. At the same time that we were pondering these possibilities, we also had to prepare for the mid-December session to count the electoral votes. Traditionally, the Speaker and the Vice President chair that session jointly, but the Vice President has the right of recognition. What that meant for me was that if someone stood to challenge a state's electoral count, Gore would decide what would happen next. That prospect didn't exactly fill my heart with joy.

If Gore were to rule that Florida's votes didn't count, neither Bush nor Gore would have an electoral majority, and the contest would then go to the House of Representatives. According to the law, state delegations decide with each state having one vote. California, for example, had fifty-two electoral votes, but in this race it could cast only one vote. It would vote for Gore because the Democrats had the majority of House seats in the California delegation. Overall, however, Bush would have won that contest easily because Republicans controlled the majority of state delegations.

But that never happened because on December 12, a narrowly divided Supreme Court–voting five to four–issued a ruling that stopped the recount in Florida. That cleared the way for Bush. And three weeks later, in the House chamber on the afternoon of January 6, 2001, Gore presided over the formal ratification of the results of the 2000 election, an election that he lost even though he had triumphed in the popular vote.

During that session, House Democrats raised some twenty objections, all aimed at blocking the counting of Florida's twenty-

five electoral votes. He was then able to disallow those objections—
"the gentleman will suspend"—because they weren't also signed by
a senator, as required by law. In fact, I believe Gore discouraged
these objections. When the count was finished, he announced the
result: Bush 271, Gore 266. Then he said, "May God bless our new
President and our new Vice President and may God bless the
United States of America." There were cheers in the chamber, and
he reached over to shake hands. In my view, he had been a real
statesman that day.

CHAPTER NINE

DOWN THE TRACKS

"It is not the critic who counts; not the man who points out how the strong man stumbles, or where the doer of deeds could have done them better. The credit belongs to the man who is actually in the arena, whose face is marred by dust and sweat and blood; who strives valiently; who errs, and comes short again and again, because there is no effort without error and shortcoming, but who does actually strive to do the deeds; who knows the great enthusiasms, the great devotions; who spends himself in a worthy cause; who at the best knows in the end the triumph of high achievement, and who at the worst, if he fails, at least fails while daring greatly, so that his place shall never be with those cold and timid souls who know neither victory nor defeat."
—THEODORE ROOSEVELT, ADDRESS AT THE
SORBONNE IN PARIS, APRIL 23, 1910

IN HIS FIRST SPEECH AS PRESIDENT-ELECT, DELIVERED IN AUSTIN, Texas, George W. Bush sounded the theme he wanted to elaborate on as soon as he arrived in Washington: "I was not elected to serve one party but to serve one nation," he began. "The President of the United States is the President of every single American, of every race and every background. Whether you voted for me or not, I will do my best to serve your interests, and I will work to earn your respect."

His Cabinet selections were outstanding, and I was encouraged by his ability to hit the ground running here. Republicans had the White House and both houses of Congress. We had to perform. Soon after he took office, Bush laid out a common-sense budget blueprint that would fund our priorities, reduce our debt, and deliver tax relief to the American people. I asked my colleagues to pass that budget promptly.

The House went to work, especially in the area of providing tax relief. Under the law at that time, couples who decided to marry had to pay an extra $1,400 in taxes. To me, that seemed absurd. Societies don't prosper by discouraging marriage, but that's what we were doing to ourselves. I was delighted when the House eliminated the marriage penalty, expanded the child tax credit from $500 to $1,000, and even abolished the onerous death tax. On top of that, we cut taxes across the board.

People seemed to like what we were doing. On April 24, as we approached the end of the first one hundred days of the George W. Bush presidency, the *Washington Post* reported on its front page that Bush "received solid marks for the way he has handled himself in office," with 63 percent approving and 32 percent disapproving of his conduct thus far. As the *Post* also reported, "Congress received high marks for its work this year, with 58 percent saying they approved of the way the legislative branch is doing its job." That rating for those of us who work on Capitol Hill was the highest in more than a decade.

Eventually, we passed—and the President signed—the education reform bill (No Child Left Behind Act of 2001). We also succeeded with a $1.35 trillion tax cut which, except for the objections of Vermont Senator Jim Jeffords, a Republican maverick, would have been $300 billion more. Then in May 2001, Jeffords bolted from our party, and, although calling himself an independent, continued voting with the Democrats. A liberal who was first elected to Congress in 1974, he was never held in high esteem in the House; when he ran for the Senate in 1988, people here shook their heads. "Anybody can be a Senator," was the common refrain, "especially if you're from a small state."

Jeffords won that race, and he's been in the Senate ever since. As *The Almanac of American Politics 2002* pointed out, "Jeffords voted as often with Democrats as any Republican senator. In July 1993 he announced he was supporting the not-yet-written Clinton health care plan, the only Republican member of Congress who ever did." No wonder Bill Clinton once called him "my favorite Republican." Jeffords had disappointed me on several occasions, but he no longer surprised me.

Because we had the Senate, we were able to pass the education measure (which lessened regulations and red tape, increased accountability, and heightened the focus on literacy) and then the tax cuts, but after we lost Jeffords, we lost the Senate, too; Tom Daschle of South Dakota became Majority Leader.

Democrats became obstructionists, and progress grounded to a halt. Tom Daschle called us a "Do-Nothing" Congress. We turned that around on him, sending him a hundred bills that piled up undebated in the Senate and dubbing him "Do-Nothing Daschle." It became obvious who the obstructionist was. (Eventually, the Democrats lost their majority because they didn't *do* anything. They were very adept at slipping a monkey wrench into the gears.)

Very early in the Bush administration, the President slapped a tariff on foreign steel. I didn't agree with that. At a meeting in the Oval Office, I told him so. But I didn't win that argument. Despite

our occasional disagreements, Bush has always been approachable
for me. I could go to the White House if I needed to sit down and
say, "Here's how things really are." We could have a good conversation, and I could walk out of there thinking I had accomplished something. Every time I had a problem, I could walk out
with something for the troops. I found him very sharp, very
focused, even-handed, and up to any challenge I could imagine.

∽

In that summer of 2001, I was completing my fourteenth year in
the House and my third year as Speaker. I was getting used to the
rhythms of the place and the demands, challenges, and special
pleasures of the job.

People often ask me what's the most enjoyable aspect of the
work I do. I say it's when you're able to pass legislation that makes
a difference in people's lives. I worked on rewriting the Public
Utility Act in Illinois in the mid-1980s and that was very rewarding to me. I felt the same way about the nine-year undertaking to
get rid of the earnings test on Social Security. And here we'd just
passed the Bush tax cut of 2001. I knew it would make a difference
because I sensed the economy would respond, that it would start
roaring back. In this business there are times when you ask, "Are
we doing the right thing? Is this the right policy for this country?"
Then, all of a sudden, things start to move forward. You see you're
on the right track, and that's a rewarding time.

Another special pleasure of this job is the opportunity it gives
me to award Congressional Gold Medals. I call that part of the
job "hanging tinsel." Of all the recognitions Congress can
bestow, the Gold Medal is considered the most distinguished.

I've felt humbled and honored to be able to present it to some extraordinary recipients—Rosa Parks, Mother Teresa, Nancy and Ronald Reagan, Billy Graham.

When I became Speaker the Congressional Gold Medal was basically given out to any person sponsored in a bill to do so. Most of them were deserving people, but it didn't seem that a lot of forethought was given to the selection process. When considering who really shaped the twentieth century, we thought Ronald Reagan, Margaret Thatcher, and Pope John Paul II were candidates for the medal. By forward thinking, we weren't excluding anyone else, but just thinking about who it should be.

The bill to award Congressional Gold Medals to Ronald and Nancy Reagan passed easily in the House. There was a ceremony here in Washington attended by an appreciative Nancy Reagan, and I delivered a speech at the Reagan Library in California.

Another bill was passed with only positive debate to award the medal to Pope John Paul II. But it was very difficult to schedule a time to award the medal. It had taken us over a year. We had very good relations with the Vatican and with the papal annuncio in Washington, yet we just couldn't work everything out. We were getting a little frustrated; we had this honor to bestow, and we couldn't do it. Weeks after the presidential election of November 2000, we thought we would try one more time to schedule the event, and if this didn't work out then we were just going to present the medal to the papal annuncio in downtown D.C. During the course of our discussions, February of 2001 came up as a possible date for the presentation. We mentioned this would not be great timing because the new Congress would be beginning, and we would have a new President—not a good

time to be sending a congressional delegation to the Vatican. It
was then that it became clear that it was a surprise to the Vatican
that a congressional delegation would be giving the award—not
the President.

For some time, Democrats had been writing the legislation in
such a way that the President would award the medal. I don't know
why they did that, but we figured out that this was not the way
things had been done throughout history—and that all that needed
to be done was change how the bill was written. So we changed it
back to the original tradition. We explained this to the Vatican.

Suddenly they were available in January. They never said anything to us about why, but it was clear to us that they were happy
to receive a congressional delegation, but perhaps not so happy
about receiving the medal from President Clinton.

It was a memorable trip to the Vatican. I was honored to present the award to a truly distinguished honoree. "Today, I'm
pleased that Congress has bestowed this honor to you, John Paul
II, and that you have agreed to accept it," I said. "This award cel-
ebrates your life . . . as a peacemaker, healer, and beacon of light to
the whole world." We were told Pope John Paul II would only be
staying for fifteen minutes. We limited our remarks and listened to
his from a prepared text. Then he went off text and talked to us
for quite a while in a very heartfelt way. As he was leaving, after
nearly an hour, he turned back around and said, "God bless
America." I was truly moved.

But with pleasures such as these came demands and expectations that always kept me on my toes. As I told David Broder of
the *Washington Post,* "When I was a coach, we were state champions. But every year, we had to prove ourselves." I was finding out

that it's the same way here. Just because you passed a tax cut a few months ago doesn't mean you can live on that forever. In politics, it's always, "What have you done for me lately?"

Being a coach and being Speaker both require "people" skills. That's what it boils down to. If Tom Jarman is in the National Wrestling Coaches Association Hall of Fame, it's because he understands people and can motivate them to do extraordinary things. I have always said that you *can* get ordinary people to do extraordinary things. That's what you do in coaching, and it's exactly what you do in politics.

As a coach, you start with kids before they're freshmen, and, hopefully, what you teach them starts blooming when they're juniors or seniors. Similarly, in politics, there's a lot of thinking and planning that goes into the process before you even get to Election Day. To be successful, you have to find good candidates. You have to be sure that your Members—who have to run on their records—have something they can be proud of and point to in terms of accomplishments. You have to think it through and determine if your legislation is really in touch with your base. That's a tall order, much taller than it seems. But then we also have to look over the horizon, to come up with new ideas that can excite people and get their imaginations involved.

Another challenging part of my job as Speaker is resolving high-level disputes, and nothing I learned as a coach quite prepared me for it. For example, I had to settle an argument between Representative Bill Thomas, the talented but headstrong California Republican who is Chairman of the House Ways and Means Committee, and his counterpart Billy Tauzin, Republican of Louisiana, the veteran Chairman of the House Energy and Commerce Committee.

Now these are strong-willed men, and I know I'll have to go back to them again and again. I *depend* on them, so I can't alienate them. But at the same time I have to be the judge.

I listen to their case and say to one of them, "Okay, it's your decision today." Then I turn to today's "loser" and tell him, "Another decision may come down tomorrow, and it may go your way..." What I'm trying to do is develop a confidence level where people know I'm fair and that I don't go into this with a tilt one way or the other. People have to know they'll get an objective decision from me.

Among people new to Washington, there's a lot of talk about sex and power in the Capitol. I haven't gotten into marriage counseling yet—and I don't plan to start—but I make it plain to freshmen when they come in that they're going to have to make up their own minds about the kinds of circumstances that are out there. I tell them, "There are all kinds of temptations in this business. You know what you can do." And when we find some guy spending too much time socializing every night, we have our own way of saying, "You'd better straighten up or you'll get in trouble." The message doesn't have to come from me. But you want to get a message out that says something like, "Being out in the bars every night is probably not the best thing for you to be doing." The smart ones will hear you and act accordingly. The others won't, but they won't be here long.

Rumors are one of the ways people try to get things done in this town. Not too long ago, the *Washingtonian* magazine reported that I was going to retire. (No one had asked me, of course.) My aunt Doral Swan called to say, "I hear you're going to retire." There are some people in our Conference who'd like to see me do that, I know, and there are a lot of Democrats who feel the same way. I told my aunt, "Don't believe everything you read."

Lobbyists spread rumors, too. To some people, "lobbyist" is a bad word because it connotes the improper use of political influence. In Washington today, lobbyists prefer to be called "government consultants." Our son Josh is one, and he enjoys it a lot. I never dreamed that Josh would ever want to do something like that. When he was growing up, he was sort of an anti-government guy. Now Ethan, our younger son, is at Northwestern University Law School. Am I going to have to take back all the things I've ever said about lawyers over the years?

By 2001, the third year of my Speakership, I had long since decided that I didn't have to be on television every week. That was not my thing. I need to be there because every once in a while someone will try to fill that slot with a Republican who may have his or her own agenda or a point of view that is inconsistent with that of our conference. Some of our Members tend to be lightning rods and no matter how good they are at explaining policy or answering questions, the media tend to isolate them on soundbites and blow our message out of proportion. Sometimes it's just my job to go on television and say where we stand on issues important to our majority.

Reporters focus on Tom DeLay. Tom is impulsive. He says and does the things that he thinks are right. He doesn't say, "I need to sit back and think about it." Tom says what he says and lets the chips fall. There is a perception in the liberal press that DeLay calls the shots, and I march to his instructions. That's what the Democrats would like people to believe. What they did to Newt, they'd like to do to DeLay. They try to demonize Tom all the time and that just makes things a bit easier for me. He goes out and becomes the lightning rod. In the meantime, I am free to move the agenda.

∽

It used to be I'd go someplace, and no one would recognize me. Not anymore. But you know what? I'm not scared to have people see me walking around doing everyday things. My doctor says I'm too heavy, that I need to walk more and get more exercise.

I have never smoked cigarettes in my life. (As a kid, I bought an old burr pipe, and I smoked that thing. My mouth tasted bad; my throat was sore. Common sense told me I'd probably get used to it, but I wondered: why bother? And that was it for me.) Once in a while I'll have a drink, a manhattan, a margarita, or, very occasionally, a beer. I don't drink a lot. I'm not being a prude, I've just never developed much of a taste for it or spent any time in a bar. When I was coaching, I didn't have much time to do that. In this business, you *never* have time for it.

People ask what I do to relax. First, I do what Jean asks me to do around the house. I enjoy gardening with her. Jean points to where she wants to plant, and I dig. I also enjoy exploring our property. We only go to a few movies a year. I don't watch television much—sports and news occasionally. I drive Jean crazy because I'll skip through the channels for an hour and a half and then go to bed. Part of it is that I just don't have the patience to sit through that. Life is so fast-paced.

I enjoy fishing where and when I can. Our son Ethan does, too. Attending wrestling matches also helps me relax. I can sit there and feel the weight of the world slipping away. It takes me back to my roots and all the great folks I worked with before I got into politics. And I go to fairs. The annual Sandwich Fair in Sand-wich, Illinois, attracts people from Kendall, Kane, and DeKalb Counties. It's down-home, apple pie, stock car races, and country singers. I've worked the DeKalb County Fair at Sandwich for almost thirty years. Entire families are out there and you see a lot of people you know. You look at livestock, watch the tractor pull, and eat barbecued pork chops.

I love getting in my truck and driving past the places that were important to me when I was growing up. Yorkville had a popula-tion of 2,500; it didn't even have a single stoplight then. (But Kendall County is one of the ten fastest-growing counties in the nation, the Census Bureau reports, and Ethan tells me that Yorkville is supposed to have 36,000 people by 2006.) Change is everywhere. The high school where I taught is now a middle school. Room 204, where I drilled those kids in history, econom-ics, and a few other things, is still there, but the halls are full of signs about the importance of character now and the elevator is new. The chairs in the hall outside the principal's office are gone. The "Pit" where my wrestlers performed so well for so many years is now the gymnasium of the private Parkview Christian School.

On June 7, 2001, less than one month after Jeffords's defection to the Democrats, President Bush signed the Tax Relief Act into law. Five days later, I urged my colleagues to move on issues important to seniors—prescription drug coverage and a patient's bill of rights. Then on June 28, after summing up what the GOP House had done over the last six months (education and tax relief were exhibits A and B), I set the stage for the rest of the year. We still had to pass an energy package to provide price stability for consumers while protecting our environment.

Wall Street Journal columnist Paul A. Gigot, an astute observer and Pulitzer Prize recipient, took note of what was going on: "Democrats who once quipped that they'd miss Newt Gingrich had no idea how right they were," he wrote on August 3. "Speaker Dennis Hastert has proven to be a tougher foe than they ever imagined.

"That's the big story this week as Mr. Hastert's Republican House majority piled up victories that weren't supposed to happen. It passed President Bush's energy plan more or less intact, including Alaskan oil and gas drilling. It also struck a deal on HMO regulation that united Republicans and left Dick Gephardt sputtering. Add those to a six-month list of House accomplishments that include the tax cut, a cloning ban, modest education reform, faith-based welfare, and the delicious demise of campaign finance reform at the reformers' own hands. Not bad for a six-vote majority."

In politics, I've found, few people care about or even remember the nice words that columnists employ every now and then. All politics is local, as House Speaker Tip O'Neill is reported to have said, and the question of the day is, "Why didn't you see that big problem coming down the track?"

Well, there was a big problem—the sagging economy. It was coming down the track, and I did see it. Indeed, I had some thoughts on what to do about it.

There were at least half a dozen steps that we in Congress could take to give workers and businesses the lift they needed now. On Monday, September 10, 2001, I flew into Washington early to see the President and talk about the stimulus package we needed to offset the downturn of the economy. I was going to bring in some economists later, but this meeting was just the two of us in the Oval Office. He was leaving the next morning for Florida.

∾

The atrocities of the following day would leave our nation grieving. The sheer horror of what had happened to us on September 11, 2001, was undeniable. But I wanted to act. We had work to do, legislation to pass, steps to take to make sure that this sort of attack never happened again. Yet the events of that day are never far away for me.

I know people try to do it, but I don't think you can put an accurate dollar value on human lives. You can't even come close to calculating the true cost of the physical and structural damage and devastation in a situation like this, but already we heard voices asking, "Who's going to pay for this? How much will it cost?" The unseemly scramble for dollars had begun.

A day or so after September 11, the President was talking with the New York delegation about money for New York. I was talking to Oklahoma Republican Don Nickles, the Senate Minority Whip, in the Capitol rotunda that day, and he told me, "Geez, this thing may be $5 billion."

"Hold onto your hat," I said. "It may be more than that." Well, as it turned out, the number was $40 billion, with $20 billion for New York. But that wasn't an easy sell. We were having a leadership meeting in the Lincoln Room of my office, and New York Senators Chuck Schumer and Hillary Clinton wanted to be in there. (Schumer isn't exactly a shrinking violet about publicity; media people tell me the single most dangerous place to be in

Washington, D.C., is in the line of sight between Schumer and a television camera.) Hillary was not happy about being excluded—and expressing it. The truth is that Senate Majority Leader Tom Daschle didn't want them in the room. He thought they'd screw up the deal, and he stepped outside to tell them: "This place has got three Texans—Phil Gramm, Dick Armey, and Tom DeLay—and if you come in here, you're not going to help yourself."

A day or two after September 11, I started asking the President to come up to Capitol Hill. "You need to come up here and talk to the American people about this," I said, "and about what you're going to do. You have to bring them into this process, and only you can do it."

I had heard that his staff didn't want him to come, but he said he would. At nine o'clock on the evening of September 20, nine days after those shattering events, the President addressed a Joint Session of Congress. Everyone was there: the dean of the diplomatic corps (ironically, it was His Royal Highness Prince Bandar Bin Sultan Bin Abdul Aziz, ambassador of the Kingdom of Saudi Arabia, the same country that had sent most of those hijackers to the United States) and other accredited diplomats, the Chief Justice and Associate Justices of the United States Supreme Court, and the members of the President's Cabinet.

British Prime Minister Tony Blair, our nation's closest friend, had flown across the ocean to show his unity with America that night.

"Great battles," Winston Churchill once remarked, "change the entire course of events, create new standards of values, new moods in armies and in nations." (This according to historian Victor Davis Hanson and his new book, *Ripples of Battle.*) I believe they do, and I was waiting to see if and how the President would acknowledge that. He did not disappoint.

"Tonight we are a country awakened to danger and called to defend freedom," he pointed out. "Our grief has turned to anger and anger to resolution. Whether we bring our enemies to justice or bring justice to our enemies, justice will be done." Everyone rose and applauded that.

"Americans are asking: How will we fight and win this war?" the President continued. "We will direct every resource at our command, every means of diplomacy, every tool of intelligence, every instrument of law enforcement, every financial influence and every necessary weapon of war to defeat the global terror network.

"Great harm," the President concluded, "has been done to us. We have suffered great loss. In our grief and anger, we have found our mission and our moment. Freedom and fear are at war. The advances of human freedom now depend on us. Our nation, this generation, will lift the dark threat of violence from our people and our future. We will rally the world to this cause by our efforts and by our courage. We will not tire, we will not falter, we will not fail."

He spoke for about forty minutes, and I thought it was a great speech. It laid out what he was doing and where he was going in his presidency. Up to that point, critics were saying that he didn't have a clear mandate. But the leadership he exhibited after September 11 was extraordinary. What I especially liked about his address was that he talked about a commitment—and the commitment was not just weeks or months but years against an enemy that doesn't have flags or generals, an enemy that is a world organization of terrorists who threaten freedom everywhere. We're going to have to see that commitment through because so long as those types of governments–and terror–exist, no one in the world is safe.

What happened on September 11 changed the way we think as a country. Or at least I thought it did. That's why I couldn't understand why some Democrats wanted to treat this as a police action or didn't want us to commit the forces we needed to win. In the Arab world, weakness is despised. From time to time the President has asked me to intercede personally with some allies–the Turks, for example–and help explain to them why we want them to do such and such. As the months have passed, I've been to the White House many times, and I've seen the President lead. I'm convinced he understands what we have to do and that he doesn't much care if doing the right thing costs him reelection to a second term.

There were constant reminders, especially on Capitol Hill, of the new dangers we faced. On Wednesday, October 15 (I remember that date because Jean was coming to town to join Josh, Ethan, and me for the photograph that would be on our Christmas card that year), as puffy white clouds scudded overhead, we had one of our regular breakfast meetings with the President in the White House. That's when Senators Daschle and Lott came in and said there was some friable, highly toxic anthrax in the Senate office buildings.

Daschle's office had just received a letter containing "weapons-grade"–that was the term he used–anthrax; people in his office had possibly been infected. Workers at one of the U.S. Postal Service's distribution facilities had inhaled the stuff and had become very, very sick. The concern now was that the tiny spores had gotten into the air ducts. They said they were considering shutting down the Senate, and they wanted to know if we would go along with them.

"Fine with me if you want to shut down," the President said. "It's [anthrax] a real risk."

Minority Leader Dick Gephardt and I didn't know of any similar problem in the House, but it could be coming through the post office. An ounce of prevention is better than a pound of cure. So we told our Senate counterparts that we would shut down if they shut down.

Back on Capitol Hill, I stepped before the Republican Conference and said, "The Senate's found some anthrax. We think the best thing to do is shut down our buildings today." Gephardt said the same thing to his troops. So we shut down the House. When we did that, we also stopped our mail delivery, which came through the Gerald R. Ford Building. We said, "We have *kids* opening that mail." I'm responsible for the people who work in these buildings on Capitol Hill, so I decided we were better off shutting down and sending everyone home.

The Senate didn't meet until an hour later that morning, and its Members resisted efforts to close. "No, we're not going to shut down," they declared. "Let those House guys shut down." Senators denied that they'd ever claimed to have anthrax in their buildings, and they insisted they'd never said it was in the ventilation system. This after telling us, and the President, that it was high-tech, very well engineered.

The *New York Post* had fun with this. They published a photograph of Gephardt and me under the headline, "WIMPS." Gephardt was livid, furious at Daschle for undercutting him, and so was his staff. Gephardt and I didn't agree on many things, but we did agree that shutting down was the right thing for the House to do. Later, we did find anthrax in our post office, but, because we acted when we did, damage was minimal; there were only a few offices in the Longworth House Office Building that had to be closed for a while. The Senate closed its entire complex, but only after people had been exposed to anthrax. One of its buildings was shut down for three months. Two workers at the U.S. Postal Service distribution facility died as a result of the anthrax.

Meanwhile, we were trying to reboot the economy by passing a $100 billion economic stimulus package. Since September 11, hundreds of thousands of jobs had been lost. We needed to get consumer confidence back up so people would feel they could go out and buy a car or a refrigerator or make the house payment without worrying. I asked Federal Reserve Chairman Alan Greenspan and former Treasury Secretary Robert Rubin to come in with our guy Lawrence Lindsey, Director of the National Economic Council, to talk about what we should do. Greenspan said, "You have to keep interest rates low and keep the housing market going because that's the thing that drives our economy." He thought a rate reduction might be in order soon.

And Rubin said, "Well, you have to pass something to put money in poor people's pockets. They'll spend it, and that'll be a spur to the economy." Lindsey had his own views, and I thought, well, obviously, you bring in five economists, you're going to get five different opinions.

But they all agreed on one thing: Our economy was in, or was about to be in, a recession. That demanded action from us. I think we put together a pretty good package for the stimulus bill. It contained some incentives for people to invest; it also had some things in there to boost consumer confidence. Most important, it created jobs. That's because its key points followed common sense.

People wanted to buy things, both finished and capital goods. Think about that for a minute. If you want to buy a pickup truck, someone has to build it first; someone else has to deliver it. A third person has to sell it and so on up or down the line. There was job creation there, plus an expensing package we had put together giving tax credits to businesses that spent money on capital goods, again creating jobs.

We passed the bill in October 2001. The Senate couldn't muster the votes it needed to pass it in that chamber, so nothing happened. We became a bit frustrated. The House passed the bill again in November—this was after Thanksgiving and we didn't think we were still going to be in session, but we were—but we just couldn't get the Democratic-controlled Senate to move.

That's when we came up with the idea of what we called a "virtual conference." Even though the Senate hadn't passed the bill—and they were insisting that they needed sixty votes to do so, a majority that had never before been required for routine legislation in the history of the Senate—we had them act as if they *had* passed it and select four or five conferees to go to conference with their counterparts from the House. Procedurally, we were hoping to add the result to another bill we had over there.

Unfortunately, we couldn't reach agreement with Daschle about this. Daschle named Senator Jay Rockefeller, a Democrat from West Virginia, as his watchdog here. Every time we got close to an agreement, Rockefeller would pull the plug. By November, I was beginning to think that Daschle never intended to strike a deal with us and that he didn't want to find a solution to the problems we faced. In my opinion, he wanted to see the economy deteriorate. Democrats had made up their minds that this would be better for them, that it would put them in a better position politically.

The holidays were upon us then; we went home for Christmas.

In his State of the Union address in January 2002, the President repeated his request for a stimulus package. In February, I went to him and said, "Mr. President, you talked about the stimulus package. We still want to do this. Can you get it through the Senate?"

The fact was that the Senate had pretty much waved the white flag. They couldn't, or wouldn't, do it and the liberal press was beating up on us saying we were obnoxious for even trying to pass this thing, again, a fourth time.

I told the President, "Let's try one more time." We put the bill together on a Thursday morning in February, and went to the Rules Committee and then to the floor. That's when a strange thing happened. Between forty and sixty House Democrats approached their leadership and said, "You've been holding us off this bill, but we want to vote for it. We think it's the right thing to do," and when that happened, the whole dam broke loose. The bill that passed the House that Thursday afternoon had more than four hundred "yes" votes.

When you run the House on a five-vote margin and you get four hundred–plus votes on a bill, that's a real victory. We were running all over Ohio giving Lincoln's Day speeches on Thursday and Friday. I finished my remarks at this dinner in Bowling Green, stepped off the podium, and someone handed me a note saying, "Call the White House—Immediately."

Well, if it's 9:30 on a Friday night and you've been on the road all day and you're finally headed home, this is not the kind of message you want to receive. I called the White House, got a hold of

Nick Calio, the President's liaison man to Capitol Hill, and asked, "Hey, what's going on? What's this message about?"

"You have to sign the bill before it goes to the President," he said.

"What bill?"

Well, it was the stimulus bill. The Senate had just passed it by voice vote. And the President was going to sign it in the Rose Garden tomorrow. "You have two options," Calio was telling me. " We can send someone to Ohio or to Illionis."

"Wait a minute, wait a minute," I shot back at him, raising my voice to make sure he heard what I had to say: "I'm halfway to Washington now. I'm going to come down, and we'll sign the bill in Washington tonight. I want to be in the Rose Garden when the President signs it tomorrow because we passed that bill in the House four times. The liberal press said it couldn't be done, and the Democrats wouldn't lift a finger in the Senate to help." I was sure that Daschle would be there to take credit for the bill. I wanted to be there, too.

CHAPTER TEN

LESSONS IN THE 108TH

Turning and turning in the widening gyre
The falcon cannot hear the falconer;
Things fall apart; the center cannot hold;
Mere anarchy is loosed upon the world,
The blood-dimmed tide is loosed, and everywhere
The ceremony of innocence is drowned;
The best lack all conviction, while the worst
Are full of passionate intensity.
—WILLIAM BUTLER YEATS, "THE SECOND COMING," 1921

TERRORISM WAS SOMETHING WE THOUGHT WE'D NEVER SEE IN THE United States. Terrorism happened in the Middle East or Northern Ireland, but vast oceans separated us from those places. We thought we were safe. Then we learned that wasn't true and that we were in just as much—if not more—danger as everyone else. "We shall draw from the heart of suffering itself the means of inspiration and survival," Winston Churchill once wrote, and no sooner had the terrorists hit us on September 11 than we swung into action to find and destroy them. By early 2002, we had liberated the people of Afghanistan from the Taliban's cruel grip.

The President had told us from the beginning that terrorism was something you didn't wipe out in a couple of weeks or months. We've been successful in Afghanistan and Iraq because we have a President who hasn't been afraid to lead, a man who didn't stick his finger in the wind or have to read the latest poll before he gave a speech or made a decision that might send young Americans into harm's way. He knew—we all knew—that we'd take casualties and that the nation would grieve over each and every one of them, but he also knew that acting against terrorism was the only way to keep our country free.

The fact is that September 11 happened, and we had a choice to make. Either we were going to stand up and stop terrorism, or we were going to wait for it to hurt us again. I think the consensus of the American people is that we're probably better off fighting terrorism over in Iraq and Afghanistan than here in the United States, and that's what we're doing today.

There was no doubt in my mind that Iraq's Saddam Hussein was a cruel dictator. He was a butcher who had tortured and murdered tens of thousands of his countrymen. We knew he had gassed his own people and that he had lethal chemical and biological weapons, and that if no one stopped him he'd likely use them to terrorize the world. While Saddam Hussein controlled Iraq, al-Qaeda terrorists trained in northern Iraq, and Hussein put his scientists to work on developing nuclear, chemical, and biological weapons. That's why the Bush administration made the decision early in 2003 to go in there, arrest Saddam, and liberate Iraq.

People ask me, "Couldn't we have given the weapons inspectors more time? Shouldn't we have taken this dispute to the United Nations first?"

Well, the weapons inspections struck me, and many of my colleagues, as little more than a shell game. And defending America from terrorist states is our responsibility, not the UN's.

Besides, the UN had already passed sixteen resolutions calling on Iraq to give up its weapons of mass destruction; would the seventeenth have made a difference? Saddam Hussein had already defied the world body sixteen different times and had gotten away with it. His behavior had challenged the very legitimacy of that organization in much the same way that Hitler's defiance of the League of Nations in the 1930s had rendered that body useless and impotent.

I thought back to the words President Bush had used after September 11 when he had addressed West Point cadets—words that bear repeating and repeating again: "The gravest danger to freedom lies at the perilous crossroads of radicalism and technology... Enemies in the past needed great armies and great industrial capabilities to endanger the American people and our nation." Then came the money paragraph: "Our security will require all Americans to be forward-looking and resolute, to be ready for preemptive action when necessary to defend our liberty and to defend our lives."

On March 17, 2003, just forty-eight hours before our troops (together with those of Britain and our other coalition partners) began their push toward Baghdad, Senator Tom Daschle addressed a group of labor union leaders. "I'm saddened that this President failed so miserably at diplomacy that we are now forced into war," he said.

Well, I was disappointed myself to hear of Daschle's remarks. They might not undermine the President's remarks; they might not give aid and comfort to our adversaries—but they sure came close.

Our assault itself was successful and Baghdad fell to coalition forces on April 9, 2003. The dictator, Saddam Hussein, was gone, and I thought President Bush deserved a lot of credit for freeing the people of Iraq. But that wasn't what Democrats and the media wanted to focus on. They kept asking, "Where are the weapons of mass destruction?"

A fair question. I wondered about them myself, and I don't have any answers now. But I do know one thing: The best intelligence we had, the best intelligence the Democrats had ("Without question, we need to disarm Saddam Hussein," Senator John F. Kerry had said on January 23, 2003, "The threat of Saddam Hussein with weapons of mass destruction is real."), the best intelligence the UN had, all pointed to those weapons of mass destruction being there. Israeli intelligence, one of the best services in the world, concurred with that view. So did Russian, German, and French intelligence. And it's a big country. Those weapons may still be there—and sixteen UN resolutions gave them plenty of time to hide them well.

Democrats as well as Republicans who have been to Iraq have come back and told me we're doing the right thing. Seventy percent of the people in Iraq, they point out, have gotten on with their lives. Kids are going to school. Oil is pouring out of their wells. Farmers are harvesting wheat. Terrorists are still fomenting trouble and trying to spread religious strife and hate. They can—and will—cause problems as the transfer of authority/sovereignty continues, but the thing to remember is that most Iraqis see hope in their future where they saw none before. They didn't like our occupation (I don't blame them, who would?), but at the same time they don't want us to leave. Iraq is a long-term commitment. We need to finish the job that we started there.

∾

In my opening remarks to the first session of the 108th Congress in January 2003, I congratulated Members for enacting landmark education and election reform while passing the most significant tax relief in a generation. I thanked them as well for the measure they passed–Dick Armey's baby–to create a Department of Homeland Security, which was the single most significant restructuring of the federal government in the last fifty years. I extended my colleagues' best wishes to Dick Armey and Dick Gephardt, my old nemesis, both of whom had decided to make the 107th Congress their last as leaders of their respective parties. I thanked retiring Republican Conference Chairman J.C. Watts as well. Then I listed what I hoped the members of the new Congress would accomplish in this turn at bat.

Overseeing the creation of the new Department of Homeland Security was a top priority. Supporting our armed forces and intelligence services–and providing them with the resources they needed to get the job done–ranked high along with that. So did improving the nation's economy. In too many parts of the nation, that recovery was still anemic, and the economy was just stumbling along. We could keep extending unemployment benefits for another thirteen or twenty-six weeks, but for a working family, I think all of us knew there was no substitute for a permanent job.

Then I rounded out the list: We had to simplify our tax code, rein in skyrocketing health care costs, find ways to provide health insurance to those who wanted it but couldn't afford it, and finally, improve upon the landmark No Child Left Behind Act and make our public schools the best in the world.

Five months later, in May 2003, the House had chalked up a record of accomplishment. We'd passed the President's welfare reform bill, a medical malpractice reform bill, a bankruptcy reform bill (Have you noticed yet how measures labeled "reform"

seem to get passed around here much more frequently than those
that are not?), the President's energy bill, his Global AIDS Initiative, and his IDEA Education bill. We had also completed work
on the President's budget, and we'd gone through his supplemental budget request and returned it to the Oval Office for his signature in less than three weeks. And we'd done all this while the
President was leading the nation in a war to remove Saddam Hussein. We'd been successful there, too. And what was the response
of the Democrats? They kept complaining about the President's
flying out and landing on an aircraft carrier to personally thank
the servicemen and women involved in this effort. Their carping
caused the cable channels to run and rerun footage of the President acting like a President should. That didn't sound like a smart
strategy to me.

Then in January 2003 there was an incident that underscored
how much the two parties disliked and distrusted each other. The
trouble started, back at the beginning of the session when Bill
Thomas, the California Republican who chairs Ways and Means,
tried to reduce the size of his committee from forty-one members
to thirty-nine to make it easier for him to control. The Steering
Committee agreed with him, and we asked Majority Leader Tom
DeLay to call Minority Leader Nancy Pelosi to tell her that we
were reducing the committee's size.

He couldn't get through to her; she wouldn't take his call. The
next thing I knew, the Democrats had issued a press release tout-
ing the fact that they had just appointed an African American
woman from Ohio named Stephanie Tubbs Jones to Ways and
Means. This put us in an awkward position. If we went ahead and
slimmed down that committee, we'd be depriving this African

American woman of an opportunity. They were trying to paint House Republicans, and Thomas in particular, as racists. It was a no-win situation, so I told Thomas, "Bill, back off. It's not worth the fight. We're not going there."

Thomas played a role in the next incident as well. A bipartisan, non-controversial bill to reform employer pension plans had been on everyone's computer since January. Thomas had changed it and brought it up for consideration at eleven o'clock one night–a typical Thomas performance, and said that Members would be expected to be ready to vote on it the next morning. Well, all hell broke loose. (It didn't matter, of course, that in the old days when he was chairing that committee, Dan Rostenkowski never gave anyone notice. The Democrats marked up bills without paper there.) Charlie Rangel, a veteran Democrat from New York who knows how to provoke Thomas, was first out of the gate. This bill came to him at midnight; he hadn't had time to read or analyze it, he said, so he asked for a full, line-by-line reading of the measure now.

Usually, because it can take five or more hours to read a bill in its entirety, you ask for a waiver. But in this case, the clerk started reading the bill. Thomas, furious, interrupted. "In the House, the minority can delay," he said. "They cannot deny."

The Democrats walked out, stepped into a library next to the hearing room in the Longworth House Office Building, and left Representative Fortney (Pete) Stark, a liberal from California who'd been in Congress since 1973, sitting there to make sure we didn't shortcut the reading of the bill.

I think the Democrats were spoiling for a fight and, unfortunately, Thomas took the bait. Democrats were taunting Thomas and provoking the incident. They wanted photographs of police escorting Rangel out. He had his staff call the Capitol Police to eject them from a room where they weren't supposed to be in the first place. (He didn't tell fellow Republicans what he was trying to do.) Then he asked the clerk to dispense with the reading of the bill. Stark wasn't paying attention, so when the reading stopped, Thomas moved the bill—bang, bang, bang—just like that.

Stark looked at Thomas and said, "You f–ing a–hole."

Representative Scott McInnis, a Republican from Colorado's Western Slope, a member of the Ways and Means Committee and a former cop, told Stark to shut up.

Stark looked at him and said, "You think you are big enough to take me, you little wimp? Come on. Come over here and make me. I dare you. You little fruitcake. You little fruitcake. I said you are a fruitcake."

Fortunately for us, the Capitol Police didn't heed Thomas's request to eject the Democrats. And we were lucky, too, that Stark blew it. McInnis didn't take up his challenge, and tempers never got to the point where the police had to be called to escort Rangel from the room. But he was *in* the room. The Democrats were inviting the press in for interviews, tossing around terms like "police state," "un-American," and "tyranny," and when Pelosi came to see me to protest, she was, in my opinion, reading from a script.

I figured this was and had been a set-up from the start. They were just trying to slow us down and paint us as racist at the same time. Two days later, I called Thomas in and told him I wasn't happy with what had been going on. Then I got Jim Nussle, a Republican from Iowa, Ohio Republican Rob Portman, Louisiana Republican Jim McCrery, and a couple of other guys from Ways and Means—the same people who had supported Thomas to be their Chairman over the more senior Representative Philip Crane—to come by the office, and I told them to talk to their Chairman and tell him he needed to do a mea culpa on this.

Basically, they did that. Thomas issued a mea culpa; he said he was sorry for embarrassing the institution, and he did it with grace. And everyone clapped except Pelosi. She sat in her chair and stared straight ahead.

The Founding Fathers must have been shaking their heads.

There is a real difference in philosophical points of view between Nancy Pelosi and me. Indeed, there's a huge difference between Democrats and Republicans. Democrats just don't believe in what we're trying to do—put more money in people's pockets and give them more say in the decision-making process. They want *government* to have more money and *government* to make more decisions for people. They don't trust people to spend money wisely. As Hillary Clinton once told me long before she became a Democratic Senator from New York, people are basically greedy and won't make the tough decisions. They won't take their kid to the hospital when he needs to go because they want to keep the money for themselves.

I don't see human nature that way. As Mike Stokke points out, the Democrats' philosophy collapses of its own weight. They don't trust individuals to make the right decisions, so they turn it over to big government. But it's still some person, some individual inside big government who's making the decision for them.

Now Democrats complain that we leave them out of the legislative process. Representative David Obey, a Democrat from Wisconsin and the third most senior Member of the House, is someone I like and respect; I know where he's coming from. He compares the way the House is run today to "the old Soviet Congresses–stamp of approval and ratify" rather than using your own judgment. Well, Obey was here when Democrats ran the place (he replaced Melvin Laird in April 1969 when Laird left Congress and became Secretary of Defense). Talk about rubber stamps and domination by a party that had lots of votes and squish room. They were ruthless. They did things like the old Soviet Congresses, such as removing offenders from their hideaway offices, grabbing their office furniture, and taking their parking spots away.

At a conference on Capitol Hill last fall, I heard former Speaker Tom Foley, a Democrat from Washington, speak wistfully about Ohio Democrat Michael Kirwin, an Appropriations Cardinal (subcommittee chairman) who had told new Members in 1964 that the greatest danger in that place was thinking for yourself. He went on to say that in his experience, more people had gotten into trouble in Congress by thinking for themselves than by stealing money. Foley concluded, then and now, "Members do think for themselves."

I'm not going to say that we haven't committed wrongs ourselves or seemed overbearing at times, but as a former coach I know the importance of fairness and I take it seriously. Still, in our system, the majority rules, and I consider it my job to make sure we retain our majority. As I have pointed out, the hallmark of effective leadership is one that can deliver the votes. And we have been an effective leadership.

Sure, the accusations of foul play hurt. I know Democrats feel the same way. In truth, both parties are culpable here and calling each other names isn't going to help. At the end of the day, everyone looks bad. What bothers me is that this venom infects our daily discourse, interferes with what we're trying to accomplish here, makes the House look like a snake pit, and contributes to the breakdown of civilized behavior in the political world. As Ronald Brownstein, an astute observer for the *Los Angeles Times*, pointed out in a column last year, "If there ever was a Geneva Convention in politics–a set of rules that governed even the fiercest combat–it has lapsed. The only rule is that there are no longer any rules. In American politics, we now live in an age of total war."

I don't think that's what the American people want. Indeed, during the 2000 election campaign, one of candidate George W. Bush's most appealing lines was his pledge "to change the tone of Washington to one of civility and respect." Four years later, everyone in politics seems to be angry all the time. Members of both parties are at each other's throats, and some of the overheated rhetoric has soared into the danger zone. Consider this (as reported by the *Orlando Sentinel*) from an African American state legislator, *an elected official*, in Jacksonville, Florida, in May 2004: "The Bushes are like weeds," he told an outdoor crowd. "What do we do with weeds? We cut them down."

I believe in free speech, but that's way over the line. It strikes me as an incitement to violence. I know that if and when it becomes commonplace–and acceptable–to call President Bush, Vice President Cheney, Defense Secretary Donald Rumsfeld, or other elected officials liars and/or war criminals, we will have passed a point of no return. I hope and pray it doesn't come to that, but I'm not holding my breath.

On September 11, 2003, the second anniversary of the devastating attacks upon the United States, I spoke from the West Front steps of the Capitol and said that as a nation we mourned with "those who lost loved ones on that fateful day even as we drew inspiration from the courage of the fallen." Then I concluded with some words from Churchill, who has always inspired me, "We shall not falter or fail; we shall not weaken or tire. Neither the sudden shock of battle nor the long drawn trials of vigilance and exertion will wear us down."

The truth was we faced tough challenges not only overseas but also here at home. At that point in time the 108th Congress had either already passed or was about to pass measures to make this country a better place to live. By substantial margins, we had approved the Do Not Call and Do Not Spam bills aimed at stopping consumers from being harassed through their phone or computer lines. We passed the Amber Alert bill to help keep our kids safe from kidnappers, and we okayed spending to combat AIDS at the highest level yet.

And that was just for starters. How about the economy? We passed the tax cut in 2001, the stimulus bill in 2002, and what turned out to be the third largest tax cut in American history in 2003. We reduced the capital gains tax and the dividends tax to help the markets bounce back. And bounce back they did. The Dow Jones reached its highest level in eighteen months. The jobless rate was at its lowest point in two years, and manufacturing output was snapping along at its highest pace in nearly two decades.

We couldn't let these trends stop. We needed to make sure that American consumers had more money in their pockets so they—rather than some bureaucrat in Washington—could spend it. Second, we still needed—more than ever now—to create jobs. To do that, we needed to get people to make capital investments in the economy again. That's a tough proposition, so we had to offer incentives.

To me it was clear that for the 108th Congress to succeed, we'd have to pass an energy bill and take advantage of an opportunity–one that wouldn't come again soon–to reform Medicare.

Take energy first. From the rolling brownouts of California to the blackouts of New York City, to the utility company screw-ups that shut down most of Montgomery County, Maryland, for nearly a week last September, to the turbulence of the natural gas market, to the high prices all of us had to pay at the gas pumps, energy policy was fast becoming a front-burner issue. We needed a strong new energy bill and have needed for a long time to become more energy independent. When we're 72 percent dependent on offshore petroleum, there's a problem.

By a large bipartisan margin, the House passed the energy bill conference report and sent it over to the Senate. There, it seemed to stall. Then, even before the Senate could get the conference report up for a vote, the trial lawyers moved in for the kill.

This put Senate Minority Leader Tom Daschle in a difficult spot. He endorsed the energy bill, but he couldn't–or wouldn't–stop a Democratic filibuster, which, along with the defections of some pro-trial-lawyer Republicans like Pennsylvania's Arlen Specter, pretty much doomed the bill for the first session of the 108th Congress. All that work on a bill of some twelve hundred pages had gone up in smoke. Once a bill of that magnitude falls apart it is almost impossible to put back together again. You could call it the Humpty Dumpty effect.

Enter Medicare. When I first got involved in politics, half the dollar cost of Medicare went to hospitals. Doctors accounted for the rest. (Medicare didn't cover pharmaceuticals.) Today roughly 40 percent of the money we spend on senior health care goes for the drugs that keep them healthy and out of doctors' offices and hospitals. Life expectancy for our seniors has soared. According to the U.S. Census Bureau, life expectancy for women increased 7.73 years between 1970 and 2002, while life expectancy for men shot up by 9.54 years.

To my way of thinking, we were at a place we hadn't been before and might not be again soon. We had $400 billion set aside over ten years to pay for Medicare reform. It was now or never; nothing would happen in 2004 because that was an election year, and we had all those prancing ponies of politics on the other side of the rotunda who wanted to be President. If we didn't act now, indications were that in another twenty years, taxes would rise so high that working people would be paying one-third of their income just to sustain Medicare. That wasn't workable. We needed to make the changes now so Medicare could begin to sustain itself.

Still, it wasn't going to be an easy sell. Back in June of 2002, the Democrats just picked up and walked out of the House chamber when we addressed prescription drugs. I didn't know how they'd react this time.

Some of Medicare's systemic decisions defied common sense. As Representative Heather Wilson, a Republican from New Mexico, asked on the floor, how can you justify paying up to $28,000 to amputate the feet of a diabetic if you refuse to pay $29.95 a month for the Glucosage that will help the man keep his feet? That was just one example. There were many more. At that moment, Medicare covered thirty-five million seniors sixty-five or older, along with six million younger people with permanent disabilities.

The total enrollment, experts told us, was expected to rise from forty-one million to seventy-seven million by the year 2031.

Soon we got to work on common-sense legislation again. And this brought a pleasant surprise, a chance to get to know and work with Senator Bill Frist, a Republican from Tennessee. After Trent Lott had been forced to step down as Senate Majority Leader in the furor surrounding some remarks he made at Senator Strom Thurmond's one hundredth birthday party, Frist had succeeded him. I found him to be a pleasure, a trustworthy leader who would listen before expressing an opinion on anything. We worked together extremely well and soon joined forces trying to craft legislation.

Early in June 2003, the Senate Finance Committee, chaired by Iowa's Chuck Grassley, okayed the Medicare/prescription drug measure by a vote of sixteen to five.

The vote was set for the early morning hours of June 27, a Friday. In preparation for that vote, the Whips made their rounds and divided everyone into one of five categories: yes, no, lean yes, lean no, undecided. Then the Whips went after the waverers.

It became obvious fairly quickly that we'd have to stretch out debate time. I held up the final roll call until 2:45 in the morning when I felt sure we had enough votes to win. As it turned out, we did win, by the slimmest of margins, 216 to 215, but the outcome was still in doubt until the very end. (The Senate vote in our favor was 76–21). Sometimes it's pretty; sometimes it ain't. But we got it done.

But the House vote was just round one in this fight, and all of us knew it. The two chambers had to hammer out their differences before sending a compromise to the President's desk. And there *were* differences. The House-passed bill, according to the

Congressional Budget Office (CBO) would cost $395 billion over the next ten years; the Senate bill, at $461 billion, would be even more expensive. And cost was not the only problem. On July 15, AARP, the powerful seniors' lobby that claims thirty-five million members age fifty and older, urged Congress to "produce a better bill" than the one we had already approved. "The more people hear about it, the less happy they are," the letter from Bill Novelli, its executive director, exclaimed.

Trent Lott had scoffed at AARP as "a wholly-owned subsidiary" of the Democratic Party. Bill Frist saw an opening there, and pounced. (Frist also met with Ted Kennedy.) I took Novelli and AARP very seriously—as had Newt Gingrich when he was Speaker before me—and Republicans had been courting AARP for quite some time, listening to them, engaging in a give-and-take dialogue that none of the capital's pundits even suspected was going on. Indeed, when they found out we'd been talking to AARP, the Democrats were flabbergasted. It was almost as if they believed we didn't have the right to talk to them. Just because we were talking, however, didn't mean that they agreed with us. Not by a long shot. We still had a lot of work to do.

Start with the conference committees that allow the two chambers to settle their disagreements and pass identical bills—as the Constitution requires—before sending them on to the White House for the President to sign. Because they play host to all this hammering, they are, in a sense, Congress's third house.

To represent the House in its conference with the Senate, which was supposed to reconcile differences between the two bills, I appointed Ways and Means Chairman Bill Thomas, Energy and Commerce Chairman Billy Tauzin, Connecticut's Nancy Johnson, and Florida's Michael Bilirakis, a twenty-year veteran from the area just north of St. Petersburg who had a lot of health care expertise. I had expertise, too; I was very proud that I'd succeeded twice before in pushing Medicare legislation through a divided House, so I thought of naming myself to the list of conferees. But there was no precedent for a Speaker doing that. Then it occurred to me that Tom DeLay would be ideal. It wouldn't take him much time to gain substantive knowledge of the policy details, and he'd know almost instinctively how to work the personalities and the turf. More important, he could—and would—work with Bill Thomas and be effective.

On the Senate side, Frist named himself as a conferee. Altogether fitting, I thought; he's a heart surgeon. Talk about expertise. Among others at his table were Iowa's Chuck Grassley and two Democrats, Louisiana's very able John Breaux and Max Baucus of Montana. Everyone hoped we could agree soon and put a bill on the President's desk before starting our August recess.

Soon we got bogged down. We lost ground. Yet for every retreat, we moved forward in other areas. Late in August, for example, Grassley pulled his troops from the conference table. Ostensibly, he was upset that conferees were devoting too little time and thought to rural health issues that were important in a state like Iowa. Then Grassley said something that indicated the real reason for the walkout. He was miffed at the working schedule Thomas had laid out for the conferees. Thomas, he said, "ought to show a little more respect to a person of equal rank." Grassley just wanted to show that you couldn't slight him and get away with it. This was beginning to remind me of some exercise you read about in some ancient Japanese royal court.

Late in August, former Speaker Newt Gingrich entered the debate. As always, he was full of ideas, most of which were very good, and he added experience with a certain intensity. Then, in September, two steps forward. By voice votes, conferees agreed on providing a discount card for seniors and more aid to rural health care providers. Grassley had to be happy about that.

Late in October, conferees rejected provisions in the bill that called for Health Savings Security Accounts that were to cost an extra $163 billion over the next ten years. That was something conservative voters really wanted. So did I. I wrote one of the first Medical Savings Accounts plans in 1991. I signalled to the conferees there wasn't going to be any bill without HSAs in it, so language for them was left in the bill. We could say we still had our foot in the door. Nonetheless, the mood around here was grim. As *The Hill* newspaper exclaimed on November 6: "Chances of Medicare breakthrough are all but exhausted this year."

The proposal for competition, known in Hill vernacular as "premium support," was the sticking point once again. Thomas suggested a compromise: Competition would be allowed to begin only if future federal spending on Medicare improvements increased faster than Congress had envisioned. Talk about safe bets. Costs *always* rise faster than Congress thinks they will, so I wasn't surprised when the Democrats said no.

Then, with one-third of November gone, Frist and I intervened and proposed a new compromise. Under this approach, Republicans would scale back our demands for direct competition across the board and experiment with the idea in selected markets first, say four metropolitan areas and one region of the country. It would start in 2008, last for just three years, and offer billions of dollars in incentives to discourage private businesses from dropping health care coverage for their retirees.

That's when we heard thunder from the Ways and Means Chairman. Thomas felt undercut by our proposed compromise. He stormed out of the Capitol on the afternoon of November 12 to catch a six o'clock flight home to California. Fortunately, Frist and I reached him on his cell phone and somehow convinced him to turn around. We told him that we needed him, which was true, and that must have been pretty persuasive because we didn't have anything tangible to offer him.

Two days later Novelli was very clear: He wanted a deal before the budget deficit grew so large that it made program expansion impossible both politically and financially. Pointedly, AARP also made clear that it would allocate funds to get the Medicare message out. Next day, November 15, conferees rejected a House-passed bill—per my promise to Missouri's Jo Ann Emerson of five months before—to allow the re-importation of drugs from Canada.

One by one, the obstacles were being swept away. The fog was dissipating and the outlines of an agreement were becoming clearer every day. To me, this bill, if we could get it done, would mean that low-income seniors would never again be confronted with the choice of putting food on the table or paying for life-saving prescription drugs.

On November 17, AARP approved our bill. That public endorsement was huge—a Good Housekeeping seal of approval—and I had a lot of key people to thank. Among them was Tom DeLay. As I had suspected he would, he had represented both the leadership and conservatives at the bargaining table. He had mastered the details of this complex bill, stood up to Bill Thomas when events dictated he should, and played a vital role as a conferee.

Other pieces were starting to fall in line. On November 20, former Speaker Newt Gingrich had an op-ed in the *Wall Street Journal.* "Conservatives should vote 'Yes' on Medicare," the headline
said.

This was the biggest piece of legislation that I'd seen happen
in this place in twenty years, but I was under no illusion that this
was going to be a slam-dunk of any kind. A dismaying op-ed
appeared in the *Wall Street Journal* on Friday, November 21. "Say
'No' to the Medicare Bill," was the headline. The author was Dick
Armey of all people. Dick helped us put together the last two prescription drug bills that weren't nearly as good as this one was.

I knew the night before that Armey had written a piece, so I
tried to call him. I called his home in Texas: no answer. I called his
number in Washington, D.C., still no answer, so I called again and
left a message in his voice mail: "Dick," I said, "this is your old
friend Denny. I'm trying to get a hold of you. I've got another
'Armey's Axiom' (the title of his most recent book) for you. It goes
like this: 'In this business of politics, you don't have to worry about
your enemies. You have to worry about your friends stabbing you
in the heart.'" He and I are good friends. I just wanted him to hear
that message from me.

I go to sleep almost every night with problems still to solve and
people's names and faces pop up in my dreams for reasons I can't
always explain. I woke up that Friday morning, November 21,
2003, and Trent Franks, a freshman Republican Representative
from western Arizona, was on my mind for no apparent reason. He
wasn't on my whip list or anything else. So I told Mike Stokke
before I left the house: "Have Sam (Lancaster) call Trent Franks.
Have him come into my office before I start my regular meetings."

Franks came by about eight o'clock, and I said, "You know, you're not on my list, and there's no reason I need to talk to you, but I woke up at four o'clock this morning, and you were on my mind. Is there something I need to talk to you about?"

"I'm really struggling with this legislation," he replied. "I'm just against it, but I have all these seniors down in Sun City." He didn't need to tell me they were *for* it; I knew. Just listening to him, I could tell how conflicted he was. He's a wonderful young man, very religious and committed to saving the lives of the unborn. That's why he is in Congress, to try to preserve the lives of the unborn.

We had a really good talk. "I'm not trying to whip you," I said.

He looked me in the eye. "I don't want to vote for this bill."

"I'm not here to persuade you. You're not on my whip list. You're just on my mind." I knew I was beginning to repeat myself. "So I just wanted to talk to you."

"Thanks for asking me to come in," he said. And that was it.

∾

In late fall, no matter what the most pressing issue is, the days are full around here, and this day was no exception. There was a lot of other business we just had to get done before tackling Medicare. And we were going to do that before going home, no matter how long it took. With every passing day, I was becoming more convinced that if we failed to act now, we wouldn't have another chance to reform Medicare until after the program went bankrupt.

Our appropriations process was stuck over in the Senate, and a comprehensive energy bill that had passed the House and Senate was almost ready to go to the President's desk but was hung up by trial lawyers in a procedural issue in the Senate. I ducked out of my office for a few minutes to go talk to Ted Stevens, President Pro Tem of the Senate and Appropriations Chair. I wanted to untangle an appropriations problem. After our discussion, I went back to my office to rework the Medicare votes. I knew I had a long night ahead of me. I had no idea how long.

Realistically, our chances of prevailing appeared grim. On paper, Republicans had 229 votes (to Democrats' 205 and one Independent)–well above the 218 we needed to win, but Republicans simply weren't united behind this bill. A whip check at ten o'clock that Friday night showed twenty Members of our Conference voting no, with another nine leaning no and just four undecided. As if it were any consolation, three Members said we could call on them "if needed" and they would respond.

We knew we didn't have the votes ourselves. What we didn't know was how many Democrats we could count on to vote for the bill. I asked a number of them if they could help us on this, but they said it just wasn't worth it; there was so much pressure on them over there. Minority Leader Pelosi had made this a "party vote," which means that either you vote the party line or you're apt to be thrown out of the caucus, lose your committee assignments, or any other perks you might have. I'd been told that she relied on heavy discipline to keep her troops in line; if what I'd heard was true, I didn't think we'd make much headway there.

Already, I'd talked to all our Members who were no or leaning no. I knew all of them, some fairly well; I'd been to their districts to speak, raise funds, and campaign for them. I listed the reasons why I thought this vote was crucial for America's seniors, for Medicare, and for the Republican Party. For some reason, I wasn't making the sale.

What you learn around here is that there is seldom a single reason for Members to vote no. Some are no on principle. Others because they're unhappy about something else or because they want to leverage you to do this or that. It's helpful when there's a variety of reasons for saying no because it gives you more chances to figure out how to unlock the puzzle. Unfortunately, that logic didn't apply here. Almost all of the Republicans who were listed as definite "no's" were conservatives. They viewed Medicare as an ugly child of LBJ's Great Society, not something they wanted to make better. They had an almost philosophical disagreement with our approach on the bill, which was going to make changing their minds very difficult.

My argument to them was: "Give us a chance to reform it."

Some Members had given speeches back home that criticized our bill. They felt that if they changed their votes now, they wouldn't be keeping their word. Representative Steve Chabot, a Republican from Cincinnati who is perhaps best known for his advocacy of crime victims' rights, insisted that he would never vote for any means testing. Well, one of the *cost containments* (ways to save money) in this bill was means testing.

"I can't vote for it," he said.

I tried to point out that what we had in the bill wasn't really a means test; it was an earnings test. Chabot didn't draw the distinction there. Means testing was whatever he took it to be, so that was a vote for the Medicare bill that we weren't going to get.

Hours before the actual vote, Members started to line up in the hall outside my office on the second floor of the Capitol waiting their turn to come in and talk about the bill. For some of the more than two dozen there, this was their second time. At one point my side had 185 votes. We had to get to 218. Going over the names, all I had left were no's.

When you face a problem like that, you don't accept its apparent hopelessness. You don't let it overwhelm you. You go after it incrementally, talking to Members about their votes individually, persuading them to change. Republican Mike Simpson, a dentist from Idaho, had been leaning no. After we talked, he committed to supporting the bill. I talked to Representative Zach Wamp, a Republican from Tennessee, but he was gone. Representative Don Manzullo changed his mind from no to yes. Representative Dana Rohrabacher switched from a definite no to a yes to help us out, and—because he's well liked in the House—his was an important vote change.

Earlier that day we had agreed on what we thought would be a winning strategy. We knew we had to get at least 206 Republican votes. Once we had them, we could attract enough Democratic votes to put us over the top at 218. This violated one of my old coaching principles: "Never rely on your opponent to help you win," but we didn't have a choice. Now, however, since Leader Pelosi had made this a "party vote," it was clear that 206 wouldn't be enough. We'd have to get 218 before she would even consider releasing any Democrats to vote with us.

The key to victory was to persuade the handful we needed at the end that if we failed this time, the bill was coming back. I believed the Democrats would write their version of the bill at a cost of over one trillion dollars and probably get the votes to pass it. It wouldn't just vanish from the radar screen. The measure would return in far more expensive clothes and be even less acceptable to our conservatives than what they were considering now. Leader Pelosi, we'd been told, had informed her own people that she'd use the discharge petition process to reconstitute her version of what a Medicare bill should be. They knew what I meant; I didn't have to spell out the details.

When the roll call vote started it was about three o'clock Saturday morning. I was watching the red and green lights on the voting board in the House chamber. I counted more red than green, so I decided to prowl the aisles myself to look for additional votes.

Some members had assured me that they would be with us, but when the crunch came, they weren't. One prairie state Member, a fourth-term Representative from a solidly Republican district, voted no, then ran and hid. I sent people to find him; they couldn't. Representative Tom Osborne, a Republican from Nebraska, went to look for him to no avail. Representative Bill Janklow, a former Governor of South Dakota, voted late, but he voted with us. We were still in the game.

Our rules say that Members shall have a minimum of fifteen minutes to vote; they say nothing about a maximum. Actually, the vote had continued for two hours now—already the longest-known roll call in the history of the House and one that was still continuing—and it seemed stuck with us two votes behind. The Democrats were very orderly and disciplined on their side. They weren't trying to hurry the roll call. They weren't jeering or shouting, "Regular order," or anything else.

During those early morning hours, we were at our wits' end. We had to stop and come together three or four times and try to figure out where we stood and what our options were. I was helping make these decisions. So were DeLay, Thomas, Tauzin, and Majority Whip Roy Blunt, a Republican from Missouri who was developing an expertise in counting votes. We kept asking, "What are our parliamentary options on this?" We'd never had to do anything like this before. The vote totals weren't moving either way. We were still behind and we didn't know if we could turn anybody else. On the other side of the aisle were several Members who hadn't voted yet. Would they be with us when the gavel came down? We just didn't know.

One option was to close the roll call immediately. Have one of our people vote for the prevailing side and then move for a vote to reconsider. That would mean asking Ways and Means Committee Chairman Bill Thomas or someone else to change his vote and go over to the other side. It sounded like a flawed strategy, and it was. We weren't sure that our guys would vote with us on the motion to reconsider, and if they didn't, we'd lose.

Another factor: We had at least ten Democrats with us; if we stopped the vote and tried to reconsider, we'd lose all our momentum. Worse, Leader Pelosi and her lieutenants would beat up on those Democrats, and we could never keep them if we had to come back to vote at a later time. For every option that came up, there were solid arguments against, and then someone would say, "I think so-and-so is gettable." So we'd back off the options and concentrate on winning that person's vote.

Representative Barbara Cubin, a Republican from Wyoming who was in her fifth term, had been serving as Conference Secretary, a member of our leadership team, but family responsibilities had compelled her to step down from that post. Her husband, Fritz, a physician and great guy, was ill. Then Barbara herself came down with a viral infection and meningitis as well. She had considered not running again in 2002, but her husband wanted her to serve and so did I.

In my book she's one strong, very gutsy lady. There on the floor of the House just before dawn, I spotted Barbara talking to Representative Butch Otter, former Lieutenant Governor of Idaho. Butch is a cowboy, a roper and rider who doesn't say very much. He had switched to provide a crucial vote for us when we passed the Medicare bill in June, but he had said he wasn't going to vote for it this time. He didn't believe in it, and his name was on my whip list as a definite no.

I have no idea what Barbara said to him, but all of a sudden there was movement on our side. Otter and Trent Franks went into a huddle, conferred with some of their colleagues, and both switched their votes. That put our total at 218. Talk about Providence or Divine Intervention. Less than twenty-four hours before, Franks had come by the office to tell me he couldn't vote for this bill.

The final vote on the Medicare bill was 220 to 215; sixteen Democrats voted with us, while twenty-five Republicans voted no. This would not have passed without the efforts of Chairman Thomas and the Blunt Whip team. (Two days later, the Senate approved the measure by a vote of fifty-five to forty-four; the bill went to the White House where the President signed it into law.) The roll call lasted for two hours and fifty-one minutes, a record. Republicans cheered. Democrats were furious and hurled nasty charges at us. "They criticize me for keeping the vote open so long," I told reporters, "but I've been working this issue for twenty years and seniors have been waiting through three Congresses for a prescription drug benefit, so I don't think that waiting an additional three hours to get it done is too much."

After the vote was final, I returned to my office, sat down, and took a deep breath. Someone handed out some beers, and I grabbed a Heineken. Then I walked out on my balcony and watched the sun come up. It was a beautiful morning in Washington. I was going to join Mike Stokke and some other people for breakfast at Eastern Market; then I was going to go home and get some sleep. But first I wanted to stand on that balcony and just savor our victory. The lesson of the Granby Roll, which I'd taught my wrestlers so many years before, applied to people in Congress counting votes the same way it did to high school students on the mat. And that lesson is: You can start at a disadvantage, in the bottom position, but if you keep your wits about you and use your head, you can score points from the bottom. You can win.

CHAPTER ELEVEN

THE MORE THINGS CHANGE

Make no little plans; they have no magic to stir men's blood...
Make big plans; aim high in hope and work...
—CHICAGO ARCHITECT DANIEL H. BURNHAM, 1910

TO MAKE CHANGE, YOU NEED A PLAN. HERE'S MY OWN PLAN FOR reforming taxes, health care, education, campaign finance, and our out-of-control legal system, and keeping our nation safe, so that the big issues of today don't become crises of tomorrow. I guess you could say they fall into two categories—economic security and national security. They also come together to create a vision for a stronger America—so that we can leave America better off than when we began.

TAXES

Since President Bush took office in January 2001, we've seen millions of jobs move overseas. (Forget for a moment how many new jobs have been created here and that the slumping economy Bush inherited and the September 11 attacks played a big role in this.) What kinds of jobs? We're talking tool and die makers, pattern makers, and computer operators. Salaries are one reason. The wage scale in less developed nations is a lot lower than it is here, so manufacturers export raw materials to, say, India or Bangladesh. They build their widgets there and then send them back to the United States. But a lower wage scale in developing nations isn't the only reason this is happening. It is also being driven by tax policy.

We build all sorts of products in this country and pay all sorts of taxes—corporations pay corporate taxes, employment taxes, etc.—and the cost of these taxes is added to the product's cost and hence to the price. How big a slice of the pie are we talking about? Well, taxes account for between 23 to 27 percent of the cost of our goods and services, but when our products go overseas—to France, Germany, or Japan—our taxes stay embedded in our goods or services. These countries may even slap on a Value Added Tax (VAT) on top of our costs. That means our products don't compete well overseas. But when our trade partners' products come here, their VATs drop off the moment they leave their home country. Their products may pick up a small tariff coming across our borders, but they're not encumbered with a significant burden of embedded taxes (like our outgoing competitive products). This gives their products a huge advantage in competing with ours. Our widgets have a tax burden. Their widgets don't.

That has caused billions—maybe trillions—of our dollars to flee overseas. For us to return capital and jobs to the United States, we're going to have to change our present tax system and adopt a flat tax, a national sales tax, an ad valorem tax, or a VAT. In my view, that would bring capital and jobs back, and it's one of the most important things we can do over the next few years.

The Democrats are making a big deal about outsourcing. To them, it's a simple matter of greedy corporations moving offshore in order to pay less for labor. But it's just not that simple. The fact is our labor costs are higher because of three unproductive burdens:

taxation, litigation, and regulation. The Democrats don't like to talk about these three items because they are largely to blame for these costs being added on to business in the U.S., therefore making us less competitive and more likely to need to outsource jobs. I say we must face these issues if we are going to be economically competitive overseas, and we must start with tax reform.

It's not just the burden on foreign competition that makes me say we need to change our tax code. I think most of us can agree our present tax system is archaic and over-encumbered. According to some figures I saw recently, Americans spend nearly 6.1 billion hours on their taxes annually, and two-thirds of them agree the system is far too complex. Yet every time we try to change it and make it easier to figure out, we just rearrange the chairs on the deck. We make it more confusing for people who are only trying to obey the law.

Did you know that half the people who work in this country today don't pay *any* federal income tax? If you have a family of four and you earn just under $40,000 a year, you probably don't have a federal income tax liability. (You do have a state tax bill to pay, of course, and you may have Social Security or Medicare responsibilities, but your outlays there are funds you may get some return on in the future.) In an effort to shift the tax burden to middle- and upper-income Americans, we've raised the average income level of people who are now exempt from paying any federal payroll income taxes at all.

If you own property, stock, or, say, one hundred acres of farmland, and tax time is approaching, you don't want to make a mistake, so you're almost obliged to go to a certified public accountant, tax preparer, or tax attorney to help you file a correct return. That costs a lot of money. Now multiply the amount you have to pay by the total number of people who are in the same boat. You can't. No one can because precise numbers don't exist. But we can stipulate that we're talking about a huge amount.

Now consider that a flat tax, national sales tax, or VAT would not only eliminate the need to do this, it could also eliminate the Internal Revenue Service (IRS) itself and make the process of paying taxes much easier. And it could do this while still giving lower- and middle-income Americans a rebate on, say, the first $35,000 of their purchases. People ask me if I'm really calling for the elimination of the IRS, and I say I think that's a great thing to do for future generations of Americans.

Representative John Linder, a Republican from Georgia, is pushing a national sales tax that would eliminate income taxes and the IRS–a very interesting proposition. Freshman representative Michael Burgess, M.D., a Republican from Texas has introduced a bill that would replace the income tax with a flat tax over a three-year period. Both of these ideas are worthy of consideration.

By adopting a VAT, sales tax, or some other alternative, we could begin to change productivity. If you can do that, you can change gross national product and start growing the economy. You could *double* the economy over the next fifteen years. All of a sudden, the problem of what future generations owe in Social Security and Medicare won't seem so daunting anymore. The answer is to grow the economy, and the key to doing that is making sure we have a tax system that attracts capital and builds incentives to keep it here instead of forcing it out to other nations. At the same time, our tax code must be made simpler and fairer for all Americans. Pushing reform legislation will be difficult. Change of any sort seldom comes easy. But these changes are critical to our economic vitality at home and our economic security abroad. I'd like to start moving on it soon.

EDUCATION

Education is the basis of this country's future. It's dear to my heart because I spent so many years as a teacher and coach myself. Every child is precious and deserves the best education possible. Thomas Jefferson, in his philosophy of education, cited a direct correlation between literacy, citizenship, and successful self-government.

We have to make sure that every person in America has access to a good education. We must ensure that kids who have special aptitude and skills in math and science can use them to unlock the secrets of the future. I'm a social science guy, but one of the things I'm proud I pushed for as a state legislator was the first math and science academy in Illinois. I wanted to assure that we would keep our best and brightest young minds in the state and not lose them to California or New York. The Illinois Math and Science Academy was established in 1985. The program offers free tuition to Illinois students who qualify. The school has over 2,500 graduates, 99 percent of whom have gone on to college–all of this on state funds.

In September 2003, the Organization of Economic Cooperation and Development (OECD) released a study that found that the U.S. spent more money on education than twenty-five other countries around the world–$10,240 per student here as opposed to an average of $6,361. "We spend more per child, but our students rank in the middle of the pack in almost every category," I said at the time.

"That is simply not acceptable. More money now is not the answer. Better results are the answer. As a former high school teacher, I know what it takes to get students to learn. You need to expect more from them; you need to demand better results."

Just as the Illinois Math and Science Academy opened doors for Illinois students, so magnet schools, charter schools, or private schools could open doors for children across America. If parents want to school their kids at home or give them a Christian education, that's a choice they ought to have and we need to make those choices available. The bottom line here is that competition is good for education.

President Bush, in my view, recognizes this. He's made a strong commitment to boost education. The very first initiative he took legislatively after assuming office was the No Child Left Behind Act of 2001.

But education is not just about accumulating goodies from federal programs or learning from books. It's also about learning—in a Jeffersonian sense—from everything around us and distilling the lessons of the past into forms that our children will grasp and understand.

Tom Jarman and I have had a continuing discussion about what constitutes a good education. We agree on the importance of three basic ideas.

First is the concept of mentorship. Ken Pickerill, our football and wrestling coach at Oswego High School so many years ago, was certainly one of the most influential people in both of our lives. But above all other things, *he was a mentor*, and he took the time to teach us not only about plays and strategies but also about life. What a gift that was. Former Republican leader Bob Michel was another mentor who was willing to spend time teaching me the ropes on Capitol Hill. How can I ever repay the mentors I had? By taking the time to push young people along. I worry that I don't do enough of that.

A second tenet is that ordinary people can accomplish extraordinary things, especially when they work together and when no one cares who gets the credit. Or, to quote Ronald Reagan, "There is no limit to what man can do or where he can go, if he doesn't mind who gets the credit."

The final point in this education theory involves service. Growing up in the Midwest, we were taught a core value that was drilled into us so often that it almost became second nature. If your neighbor needed help with chores, you walked over and helped him. You didn't expect a tip. Doing it was the only gratification you needed. Service was a constant, and we grew up with that.

Those three ideas provide a strong foundation for an education that—I hope—is still continuing.

HEALTH CARE

For as long as I've been involved in this issue, I've believed that we have three goals here. What we come up with must be affordable, available, and accountable.

To make health care affordable, we must address tort reform. If we can lower the amount doctors pay for malpractice insurance and reduce the mandated paperwork required for payment for Medicare claims, we can reduce the cost to doctors, which ultimately reduces the costs for all of us.

In many states across the country, health care has gone from unaffordable to unavailable. Madison and St. Clair counties in

Illinois have lost many of their medical practitioners, specifically OB/GYNs and neurosurgeons, not to retirement but to litigation. As the doctors in Pennsylvania noted on their picket signs, "The next time you have a medical emergency, call your lawyer." We need to make it easier for doctors to practice.

Many people who talk about health care reform get mixed up between health care and health insurance. But just as we need health care to be affordable and available, we need insurance that's affordable and available too.

We have the best health care system in the world, but it can't live up to its potential unless it includes the forty to forty-five million Americans who don't have insurance today. These aren't the poorest people in our society, because the poorest people have insurance—through Medicaid, green cards, or some type of state or federal program for the indigent. They are instead the itinerant workers or the people who run small businesses. They can't afford the expense, so they go without. In some cases, health care costs are escalating by as much as 20 percent a year. These small businesses—print shops, barbershops, small factories—found that they just couldn't afford to carry their employees' insurance.

To cut costs, they dropped family coverage. Then they dropped coverage for individuals. Jeff Farren, a former student of mine, runs a small newspaper called the *Kendall County Record* in Yorkville, Illinois. Everything was fine with him until about twelve years ago when one of his employees' wives experienced a difficult birth. Because of the extra costs, his insurance carrier presented him with an impossible choice: either he fired that employee or the company would drop his insurance. To Jeff, that was no choice. He kept the employee, of course, and let the insurance go.

Then he had to find a new company to provide insurance for his employees at a price he could afford.

Jeff's story is not an unusual one. From the time I came to Congress in 1987, I've been hearing about this problem, or variations of it, while I've been trying to find solutions here.

What people without health insurance need, it seems to me, is an insurance policy they could buy for themselves and their families. They might have to put up the first $1,000 or $1,500, but after that they would be covered—they would be safe. If they got sick, they could go to the hospital without worrying about running up a bill that would ruin their family. They would have a safety net, and medical problems wouldn't force them into bankruptcy.

It might be reassuring for me to say that Congress will draft and pass the legislation we need to accomplish this. We can't do that—health care insurance comes under the jurisdiction of the fifty states, and what different states will cover depends on where you live.

Here are some things we can do. Create association health plans allowing small businesses to consolidate to achieve the same market clout as major corporations. Nancy Johnson, a Republican from Connecticut, has a bill to make private long-term care insurance more accessible and affordable. Representative John Shadegg, a Republican from Arizona, has introduced legislation to allow individuals to shop the Internet for health insurance, putting consumers in the driver's seat. We should also be researching and developing methods for converting all prescriptions and health records to electronic files.

One of the best tools I know, and one I'm very keen to promote, is Health Savings Accounts (formerly called Medical Savings

Accounts), which will give patients a choice and some control as to how they spend their health care dollars.

I've been working on Health Savings Accounts (HSAs) for fourteen years. They allow someone to create a personal savings account to cover small and discretionary medical expenses (thereby freeing them to buy a less expensive, high-deductible insurance policy to cover catastrophic expenses). When you put the money in your savings account, you decide which doctor you want, when to go, and if you don't spend the money, you get to keep it. That's a great incentive for people to be responsible about their family's health care.

Today's third-party payer system is inefficient. Even physicians don't know the cost of procedures. For example, if a doctor thinks a patient needs an MRI, he or she just orders it. Neither the doctor nor the patient knows the cost. With an HSA, the doctor *and* the patient make that decision, and they know the cost. All of a sudden, a true market starts to work.

The money patients don't spend stays in their savings accounts, which grow year by year. If they want to cash them in when they get to be sixty-five, that's fine. They'd pay taxes on that money like everyone else. If they want to use the money for long-term care after age sixty-five or as a cushion for their family's health care, they could do that, too, tax-free. The important thing is that they could start at, say, age thirty-five and build up an HSA with several hundred thousand dollars in it. Think of the worries that nest egg would drive away—portability, long-term health-care insurance, health care costs for an elderly family member. All that money is tax-free if it's used for health care.

Since 1999, my first year as Speaker, I've seen lots of positive developments in this area. Chief among them, perhaps, was the

Medicare/prescription drug bill that Congress passed and the President signed on December 8, 2003. That was an important victory, but I think all of us realize that we still need to address these issues of affordability and availability. Senate Majority Leader Bill Frist, himself a physician, recognizes this. "That's the next big challenge," he says.

ENERGY

The House was proud of the mammoth, twelve-hundred-page energy bill we passed last fall. We would maximize use of the resources we have, like soybeans and ethanol (which is made from corn, and Illinois has lots of that), build the infrastructure we need—natural gas pipelines and a stronger, more coordinated power grid—and more fully develop our coal, oil, and gas reserves. We would have an alternative to our dependence on foreign petroleum and address rising energy prices from coast to coast.

Minority Leader Tom Daschle supported the measure, and the Senate was on its way to passing the conference report, which is the final version of the energy bill. Then the trial lawyers stopped everything.

The dispute was over waivers of liability to producers of the fuel additive MTBE (methyl tertiary butyl ether). This substance, designed to make gasoline burn more cleanly and reduce pollution from motor vehicles, was originally mandated by the federal government under the Clean Air Act to be added to the gasoline we buy at the pump. That was before we learned it's environmentally risky and physically harmful. It seeps into groundwater supplies and causes all sorts of problems.

Instead of an energy solution, the issue soon became: Who's responsible? Who pays and how much? To some trial lawyers,

MTBE is "the next tobacco." Instead of pursuing the people who illegally dumped it or misused it, the trial lawyers want to sue the producers because that's where the deep pockets are.

As a direct result of this trial-lawyer-triggered dispute, the energy bill stalled. Half a dozen Republican senators, most from the northeast, joined a filibuster led by Senator Chuck Schumer, a Democrat from New York. When Majority Leader Bill Frist couldn't summon enough votes to break it, the nation lost a chance to solve some of our most pressing energy needs.

This is inexcusable and needs to be resolved.

It would be hard for me to name a single group that exerts more influence on Capitol Hill than trial lawyers do. It's not their numbers; trial lawyers constitute a small subset of the legal profession today. It's their funding–they can and do spend millions to support or oppose candidates, mainly in favor of Democrats. They focus in on their issues with a laser-like intensity.

TORT REFORM

In Mississippi a few years ago, I was getting ready to speak at a fund-raiser for Republican Representative Chip Pickering. Senator Trent Lott was there. Before I began my remarks, my hosts invited me to step into an adjacent room and introduced me to Richard Scruggs, Lott's brother-in-law, who is one of the most successful trial lawyers in America.

"We need to talk," Scruggs began. "We need to change the current situation with the asbestos impasse. On the class action suits people get some award, but the people who are really sick aren't getting the money on a timely basis. They're dead before the money arrives. We need to change that."

"What do you want me to do?"

He said we ought to make sure we take care of people who are really sick and establish a fund to pay for those who will probably get sick in the future.

Back on Capitol Hill, I talked to Representative Jim Sensenbrenner, a Republican from Wisconsin who is chairman of the House Judiciary Committee. Scruggs's attitude was encouraging, but Jim wanted to proceed cautiously with new legislation. Because the trial lawyers' strength was in the Senate, he didn't want to expose House members to a risky vote without first having a better idea what action the Senate was likely to take. "I'm not going to move the bill until they move it in the Senate," Sensenbrenner told me.

In the House we've passed medical malpractice reform and class action reform—both of those are still in the Senate. Progress lies on a rough and difficult road, and the trial lawyers don't want to give an inch. Still, I think we're on track to getting some kind of asbestos reform legislation done. We wanted to be able to move it in the Senate first and then get it done in the House. We're making progress, but the incredible force of trial lawyers and unions moving in lockstep here just raises havoc with the legislation and our efforts to get it out.

Time and again I've met with union leaders and told them that asbestos legislation reform was in their members' best interest. "There are some thirty of your companies that have gone bankrupt or closed down because of asbestos suits," I reminded them. "They all have American workers, and if they get bought up by foreign companies, those jobs go overseas. It's your jobs that you're losing. You ought to support reform and help us get it done." The AFL-CIO is so tied into the trial lawyers that, so far at least, its reaction has been lukewarm. I hope that will change.

Why is asbestos reform important? Companies have set aside billions of dollars to address the health needs of those afflicted with asbestosis. If the bill pending in the Senate were to pass, the fund would be set up with money already set aside by corporations. This would bring certainty to an issue that has bankrupted many American companies, thus driving those jobs overseas. The money not spent to litigate these issues in the future could then be put back into the economy.

The governor of California has a new idea: taxing the excess profits from punitive damages. It's an interesting idea that we ought to look into further.

CAMPAIGN FINANCE REFORM

Even before the 2000 election, I was on the record in favor of campaign finance reform. "Many Americans have lost faith in the system," I pointed out. "It's a system that lacks transparency, that's typified more by complex laws than by the virtues of common sense. It's a system that discourages political participation." And I said this when the nation was still reeling from allegations of fundraising in the Lincoln Bedroom or in a Buddhist temple in Los Angeles. At the time I didn't think the situation could get worse. I was wrong.

As Speaker of the House, one of my responsibilities is to prevent bad legislation from coming to the floor, or–if I can't prevent it–to delay it for as long as possible. That's why I did whatever I could to block the McCain-Feingold campaign finance measure from becoming law and made my colleagues go through the hoops of signing two discharge petitions–each requiring at least 218 names–before they could get the bill to the President's desk.

That bill, the worst piece of legislation to become law while Republicans controlled Congress during my time in Washington, actually stifles free speech while enticing and empowering questionable people to do improper things. Ever since this country was founded, our two political parties have helped select and fund candidates. That always made sense to me. If you're a political party, then the people who believe in that party and its philosophy should have control over that campaign. But, under McCain-Feingold, the parties are severely restricted in doing that. The law gives special interest groups more freedom to participate, weakening the two-party system. These so-called "independent" groups, set up and funded by people like billionaire George Soros–who says that defeating George W. Bush in November "is the central focus of [his] life,"–are free to contribute untold sums to whomever they want without meeting the same disclosure requirements as the parties. Today the playing field is so tilted, so unbalanced, that one might expect the press to do its job and alert readers and viewers to this legal travesty. But don't hold your breath. The *New York Times* and the *Washington Post* actually benefit from the statute as it's written now.

McCain-Feingold makes the media the only game in town. The law restricts campaign advertising (issue advocacy) from outside groups within sixty days of an election. That gives tremendous power to those who write editorials. According to a poll (conducted jointly by the Pew Research Center and the Project for Excellence in Journalism) released on May 23, 2004, 88 percent of "national" journalists considered themselves to be moderates or liberals; 7 percent called themselves conservatives (as opposed to 34 percent of the public who described themselves that way). Additionally, 55 percent of these journalists thought the press had been "not critical enough" of President Bush. Am I supposed to believe that editorial writers for the *New York Times* will listen to Republican views on issues of the day and write about them objectively? That's not an assumption I'm prepared to make.

Ever since I was Chief Deputy Whip, and especially since I've been Speaker of the House, I've spent almost every weekend raising money for Republican candidates. Basically, I try to help anyone who's in need. During the 2002 campaign I traveled to some 178 congressional events. Back when both parties were allowed to use "soft" money, I was the single biggest funding source for the Republican Party in Illinois and for the Republicans in the state house and senate. Today, under McCain-Feingold, I can't raise or spend money (under state law) for state candidates. And that's not all. I can't even show up at events I've attended all my life because the law imposes restrictions on my ability to associate. For example: If my old friend Dallas Ingemunson, the Republican Party chairman of Kendall County, wants to meet with our mutual friend Tom Cross, the Republican Leader of the Illinois General Assembly, to discuss raising state funds, I have to leave the room. I can't participate in the conversation. My speech is limited.

According to the *New York Times*, the law has been a success. We've banished all that evil soft money. Well, of course we haven't. The other side is out there raising $500 million right now to spend against George W. Bush, and guess what? Our party can't do it. Only outside groups can. They can form entities called 527s (so named after the section of the tax code that applies to them) and raise all the money they want, with no limits. Political parties have always been banned from accepting foreign funds; some 527s are not. The law says you can't coordinate between a federal campaign and these outside entities. Right now, they insist they're not coordinating. It's just a coincidence that all these dollars went to support the same candidate, and they'll dare you to prove otherwise. That could take years. So, in the name of reform, we've shoved all the money off the table to a place where you can't tell who's responsible or even from what country it is coming.

To people who insist that we need campaign finance reform and that our political system is awash with too much money, I respond that the answer is obvious: transparency. Require all candidates to report how much they received, from whom, when, and how they spent it. Then make that information publicly available as soon as possible. That's what voters need. Everything else is chaff.

Soon after President Bush signed the Bipartisan Campaign Finance Reform Act (BCRA–the official name for McCain-Feingold) into law, I joined a suit against the federal government declaring that the bill that had passed the House of Representatives was unconstitutional. "Although the BCRA will not directly impact the Speaker's legislative role," my lawyers' brief explained, "it will curtail the Speaker's ability to participate meaningfully in the political process. Furthermore, it will prevent the Speaker and other members of the House from participating fully in state and local government elections or civic organizations." As far as I know, this was the first time any Speaker had done something like that.

Last December, the United States Supreme Court, in a 5–4 opinion, upheld the ban on soft money and said the new rules restricting advertising during political campaigns–which exempt such "mainstream" media as the *New York Times* and the *Washington Post*—were constitutional. ("This is a sad day for freedom of speech," declared Associate Justice Antonin Scalia.) When McCain-Feingold flunks its first major test in November, I hope the American people will demand that we revisit that law and dismantle it. The answer is not more regulation of speech and association; the answer is more transparency. We should look to full disclosure options like those advocated by Representative John Doolittle (R-CA). This is the direction we should go.

NATIONAL DEFENSE

In early 2004, senior officials from the Department of Defense arrived at the Capitol and laid out a very direct and disconcerting assessment of our Pentagon budget situation. This meeting confirmed what many Americans already knew: The Clinton administration decimated military readiness. In fact, Clinton reduced the total number of Army divisions from eighteen to ten; cut our twenty-four fighter wings to thirteen; and reduced the Navy from 546 ships to 314. It is a testament to the fine men and women of our Armed Forces that they have achieved so much in recent years despite Democratic underinvestment.

The scenario is similar for intelligence programs, particularly when Democrats controlled both the White House and the Congress. The Clinton budgets between 1993 and 1995 cut funding for the intelligence community by 11 percent. Meanwhile, from 1992 to 1994, the Democratic-controlled Congress sought further cuts to intelligence budget requests. Ardent House liberals like Barney Frank and Barbara Boxer authored amendments to slash intelligence funding and to hamstring intelligence collection.

Senator John Kerry, in May 1997, summed up Democratic attitudes about investment in intelligence programs, stating, "Now that that struggle [the Cold War] is over, why is it that our vast intelligence apparatus continues to grow?" Senator Kerry further admonished the Senate, "Why is it that our vast intelligence apparatus continues to roll on even as every other government bureaucracy is subject to increasing scrutiny and, indeed, to reinvention?" Sadly, even in the post–September 11 world, many Democrats still do not understand the value of increased intelligence funding: Senator Kerry himself voted in October 2003 against billions in supplemental intelligence appropriations. Republicans, on the other hand, have been working hard to rebuild both our military and our intelligence capability.

President Bush, working shoulder to shoulder with House Intelligence Committee Chairman Porter Goss (himself a distinguished retired CIA case officer), set to work in 2001 to rebuild the decimated intelligence community. And while intelligence funding amounts remain classified, it is accurate to say that Bush administration budget proposals and Republican congressional funding are billions of dollars above Clinton levels.

THE GLOBAL WAR ON TERROR

Iraq and Afghanistan are not the only important setting in the global War on Terror. In fact, there are several other, less publicized national security issues which may be equally critical to continued American national security.

President Bush and Republicans are right to continue a hard line with rogue regimes in North Korea and Iran, with whom the Clinton administration struck bad deals. It is obvious that Kim

Jong Il never intended to honor the Agreed Framework with President Clinton, despite receiving more than $400 million in U.S. aid. Yet many Democrats today call for further compromise and compensation for North Korea, and they seek European-style concessions to Iran for its aggressive nuclear ambitions.

Perhaps the most significant, yet underreported, accomplishment related to the global War on Terror is the president's Libyan policy. Deemed a state sponsor of terror for years, Libya quietly agreed in December 2003 to eliminate its clandestine nuclear and chemical weapons programs. Dictator Moammar al-Qaddafi's dramatic concession was delivered not to UN weapons inspectors but to American and British intelligence officers. Skeptics need look no further than Tripoli to see the success of the Bush doctrine.

At the UN, President Bush has refused to submit to dangerous multilateral schemes solely for the sake of consensus with the European Left. He has refused to allow American citizens and soldiers to come under the jurisdiction of the new International Criminal Court, an entity strongly supported by John Kerry and most congressional Democrats. And in an unprecedented move which caused a collective gasp in international left-wing circles, President Bush "unsigned" the Kyoto Climate Change Treaty. I was part of the official congressional delegation participating in the original Kyoto Conference in December 1997, where at the eleventh hour, negotiations were hijacked by Al Gore and rabid environmentalists. It remains a bad treaty for America, and Republicans are right to continue to fight it. But there is little doubt that John Kerry as President and a Democratic-led Senate would swiftly consent to these and other dangerous UN treaties subjugating American sovereignty to international bureaucrats.

Such international bureaucrats at the UN were at the center of the controversy surrounding the UN Oil-for-Food program in Iraq. The unfolding scandal, which appears to have lined the pockets of French, Russian, and UN bureaucrats, is troubling, especially if influential people in Russia and France were vociferously opposing action against Saddam Hussein while being paid off by him. It is shameful that some at the UN were profiting from a fund that was supposed to be used to feed the Iraqi people.

THE WAR ON DRUGS

The war on drugs is yet another item critical to our national security. The events of September 11, 2001, clearly illustrated the enemy's ability to strike our homeland. So too does the flow of illegal drugs into America. Drugs constitute a huge challenge to the very health of our nation, costing our health care system almost $15 billion annually. Every year, thousands of lives are lost to drugs–the total in 2001 was 21,683. Drug use causes crime, and drug money supports terrorists–at home and abroad–making neighborhoods less safe and less secure for our families.

Yet year after year in the House, Republicans have been forced to fend off Democratic efforts to slash counternarcotics aid to Colombia, Peru, Bolivia, and elsewhere in Latin America. President Bush's Andean Initiative is yielding significant results. President Uribe of Colombia, with whom I met recently in my Capitol office, confirms this success: Pure cocaine production potential dropped more than 21 percent between 2002 and the end of 2003. If Colombia, with U.S. assistance, achieves its 2004 goals, we are on pace to achieve a dramatic 54 percent reduction

from 2001 coca production levels. Reductions of this magnitude
will undoubtedly create substantial shortages of cocaine in the
United States, Europe, and Latin America.

And this reduction of cultivation south of the border is having real effects at home. In 2001, President Bush and Republicans
pledged to reduce illicit drug use among youth by 10 percent in
two years. During this period, there was actually an 11 percent
decline in drug use by eighth, tenth, and twelfth grade students,
translating into 400,000 fewer teen drug users then before.

Homeland Security

In a post–September 11 world, homeland security became a
much more important component of our national security. The
tensions among limited resources, our precious liberty, and the
need for real security presented difficult questions with enormous
ramifications. Shortly after September 11, the Bush administration
proposed a series of changes to law enforcement authorities that
would allow the federal government to observe and prosecute terrorists and those who support terrorists. Many of the recommendations became law under the Patriot Act in October 2001. Since
then, terrorist plots have been disrupted, and at least four terror
cells in the U.S. have been disassembled. Yet Democrats have
assailed the Patriot Act as a grave threat to our way of life. This
divide between Republicans and Democrats on the issue of trust-
ing, with oversight, the law enforcement community to disrupt terrorist plots in the U.S. is so wide that John Kerry is campaigning
on an anti–Patriot Act platform.

Unquestionably, keeping a watchful eye on how the powers
are used is the obligation of the Department of Justice, the Office

of the President, and Congress. Equally unquestionable are the value of the results. In addition to the neutralization of the four terrorist cells, over 515 individuals linked to September 11 have been deported. And 132 individuals have been convicted or pled guilty, including shoe-bomber Richard Reid, "American Taliban" John Walker Lindh, Iyman Faris (who plotted to cut the supporting cables of the Brooklyn Bridge), six members of the Buffalo cell, and two members of the Detroit cell.

Despite these tangible successes, Democrats move forward with their conviction of criticism, which extends beyond the necessary, watchful eye of oversight into the realm of uninformed hysteria. Under the President's leadership, Republicans have tried our best to fight the War on Terror abroad, secure our homeland, and preserve our freedoms. Many Democrats, including presidential candidate John Kerry, look first for a political criticism rather than what is best for our country.

What those Democrats cannot do, though, is take away the extraordinary efforts Republicans have made to promote our common defense. They cannot take away the fact that Republicans created the new federal Department of Homeland Security, in the largest government reorganization since 1947, to better protect our homeland. They cannot take away the fact that America has brought democracy to over fifty-three million people in Afghanistan and Iraq. They cannot take away the fact that boys and especially girls are going to school in Iraq, with over 7,500 schools set to be rehabilitated or built in the next few years. They cannot take away what President Bush wrote when he learned from National Security Advisor Condoleezza Rice that Ambassador Paul Bremer had transferred sovereignty back to the Iraqi people: "Let Freedom Reign!"

∞

These are the economic and national security issues we need to address. We're not going to succeed in these areas—we won't have a chance—unless we stop shouting over one another and start pulling together as a team.

That's going to be hard to do when you have people like former Vice President Al Gore aligning himself with the left-wing group MoveOn.org and screeching at the top of his lungs that President Bush "has brought us humiliation in the eyes of the world...deep dishonor to our country." The truth is that we are all in it together and have been since September 11, 2001.

On a rainy Sunday night nearly three weeks after the attacks of September 11, I stood at Ground Zero with New York City Mayor Rudy Giuliani and New York Governor George Pataki. Many of the nearby apartments had been evacuated. Although no people were there, televisions were still on in some apartments, giving an eerie look to the night. Part of one tower was still standing. I will never forget the look of determination that I saw on the firefighters' and other workers' faces. They were still excavating— their machines grinding, grating, belching, and choking. Fires were still raging under all that rubble; smoke was pouring out of it; and the scene looked like something you might imagine in Hell.

We've been waging war for the past three years, and while we've suffered reverses, we've also recorded some triumphs that haven't always been acknowledged the way they should have been. Remember Richard C. Reid, the strapping Muslim fundamentalist who boarded a Paris to Miami flight in December 2001 and then tried to detonate the bomb built into his shoe? Had he succeeded, he and nearly two hundred innocent passengers and crewmembers would have plunged to their deaths somewhere over the North Atlantic. But he didn't succeed. He was arrested, tried, and convicted for his crimes. In January 2003 he stepped before Chief U.S. District Court Judge William G. Young in Boston, Massachusetts, for sentencing. First Judge Young, a Reagan appointee, asked Reid if he had anything to say.

After admitting his guilt, Reid discussed his "allegiance to Osama Bin Laden, to Islam, and to the religion of Allah . . . I think I ought not apologize for my actions," he said. "I am at war with your country."

Judge Young imposed a sentence of life imprisonment, then leaned forward. "Let me explain this to you," he began. "We are not afraid of you or any of your terrorist co-conspirators, Mr. Reid. We are Americans. We've been through the fire before.

"You are not an enemy combatant. You are a terrorist. You are not a soldier in any war. You are a terrorist . . . and we do not negotiate with terrorists . . . we do not sign documents with terrorists. We hunt them down one by one and bring them to justice. . . .

"What I have, as honestly as I know how, tried to grapple with is why you did something so horrific. What was it that led you here to this courtroom today? I have listened respectfully to what you have to say, and I have an answer for you . . . it seems to me you hate the one thing that is most precious. You hate our freedom . . . our individual freedom to live as we choose, to come and go as we choose, to believe or not believe as we choose. . . .

"Here in this society, the very winds carry freedom. They carry it everywhere from sea to shining sea. It is because we prize individual freedom so much that you are here . . . so that everyone can see, truly see, that justice is administered fairly, individually, and discretely . . . we all know that the way we treat you, Mr. Reid, is the measure of our own liberties. . . .

"The world is not going to long remember what you or I say here. But this, however, will long endure. Here in this courtroom and in courtrooms all across America, the American people will gather to see that justice is being done." The judge paused and pointed to his right.

"See that flag, Mr. Reid? That's the flag of the United States of America. That flag still stands for freedom. You know it always will."

Then the judge turned to a marshall. "Custody, Mr. Officer," he said. "Stand him down."

I've been critical of some judges and their decisions in the past, but it seems to me that as far as the War on Terror is concerned, Judge Young got it right.

∾

My wife, Jean, taught for thirty-four years and she always said she was going to retire when some little kid tugged on her sweatshirt and said, "Mrs. Hastert, you taught my grandmother." Sure enough, that happened, and Jean did retire. Today she walks, jogs, and plays golf a couple of times a week. I should go out and walk or do something. I need to do it and I don't. But I do relax by attending wrestling tournaments, going to antique car shows, carving wooden ducks, or fishing either by myself or with family or friends.

Physically, I'm nowhere near as agile as I used to be. I'm stiff, and I need to lose weight. I'm also just getting old. I'll be sixty-three next January 2, and I'm still getting up at six o'clock, going to work at seven or seven-thirty, and working until eight, nine, or ten o'clock at night. A day when I'm just sitting around is very unusual.

I used to pick up wrestling mats and drive the school bus when others weren't available. My coach's office was exactly that, a coach's office. Now I have this handsome office in the Capitol with chandeliers, beautiful paintings, and a secure phone to the White House. I can stand on the balcony looking down the Mall and see the Washington Monument, the new World War II Memorial, and the Lincoln Memorial. I call it America's front porch. Things have gone pretty well. I'm not the assistant principal in a high school in northern Illinois. But life comes full circle or, to put it another way, the more things change, the more they stay the same—in the hall outside the door to my office sit seven or eight chairs....

I can't tell you how many times I've heard the rumor that I'll be retiring soon. I'm sure there are some people on both sides of the aisle, as well as in my own family, who'd like to see that happen. But I'm running for reelection to another term now, and I've told family, friends, and colleagues that I'd like to continue serving as Speaker as long as I am doing some good.

Both Jean and our two sons, Josh and Ethan, say that I can be inscrutable (Ethan compares me to Buddha) and that even after knowing me well for all these years, they can't always tell what I'm thinking by the expression on my face. Actually, what I'm thinking about a lot these days is how very lucky I've been and what an incredible journey I've had. And what memories—I'll treasure them forever.

Just think: Twenty-five years ago I was a wrestling coach at a high school in northern Illinois. Our system of government, as much as we like to criticize it, allowed me to step up to become Speaker of the House, and I'm deeply grateful to my colleagues and, mostly, to my constituents, for that opportunity. I've always

RONALD REAGAN— SON OF ILLINOIS

AS THIS BOOK WAS GOING TO PRESS, I RECEIVED WORD THAT President Ronald Reagan had died. As a son of Illinois and as an American I had enormous respect and admiration for him. His boyhood home in Dixon is in the congressional district I represent. I admired his optimism, his civility, his can-do attitude. Most of all, I admired the strength of his convictions and his willingness to fight for them. Yes, he was "The Great Communicator," but he was so much more than that.

Reagan didn't use any weasel words. In his inaugural address in 1981, he told us what he was going to do: "It is my intention to curb the size and influence of the federal establishment and to demand recognition of the distinction between the powers granted to the federal government and those reserved to the states and to the people. All of us need to be reminded that the federal government did not create the states; the states created the federal government."

Reagan held another strong conviction as well. America, in his view, was a special place, and it was our duty as citizens to make

297

better still. Here are remarks I delivered on June 10 when our fortieth President returned to the Capitol for the final time.

> Mrs. Reagan, Mr. Vice President, Members of Congress, Distinguished Guests:

Ronald Reagan's long journey has finally drawn to a close.

It is altogether fitting and proper that he has returned to this Capitol Rotunda, like another great son of Illinois, Abraham Lincoln, so the nation can say goodbye.

This Capitol Building is, for many, the greatest symbol of democracy and freedom in the world.

It brings to mind the "shining city upon a hill" of which President Reagan so often spoke. It is the right place to honor a man who so faithfully defended our freedom, and so successfully helped extend the blessings of liberty to millions around the world.

Mrs. Reagan, thank you for sharing your husband with us–for your steadfast love and for your great faith. We pray for you and for your family in this time of great mourning.

But as we mourn, we must also celebrate the life and the vision of one of America's greatest Presidents.

His story and values are quintessentially American.

Born in Tampico, Illinois, and then raised in Dixon, Illinois, he moved west to follow his dreams. He brought with him a Midwestern optimism, and he blended it with a Western 'can-do' spirit.

In 1980, the year of the "Reagan Revolution," his vision of hope, growth, and opportunity was exactly what the American people needed and wanted. His message touched a fundamental chord that is deeply embedded in the American experience.

President Reagan dared to dream that America had a special mission. He believed in the essential goodness of the American people—and that we had a special duty to promote peace and freedom for the rest of the world.

Against the advice of the timid, he sent a chilling message to authoritarian governments everywhere, that the civilized world would not rest—until freedom reigned—in every corner of the globe.

While others worried, President Reagan persevered. When others weakened, President Reagan stood tall. When others stepped back, President Reagan stepped forward. And he did it all with great humility, with great charm, and with great humor.

Tonight, we will open these doors and let the men and women whom Ronald Reagan served so faithfully file past and say good-bye to a man who meant so much to so many.

It is their being here that I think would mean more to him than any words we say.

Because it was from America's great and good people that Ronald Reagan drew his strength.

We will tell our grandchildren about this night when we gathered to honor the man from Illinois who became the son of California and then the son of all America.

And our grandchildren will tell their grandchildren—and President Reagan's spirit and eternal faith in America will carry on.

Ronald Reagan helped make our country and this world a better place to live. But he always believed that our best days were ahead of us, not behind us.

I can still hear him say, with that twinkle in his eye, "You ain't seen nothing yet!"

President Reagan once said, "We make a living by what we get; we make a life by what we give."

Twenty years ago, President Reagan stood on the beaches of Normandy to honor those who made a life by what they gave.

Recalling the men who scaled the cliffs and crossed the beaches in a merciless hail of bullets, he asked, who were these men—these ordinary men doing extraordinary things?

His answer was simple and direct: They were Americans.

So I can think of no higher tribute or honor or title to confer upon Ronald Reagan than to simply say: He was an American.

Godspeed, Mr. President.

ACKNOWLEDGMENTS

WRITING ABOUT ONE'S LIFE IS MUCH MORE THAN JUST SITTING down at the desk and jotting off a few notes. There are dozens upon dozens of people who helped me chronicle my days from the cornfields of Illinois to the Speaker's office in Washington, D.C. While I have attempted to list most of them below, I want to thank them all from the bottom of my heart for their friendship, counsel, and support.

Besides the help of my wife, Jean, and boys, Josh and Ethan, this autobiography would not have been possible without the tireless assistance and thorough work of Trevor Armbrister. As a professional journalist, Trevor spent countless hours interviewing me, my family, my friends, and my colleagues in order to accurately put together the pieces of my more than sixty-two years on earth.

Soon after we met, I discovered we had some common interests—namely, American history and the sport of wrestling. As far as we know, Trevor is the only writer to have assisted both a former President (Gerald R. Ford) and a Speaker of the House in the preparation of their memoirs. And when it came to discussions about wrestling, I knew we both shared the ideals of setting goals, working hard, and delivering results.

In order to pull the pages of my life from memory for chapters in this book, Trevor spent scores of hours with me transcribing stories while we traveled all across this great land we call America—from the hectic campaign trail and inspiring halls of Congress to the tranquil setting on my back porch in Kendall County, Illinois. Along the way, he's become a trusted partner and a valued friend.

I also want to thank the folks at Regnery Publishing who took an interest in cataloguing my life's story, in particular publisher Marjory G. Ross and editor Miriam Moore. I also want to say thank you to my counsel, Randy Evans, for his relentless work to cover all of the legal and ethical bases so my autobiography could come to fruition on the forthcoming pages.

I also want to thank those who have been with me since I first ran for Congress, especially Terry DesCoteaux, Sylvia Pletcher, and Scott Palmer. I also appreciate the many efforts of those who have worked for me in my Batavia, Illinois, district office since the very beginning, especially Lisa Post, Ruth Richardson, and Bonnie Walsh.

One of the things that comes with being Speaker of the House is the requirement for around-the-clock security. While this is one of my least favorite aspects of the job, I do appreciate the work of my security detail headed by Jack DeWolfe, and the assistance we receive from many police and sheriff departments around the country. In particular, I'd like to thank the Kendall County (IL) Sheriff's Department, the Illinois State Police, the New York City Police Department, the Chicago Police Department, the Phoenix Police Department, the Scottsdale Police Department, the Arizona State Police, the California Highway Patrol, the Alaska State Police, the Jefferson Parish (LA) Sheriff's Office, and the Seattle Police

Department. I appreciate their dedicated service during my frequent visits.

While I don't want to leave anyone out, I do want to personally thank the following individuals for kindly consenting to be interviewed or for providing much-needed assistance. I am grateful to all of you for helping to make this book a reality:

Jean Hastert, Josh Hastert, Ethan Hastert, Chris Hastert, Doral Swan, Wade Swan, Tom Jarman, Ken Pickerill, Bob Corwin, Bob Williams, Bob Evans, Dallas Ingemunson, Tom Cross, Jay Keller, Bob Michel, Ken Doty, and Loren Miller. Also to:

Judy Armbrister	Roseanna Harden	Helen Morrell
Dick Armey	Doris Karpiel	Bill Novelli
Joby Boland	Barry Jackson	Bill Paxon
David Bonior	Shannon Flaherty	Margaret Peterlin
Tom Brierton	Pete Jeffries	Bob Plaskas
Greg Busch	Tim Kennedy	Robert Remini
Sharon Carlson	Nancy Kervin	Dana Rohrabacher
Bobby Charles	Kiki Kless	John Russell
Barbara Cubin	Bill Koetzle	Luke Stedman
Tom DeLay	Ray LaHood	Mike Stokke
Tom Ewing	Sam Lancaster	Ted Van Der Meid
Jeff Farren	Aaron Lewis	Ralph Voss
John Feehery	Bob Livingston	Lisa Wagner
Tom Foley	Marilyn Marklein	Chris Walker
Bill Frist	Dan Mattoon	Darren Willcox
Newt Gingrich	John McGovern	Jim Wright
Bryan Harbin	Susan Molinari	Andrea Wysocki

INDEX